The Lincoln Murder Conspiracies

William Hanchett

The
Lincoln Murder
Conspiracies

Being an Account of the Hatred Felt by Many
Americans for President Abraham Lincoln during
the Civil War and the First Complete Examination
and Refutation of the Many Theories, Hypotheses,
and Speculations Put Forward since 1865 Concerning
Those Presumed to Have Aided, Abetted, Controlled,
or Directed the Murderous Act of John Wilkes Booth
in Ford's Theater the Night of April 14

UNIVERSITY OF ILLINOIS PRESS
Urbana and Chicago

This book is printed on acid-free paper.

Library of Congress Cataloging in Publication Data

Hanchett, William, 1922–
The Lincoln murder conspiracies.

Bibliography: p.
Includes index.
1. Lincoln, Abraham, 1809–1865—Assassination. 2. Booth, John
Wilkes, 1838–1865. 3. United States—Politics and government—1861–
1865. I. Title. E457.5.H26 1983   973.7′092′4   83–1065
ISBN 0–252–01046–9

To Nell

Contents

Acknowledgments

One of the foremost satisfactions in completing a book is the opportunity provided to thank those who helped in the writing of it. Years ago, Mark E. Neely, Jr., director of the Louis A. Warren Lincoln Library and Museum, Fort Wayne, Indiana, reaffirmed my conviction that public understanding of Lincoln's assassination was in a deplorable state and has ever since encouraged me in the writing of this analysis of the Lincoln murder conspiracies. He has shared the resources of his library by overworking its copying machines and has given me the benefit of his knowledge and acumen in a critical reading of the manuscript. Members of the Surratt Society, a lively organization based in the restored Surratt tavern outside Washington, have been equally generous, but I must acknowledge the special contributions of James O. Hall, who knows more about the assassination than anyone who ever lived except those personally involved in it, and John C. Brennan, an eagle-eyed genius who has alerted me to many errors committed by past writers and saved me from some of my own. I have also received valuable criticism from Professor Constance Head of Western Carolina University, from my colleague Glenn A. Sandstrom, and from students in my courses on the Civil War, who perhaps heard more about the assassination than they had expected to. Other scholars and friends who have taken time away from their own work to assist me with mine include William C. Davis, Joseph George, Jr., Robert P. Multhauf, Richard Ruetten, Gordon Samples, and Raymond G. Starr. San Diego State University has been generous with research awards and time off from teaching, and librarians Karen L. Hogarth and Ann R. Wright have spent many hours locating and borrowing rare publications.

Parts of Chapters 6, 7, and 8 have been previously published in *Civil War History, Lincoln Herald,* and the *Journal of the Illinois State Historical Society,* respectively, and are reprinted with permission. The manuscript has profited from the literary criticism of Frances H. Runner, Glenn A. Sandstrom, and Lucia H. Simons, master stylists all. Finally, I am grateful for the care and imagination of the University of Illinois Press, especially its director, Richard L. Wentworth, and assistant editor Susan L. Patterson.

Thanks. Thanks to all.

San Diego   W. H.

By Way of Introduction . . .

AUTHORS OF NEW BOOKS about Abraham Lincoln frequently begin by apologizing to their readers for publishing still another book on the great Civil War president. It is true, of course, that the field of Lincoln literature is a vast one; the Library of Congress lists more cards after Lincoln's name than after that of any other historical figure except Jesus and William Shakespeare. But quantity is not the same as quality, and, to be frank, the great majority of Lincoln titles contribute little or nothing to our understanding. Almost all Americans are familiar with the outline of Lincoln's life and can enumerate some of his major achievements, but, despite the enormous number of books and articles about him, few people really understand the nature of his greatness. Our most written-about president is by no means our best-understood president.

Very much the same may be said about Lincoln's assassination. Counting the newspaper and magazine pieces that annually commemorate the event, literally thousands of books and articles have been written about the tragedy of April 14, 1865, and about the incidents and the personalities involved in it. The assassination is so familiar to us that, as Bruce Catton put it, "the mere words 'Ford's Theatre' and 'Our American Cousin' immediately evoke the entire story for every American."[1] But not the entire story. Only what happened at the theater. For despite the number of titles dealing with various phases of the assassination, the public has little understanding of the passions of the Civil War that led to it and that so deeply affected the way with which it was dealt. We have not only been ill-informed, we have been misinformed about the assassination; there may be more popular misconceptions about the Lincoln murder than about any other event in American history.

If a true appreciation of Lincoln has been impeded by the old tradition of sentimentalizing him and turning him into a national god—as well as by a recurrent tendency to overreact against such hagiography—public understanding of the significance of the assassination has also been frustrated by the character of the literature about it. From the beginning, the assassination was shrouded in confusion and mystery, for the murder turned the controversial wartime president into a martyr and obscured the fact that his policies had created many bitter enemies in both North and South, and the killing of John Wilkes Booth at the time of his capture deprived the government of an opportunity to interrogate him. These circumstances encouraged speculation about conspiracies and tempted partisans of this or that theory into excesses. Through the years since 1865, politicians first and then writers have jumped to conclusions, presented assumptions as facts, and succumbed to the temptation of proving hypotheses by distorting the evidence. Especially since the 1930s, writers have stressed the sensational and, in order to arouse the interests of readers, have not scrupled against making outrageous suggestions, telling brazen lies, and committing outright hoaxes. In addition, errors of fact—significant and insignificant—have been repeated over and over again until they have been generally accepted as truths. Altogether, it is not surprising that what most Americans know about Lincoln's death—outside the shooting at Ford's Theater—is simply not true.

There are, to be sure, reasonable and balanced accounts of the assassination. The best of them is George S. Bryan's *The Great American Myth* (1940), which soberly and systematically tells the story of the conspiracies of John Wilkes Booth against Lincoln. Bryan also analyzes some of the myths with which the assassination became so quickly encrusted, especially the legend that Booth did not die outside the flaming barn on Garrett's farm but escaped to live in Europe or India or California or Oklahoma. In *Twenty Days* (1965), Dorothy Meserve Kunhardt and Philip B. Kunhardt, Jr., have combined hundreds of magnificently reproduced contemporary photographs and other pictures with an informed and judicious narrative of the assassination, its background and aftermath. One regrets only their claim to have identified Booth and some of the men associated with him in an enlarged (and well-publicized) photograph of the ceremonies at Lincoln's second inauguration, March 4, 1865. Stanley Kimmel's *The Mad Booths of Maryland* (1940, 1969) is packed full of information about Booth and his famous and eccentric family. Thomas R. Turner's *Beware the People Weeping. Public Opinion and the Assassination of Abraham Lincoln* (1982) is distinguished not only for its exhaustive research and meticulous documentation, but also for the fact that it is the first book dealing with the assassination written by a professional historian.

There are also worthwhile briefer accounts. One of the best is *Album of the Lincoln Murder* (1965), written by Robert H. Fowler for the editors of *Civil War Times Illustrated*. (On the last page of this short book, Fowler praises the work of some of the sensationalist writers whom he totally ignores in his text.) Another able presentation is in *The Real Abraham Lincoln* (1960), by Reinhard H. Luthin, one of the few Lincoln biographies to give the assassination more than passing attention.

Parts of some books on the assassination deserve the attention of serious students who may be left uninterested or disappointed (or appalled) by other parts. Clara Laughlin in *The Death of Lincoln* (1909) and David M. Dewitt in *The Assassination of Abraham Lincoln* (1909) present valuable descriptions of Booth's conspiracy to kidnap Lincoln and of the probable evolution of his decision to kill. In *Myths After Lincoln* (1929), Lloyd Lewis helps us to understand the process by which Lincoln became a folk-god and Booth a folk-demon. In *Kennedy and Lincoln: Medical and Ballistic Comparisons of Their Assassinations* (1980), John K. Lattimer tells—and illustrates with pictures—all that needs to be known about the wounds from which Lincoln and Booth died. Parts of other books and some magazine articles also have merit.

The trouble is that since 1937 a kind of Gresham's law has operated in the field of Lincoln's assassination: the bad books, the sensational books, drive away the good books and dominate public opinion. For this unfortunate fact, professional historians are largely to blame.

As Mark E. Neely, Jr., has shrewdly observed, professional historians allowed the assassination to fall through the gap separating the two traditional fields of historical scholarship—the

Civil War and Reconstruction. It did not seem to belong to the one or the other. Nor did it fit neatly into any of the conventional historical categories of political, social, military, or diplomatic history. Furthermore, it demanded "focus on a handful of obscure individuals, when the profession was moving more and more towards studies of great social movements." Lincoln biographers have been similarly aloof, perhaps reflecting the disdain of James G. Randall, who declared in his four-volume *Lincoln the President* (1945–55), "This biography knows only the living Lincoln."[2] The result has been a dearth of scholarly studies of the assassination upon which those who write history for the popular market could base their works. On the subject of Lincoln's murder, the popularizers have had little written history to popularize.

In 1937 the position left vacant for so many years by professional historians and biographers was occupied with a vengeance by Otto Eisenschiml, a chemist-businessman from Chicago, whose *Why Was Lincoln Murdered?* became a bible of revelation and inspiration for a whole generation of popularizers. With apparent scholarly objectivity and a mass of so-called circumstantial evidence, Eisenschiml asked whether Lincoln's assassination could not have been arranged by none other than Secretary of War Edwin M. Stanton. This sensational idea immediately turned on the imaginations and the typewriters of a host of writers who understood the potential public appetite for a scandal involving conspiracy and betrayal at the highest level of the U.S. government. Within a short time the Eisenschiml thesis and variations upon it had come, popularly, to dominate all other theories and explanations of the assassination. The books by Bryan and Kimmel continued to be admired by specialists, and, although the Kunhardts' *Twenty Days* enjoyed and deserved a large sale, its impact was in its illustrations. Probably not many people read its text.

Turner's *Beware the People Weeping* is likely to meet a different fate, for its publication signaled the arrival of a new era of assassination scholarship. Inspired by the political assassinations of the 1960s, impatient and angry with the absurdities and cruelties of the Eisenschiml thesis, and recognizing the limitations of earlier works such as those by Laughlin and Dewitt, serious researchers throughout the country began in the 1970s to make what in reality is the first scholarly examination of assassination source materials. In this enterprise they are being assisted by the easy availability on microfilm of essential government documents, private papers, and periodicals, a revolution that will bring incalculable benefits not only to the history of the assassination but also to all phases of American history. The new and imaginative research now being conducted by so many individuals has already led to the discovery and utilization of important evidence long buried in obscure and distant archives and to new insights on the assassination and individuals involved. The scholarly studies forthcoming ought to put an end to the malignant influence of the sensational books that have deceived the public for so long.

If the public is ready to accept new and honest interpretations of the assassination, the readiness is in part a by-product of the civil rights revolution of the 1960s. At that time, American activists discovered that Lincoln's views on race were not the same as their own. The resulting disillusion, nourished by Vietnam and Watergate, demoted Lincoln from his position as national deity to the level of an ordinary mortal; more than one American dismissed him as just another white racist. Though this development was disturbing at the time, it is proving to be healthy and desirable. For, in rebuttal, historians are spreading the truth that the statements and actions of individuals must be judged in the context of their own times, not other times; and that, so judged, Lincoln was far more advanced on the questions of civil rights and race than the vast majority of his countrymen. The study of the complex problem of slavery during the Civil War leads to more respect—not less—for Lincoln's leadership. At last the public's idealized portraits of Lincoln the Great Emancipator and Lincoln the Saviour of the Union may yield to a more sophisticated appreciation of Lincoln as the leader of a divided section within a divided nation and as the engineer of what was in reality an almost impossible Union victory.

When Lincoln is seen as a leader dealing with controversial problems in tumultuous times, it is easier to understand why he was assassinated than when he is envisioned as a godlike figure hovering serenely above the storm. Only a madman would kill a god. Booth was not a madman; he believed he had good reasons to take Lincoln's life. He was not alone.

In the last volume of his *War for the Union* (1971), Allan Nevins referred to the assassination as a "fitting climax of the years of anger and butchery," and said that it had impressed upon "the American mind the terrible nature of the conflict."[3] Unfortunately it did not, for the assassination was removed from its wartime context by the idolization of Lincoln, and, in the interests of reconciliation between North and South, the "terrible nature of the conflict" was forgotten.

But the nation has now been long reunited, and the time has come when Lincoln's murder, retrieved from the gap between the Civil War and Reconstruction and rescued from those who have misrepresented history, can be seen as a political act, the political finale of the Civil War. When Americans understand the assassination, they will understand—as Nevins believed they would—the "terrible nature" of the war they fought against each other. That means they will understand a great deal more about their history—and about themselves.

This book does not retell the familiar story of the shooting at Ford's Theater, or describe the scene in the crowded little bedroom across the street where Lincoln died, or report the pursuit, capture, and death of John Wilkes Booth. What it seeks to do is to bring Lincoln's assassination into focus: first, by placing it in relationship to the bitter disputes that were responsible for it—secession, the use of U.S. military force against states, political arrests, the emancipation of slaves, and the shocking new tactics of total war; and, second, by tracing the formulation and influence of the various interpretations that through the years have clouded our vision.

In order to know where to go, one must know where one is. In order to know where one is, it is necessary to know where one has been. Here, then, is the story of where we have been and where we are on the long, long road to understanding Lincoln's murder.

1

They Hated Lincoln

THE SHOCK AND MOURNING that followed Abraham Lincoln's assassination were profound and widespread, and the martyred president quickly became the most beloved of American heroes. But during his lifetime Lincoln was the object of far more hatred than love. He was hated—by Northerners as well as Southerners—for attempting to force the South to remain in the Union, for usurping cherished constitutional rights, for pursuing a policy regarding slavery that would lead to the Africanization of the United States, for degrading the presidency, for shedding so much blood, for making so many widows, and for creating so many fatherless homes. He was hated by decent and patriotic people, and it was only to be expected that some of them should have been driven close to madness by the changes his policies were bringing about in American society. Looking back upon the nature of the hatred that so many Americans felt for Lincoln, it seems extraordinary that he lasted as president as long as he did, for it was a savage time when problems were being solved by violence.

At first, hatred for Lincoln was focused upon him simply because he was the 1860 presidential nominee of the antislavery Republican party and then the Republican president-elect. "The significant fact which menaces the South is not that Abe Lincoln is elected President," observed the Richmond (Virginia) *Enquirer*, "but that the Northern people, by a sectional vote, have elected a president for the avowed purpose of aggression on Southern rights. . . . This is a declaration of war."[1] Before the end of the election month, the state of Mississippi resolved that the proper remedy for northern aggression was "the secession of each aggrieved State." Seven states did secede (to be joined by four more after Fort Sumter), and on February 18, 1861—even before Lincoln's inauguration—Jefferson Davis of Mississippi was inaugurated provisional president of a new nation, the Confederate States of America.

In his inaugural address Davis expressed a theory of government to which the people of both sections were devoted. The formation of the new nation, he declared, "illustrates the American idea that governments rest on the consent of the governed, and that it is the right of the people to alter or abolish them at will whenever they become destructive of the ends for which they were established." The stated purpose of the compact of the Union from which the seven states of the Deep South had just withdrawn was to "establish justice, insure domestic tranquillity, provide for the common defense, promote the general welfare, and secure the blessings of liberty." But when, in the judgment of the states, it was perverted from these purposes and ceased to serve the ends for which it was established, the states had the right to declare that so far as they were concerned the government created by the compact no longer existed. "In this they merely asserted the right which the Declaration of Independence of July 4, 1776, defined to be 'inalienable.' . . . He who knows the hearts of men," Davis concluded, "will judge of the sincerity with which we have labored to preserve the Government of our fathers in its spirit."[2]

Republicans, of course, denied that their program to limit the spread of slavery—while allowing it to remain untouched in the states where it already existed—violated the Constitution or perverted the purposes for which the Union had been established. But many Northerners, including even those who rejected the legitimacy of the South's secession, did not believe that the government of the United States should use force to prevent it. "A husband or wife who can only keep the other partner within the bond by locking the doors and standing armed before them," exclaimed the Boston abolitionist Wendell Phillips, "had better submit to peaceable separation."[3] Most northern Democrats felt the same way. "The fact is that our Union rests upon public opinion," said President James Buchanan in his annual message to Congress in December 1860, "and can never be cemented by the blood of its citizens. . . . If it cannot live in the affections of the people, it must . . . die."[4] Not a single state would have joined the Union at the time the Constitution was submitted to them for ratification, said a New York publisher, if it had been imagined that the U.S. government would ever attempt to hold any of them within it by force.[5]

Holding states in the Union by force meant fighting a war that it seemed unlikely the United States could win, for it was widely assumed that if the incoming president should resort to the monstrous doctrine of "coercion," all fifteen slave states would join the Confederacy, making it invincible. But even if it should be possible for the North to conquer so vast a region as the South—at a frightful cost in lives and wealth—what kind of a union would result? General Winfield Scott, the highest ranking officer in the U.S. Army, pictured it for Lincoln. It would be, Scott wrote, "fifteen devastated provinces—not to be brought into harmony with their conquerors, but to be held for generations, by heavy garrisons at an expense quadruple the net duties or taxes which it would be possible to extract from them—followed by a Protector or an Emperor." The general's advice was "say to the seceded States—wayward sisters depart in peace!"[6]

Walt Whitman's estimate that there were about as many sympathizers with the theory of secession in the North as in the South was perhaps an exaggeration.[7] Even so, it seemed that Lincoln would have no choice but to accept Scott's advice, for in 1860–61 the U.S. government was not the powerful agency that it had become by 1865. It was still a small-scale operation that had changed very little since Andrew Jackson's day. Treasury notes were still signed individually by hand by the Register of the Treasury (who suffered severely from writer's cramp once the government began to borrow large sums of money), and the wartime paper money issue, the greenbacks, were printed in long rolls and had to be cut out individually by a clerk with scissors.[8] The capital itself was still a homey little southern city with a total population, counting slaves and free blacks, of only 61,000, the majority of them secessionist or sympathetic to secession. Its character changed dramatically during the war, when its population jumped to over 200,000, but many of the newcomers were pro-southern and, with the exception of Baltimore, there was probably no city in any of the loyal states in which there were more citizens disloyal to the United States than in the country's own capital.[9]

For a great many people in the North, the Confederate attack on Fort Sumter on April 12, 1861, ended (at least temporarily) the debate over both the legality of secession and the morality and efficacy of using force to prevent it. What had previously seemed to be coercion now seemed to be self-defense, and in response to Lincoln's call men rushed to arms in a frenzy of national patriotism. They must save the Union, Lincoln told them, as the world's best hope for freedom. If it could be broken up by a dissatisfied minority, it would prove the people incapable of governing themselves and put an end to the American experiment in democracy.

To many northern Democrats, however, Lincoln himself was seen as the greatest threat to freedom and self-government. No longer merely the symbol of the Republican party, he was now commander-in-chief of the U.S Army and Navy in what these people viewed as an unjust war against the South. Furthermore, he was taking what his critics considered to be brutal, dictatorial, and unconstitutional measures against those who opposed him. His unilateral suspension of the writ of habeas corpus led to the arrest of thousands of citizens suspected of ill-defined "disloyal acts" and to their imprisonment in such "American Bastilles" as the Old Capitol Prison in Washington and Fort Lafayette in New York harbor. Many political prisoners were held without trial; others were tried, not in the civil courts, but before military commissions. No less an authority than Chief Justice of the United States Roger B. Taney warned Lincoln that such practices violated the Constitution that he had sworn to uphold.[10] An ex-president of the United States, Franklin Pierce, said in an address on July 4, 1863, that Lincoln was telling the people that "in time of war the mere arbitrary will of the President takes the place of the Constitution, and . . . that it is treasonable to speak or write otherwise than as he may prescribe."[11] Horatio Seymour, governor of New York, reminded New Yorkers how their fathers had acted in their struggle against England. "*They* did not say liberty was suspended, that men might be deprived of the right of trial by jury, that they might be torn from their homes by midnight intruders."[12] If the public permitted its constitutional liberties to be suspended, exclaimed the noted constitutionalist George Ticknor Curtis of Massachusetts, it "will be an end of this experiment of self-government."[13]

Even Lincoln's own attorney general, who would normally be the agent through whom the government enforced its authority, feared the administration and its supporters in Congress were going too far. "Surely Cicero was right," wrote Edward Bates of Missouri in his diary, "when he said that 'in every Civil war, Success is dangerous, because it is sure to beget arrogance and a disregard of the *laws of the Government*.'" Lincoln and the Radical Republicans had opened up a boundless field of power. "When the constitution fails them, they have only to say 'this is a time of war—and war gives all needed power!'"[14]

Whether they believed Lincoln to be the enemy or the protector of free institutions, many people in the North were disturbed that he was, in their view, no gentleman. His appearance was grotesque, and the awkwardness of his manner proclaimed his unlettered, western frontier origins. The pro-administration New York diarist, George Templeton Strong, commented upon the president's lack of social polish and described him as "a barbarian, Scythian, yahoo, or gorilla."[15] Strong recognized the character and competence of the man inside, but a great many scornful men and women did not. After breakfasting with President Davis in Richmond, a Southerner noted with satisfaction how great was the contrast between the Confederate chief and the "vulgar monkey who now rules Washington,"[16] a contrast obvious and sickening to many Northerners. The newspaperman Henry Villard believed that if fashionable New Yorkers did not know who Lincoln was they would be ashamed to be seen on the street with him.[17] Perhaps Villard was not far wrong, for one New York matron declared that of the whole Lincoln administration she would admit only Secretary of State William H. Seward and Secretary of the Treasury Salmon P. Chase to her drawing room.[18]

Those people who most hated Lincoln and his war—and the measures he was taking to win it—were eager to believe that he was vulgar as well as unrefined. He was reported to forsake handkerchiefs in favor of blowing his nose through his thumb and fingers, frontier style.[19] One hostile visitor to Lincoln in the White House reported he had "found him seated, in shirt sleeves, his feet on the mantelpiece, his hat on his head, amusing himself by making huge semicircles with tobacco juice that he squeezed out of his quid." A New York editor wrote in 1864 that Lincoln "is an uneducated boor. He is brutal in all his habits and in all his ways. He is filthy. He is obscene. He is vicious."[20] Others convinced themselves that he was a coward and a drunkard as well.[21]

Ironically, the policy for which Lincoln was most hated by his contemporaries was the same policy for which he was then and later most honored—the freeing of the slaves. Cogent political arguments could be raised against emancipation. The inventor and painter Samuel F. B. Morse believed that the emancipation of slaves was not only unconstitutional but also unwise, for it tended "to divide the counsels of the North, and unite the South, and [to] render the restoration of the national Union next to hopeless."[22] It was quite true that emancipation divided the loyal states, for four slave states—Maryland, Kentucky, Missouri, and Delaware—had not seceded following the outbreak of hostilities. Nevertheless, they were opposed to federal interference with any state's internal institutions.

Even outside the loyal slave states, public opinion in the North was divided. Some people, like Lincoln himself, believed slavery to be the cause of the war and rejoiced over the Emancipation Proclamation. Others believed that not slavery but fanaticism against slavery had driven the South out of the Union and that, as a Philadelphia newspaper put it, the Proclamation had given the South "no other choice but war to the knife."[23]

But without question the impetus for the most extreme attacks on the emancipation policy and the enlistment of black soldiers, which was a corollary of it, was racist. Many whites, like the abolitionists and antislavery moderates, supported emancipation because they had long opposed the institution of slavery on principle. Others supported emancipation for the reasons that Lincoln had adopted and justified it—as a means of winning the war and preserving the Union. But many other northern whites were not unfriendly to slavery as an institution (i.e., for blacks), and, though willing to fight and make sacrifices for their country, they bitterly resented being called upon to do so for the "niggers." Even worse, many people saw emancipation as the first deliberate step toward a revolting amalgamation

of the races. Unless Lincoln and the other black abolitionist traitors were stopped, wrote Chauncey Burr, editor of the New
York magazine *The Old Guard,* the United States would become a "mongrel concern of whites, negroes, mulattoes, and
sambos, . . . the most degrading and contemptible the world
ever saw." No truly patriotic citizen, therefore, could rejoice at
news of a Union victory. The people understood, said Burr, that
the Confederate government was a thousand times closer to the
spirit of the Founding Fathers than the government of "Abraham Africanus I."[24] "The simple question to be decided," declared a Democratic newspaper in Kansas, "is whether the white
man shall maintain his status of superiority" by supporting the
Democrats "or be sunk to the level of the Negro" by supporting
the Republicans.[25] A Maryland editor noted in February 1865
that a black man had preached before the state's House of Representatives. "Shall we have a civilized gorilla next?" he asked.
"How long before Lincoln will invite them [blacks] to diplomatic dinners and lead the way to table with a greasy wench
hanging on his arm?"[26]

Northerners who opposed Lincoln's war were called Copperheads—poisonous snakes who struck without warning—by their
countrymen who supported it. The Copperheads themselves, of
course, saw things differently: they believed that they were the
loyal and true citizens and that Lincoln and those who backed
him were the disloyal subversives. Some of them even turned
the Copperhead epithet into a term of honor by cutting from
the U.S. copper penny (or from ordinary copper sheeting) the
head of the representation of Liberty and wearing it as an emblem. "Every person in favor of Free Speech, a Free Press and
the Rights of White Men, is wearing the Badge of Liberty," declared a manufacturer who placed an advertisement in the New
York *Weekly Caucasian,* offering "Copperheads" for sale for fifteen cents each or $10.00 per hundred.[27]

Cherishing the Jeffersonian faith that resistance to tyrants was
obedience to God, Copperheads sought, so far as they dared, to
uphold the principles in which they believed, chiefly states' rights
and white supremacy. The truth is that most of them were not
very daring, for the power of the U.S. military was awesome
during the war, and, as the number of arrests proved, Army

officials did not hesitate to use it against civilians suspected of disloyal practices.

Yet there were unknown thousands of Copperheads—real Copperheads, not simply Democrats labelled as such by Republicans—all across the country, and some of them were members of a resistance organization, the Sons of Liberty (also known by earlier names, the Knights of the Golden Circle and the Order of American Knights). As it turned out, most members were satisfied with attending periodic secret meetings, taking solemn oaths, exchanging passwords and recognition codes, and enjoying in each other's fellowship a righteous sense of being persecuted by evil forces. Lincoln looked upon most of them with what his secretaries described as "good humored contempt." Taking oaths to shed the last drop of blood for what they believed was easy, said Lincoln; it was shedding the first drop that was hard.[28]

Not many Copperheads shed any of their own blood at all. But they staged riots against the draft, held peace meetings, encouraged soldiers to desert by promising them refuge, circulated antiwar literature, sabotaged government property, passed military information to Rebel agents, smuggled medicine and other supplies into the Confederacy, sustained hope among Southerners, and in a variety of such ways helped to prolong the war, thus causing the shedding of a great deal of other men's blood. And no one could be sure at the time that some leader or some military setback might not stir the Sons of Liberty into open resistance.

A much larger number of northern Democrats were loyal to the United States and did not hate Lincoln, though they were vigorously opposed to the policies of his administration. The administration, after all, was Republican, and that meant it was pursuing economic and political policies to which Democrats had objected since the time of Jackson. But the party was in a difficult position; it could not effectively attack those policies during the war, when prosperity was general and the nation was struggling to preserve itself. Nor could the loyal Democrats fully exploit the racial issue, for Lincoln had skillfully established emancipation as a means to victory rather than as an objective of the war. About all the Democrats could do was to attack the administration for its violations of civil liberties, making themselves sound very much like Copperheads and giving substance to Republican counterattacks that that is what they were.

By 1864, however, a new issue had arisen: Lincoln's apparent inability—despite ruthless tactics and enormous casualties—to defeat the southern armies and end the rebellion. In this reelection year many Democrats and some Republicans, too, had come to believe that the war could not be won, that the South could continue indefinitely to defend itself. They believed, therefore, that it was time to call an end to the slaughter. From the administration point of view, the Peace Democrats were as dangerous as the Copperhead Democrats.

In order to exploit the North's internal divisions and growing war-weariness, the Confederate government dispatched special representatives to Canada, where Montreal and Toronto were already centers of spying and intrigue. In February 1864 James P. Holcombe was ordered to Canada to arrange for the return to the South of some four hundred Confederate soldiers who had escaped from Yankee prisons and fled north of the border, an assignment he was to perform in addition to mysterious "other duties already intrusted," but not specified in writing.[29] In April Davis appointed Jacob Thompson of Mississippi, secretary of the interior in the cabinet of Buchanan, and Clement C. Clay, a Confederate States Senator and once a U.S. Senator from Alabama, as special commissioners, directing them to carry out in Canada "such instructions as you have received from me verbally, in such manner as shall seem most likely to conduce the furtherance of the interests of the Confederate States of America."[30] A principal objective of the well-financed mission of Thompson and Clay was to assist in the defeat of Lincoln in the fall election through the buying up of newspapers, chiefly in the West.[31]

Already in Canada, officially or unofficially, were other Confederates who were to figure one way or another in events leading to or following Lincoln's assassination. One of them was Beverly Tucker of Virginia, who was attempting to negotiate a trade, through Canada, of northern bacon for southern cotton. Another was George N. Sanders, an adventurous Kentuckian, who encouraged Southerners in Canada to engage in raids against American towns across the border.[32]

In July 1864 Holcombe, Clay, and Sanders journeyed to Niagara Falls, where from the Canadian side of the river they sent a message to Horace Greeley, whose New York *Tribune* was often critical of Lincoln and which was now quite unenthusiastic about his renomination. The three men announced that they were "ready and willing to go at once to Washington," provided that they were supplied with safe conduct passes. Eagerly sensing the possibility of reunion through peaceful negotiation, Greeley at once informed Lincoln, who promised the passes if the men involved were duly accredited by authorities in Richmond. In response, the commissioners admitted that they had not been authorized to negotiate peace, but, they declared, they had the complete confidence of the Richmond authorities and were certain they would receive the authorization "at once."

Lincoln responded to this second communication with a message destined to influence his own fate in a way that no one could have predicted. On July 18 he addressed a note "To Whom It May Concern," stating that any proposition for peace that embraced the reunion of the sections and the end of slavery—and that came to him from a source which controlled the armies at war against the United States—would be received and considered and be met with liberal concessions on all other points. Of course, the negotiators involved would have safe conduct coming and going.[33]

With carefully contrived indignation, the Confederate commissioners announced publicly that they had been betrayed by Lincoln. His first communication promising safe conduct passes had included no conditions for negotiations. His second note, rudely addressed "To Whom It May Concern" rather than to the individuals concerned, had destroyed any possibility of peace by stating the conditions of negotiation in advance. The president, they said, was simply pursuing his old and discredited policy of trying to force the South to submit unconditionally to the United States. The people of the Confederate States sincerely wanted peace, the commissioners stated, but few of them would "purchase it at the expense of liberty, honor, and self-respect." Lincoln was demanding that the people of the southern states give up their constitutions and "barter away their priceless heritage of self-government."

Still, the commissioners believed Lincoln's perfidy would have desirable results. It would convince the South that no peace was possible with a Republican administration and thus inspire Southerners to fight on with renewed spirit and energy. It would also convince the North that the only way to restore peace and constitutional liberty was by electing a Democratic president.

In short, the reply to Lincoln's "To Whom It May Concern" letter, widely publicized in the northern and southern press, was a Confederate campaign document designed to increase dissatisfaction with Lincoln in the North by making it appear that he alone was responsible for the continuation of the war. If he were removed, peace would follow.[34]

Perhaps more was at stake in the presidential election of 1864 than in any other in American history. Lincoln believed that no Democratic administration, not even one headed by General George B. McClellan, the party's nominee in 1864, could prevent the Confederacy from establishing its independence. The election would thus determine whether or not the American experiment in popular government would be preserved. It would also determine whether or not slavery would be abolished, for, of course, Lincoln's Emancipation Proclamation would be meaningless in an independent Confederate States of America. From the Republican or Unionist point of view, Lincoln's reelection was therefore vital.[35]

To the Copperheads and Peace Democrats his defeat was no less vital. Here was a president fighting a war he could not win in opposition to the fundamental American principle of government by consent, who employed repressive measures worthy of a czar in violation of specific constitutional guarantees of civil liberty, and whose policy of emancipating slaves threatened to mongrelize the American people. Many Democrats who did not believe that Lincoln was a tyrant considered him incompetent. "Can our countrymen be so blind, so stupid," asked Maria Daly in New York, "as to again place such a clod . . . in the presidential chair?"[36] In Lincoln's hometown another woman, noting that innumerable battles and frightful casualties had not brought the South any closer to submission, declared, "Our only hope is in a Democratic President, or an uprising of the people."[37]

Indeed, in 1864 there was increasing talk about popular uprisings, and there were increasing incitements to them, too. An editor in Iowa wrote that it was not enough simply to denounce the usurpations of a despot. "There is but one way to deal with arbitrary power, and that is to treat it precisely as one would do, if he had the power, with a highwayman who might undertake to rob him of his money."[38] The Chicago *Times* declared that the people had borne much from Lincoln but that "the time is close at hand when a further endurance will cease to be either a virtue or a possibility."[39]

One of the most rabid of Lincoln's antagonists was Marcus Mills Pomeroy, editor of the LaCrosse (Wisconsin) *Democrat*. Since Pomeroy's fulminations were reprinted in other Democratic newspapers, his influence was by no means only local. "May Almighty God forbid that we are to have two terms of the rottenest, most stinking, ruinworking small pox ever conceived by friends or mortals," he wrote at one time during the campaign. A vote for Lincoln, he said at another, is a vote "for taxes— for Fort Lafayette—for the draft—for usurped power—for suspension of sacred writs—for a nigger millennium—for worthless currency—for a ruined nation—for desolate cities." If Lincoln should be elected "to misgovern for another four years," said Pomeroy, "we trust some bold hand will pierce his heart with dagger point for the public good." Pomeroy proposed an epitaph: "Beneath this turf the Widow Maker lies, Little in everything, except in size." After Lincoln's election victory, Pomeroy even expressed a willingness to assassinate the president himself.[40]

Such tirades found avid readers. Yet there was little possibility that the enemies of the Lincoln administration would rise up against it so long as there was a chance they could vote it out of office, and that chance remained good until the last weeks of the campaign. The capture of Mobile Bay in August and of Atlanta in September slackened much of the hatred for Lincoln in the North by making it seem that the war might end soon, and with a military victory for the United States. This revived hope was registered on election day, when Lincoln received 55 percent of the popular vote.

But to Copperheads, what did his reelection mean except that a majority of the voters of the northern states were willing to forgive Lincoln his tyranny because he might be successful in his war? He was still a tyrant, and the war was still unjust. From

Canada, Clay reported to Richmond early in November that "all that a large portion of the Northern people—especially in the Northwest—want to resist the oppressions of the despotism at Washington, is a *leader*. They are ripe for resistance, and *it may come soon after the Presidential election*."[41] Clay was no doubt unduly influenced by what he read in the anti-Lincoln press, many of whose columns he and Thompson had inspired. But it was true that from the southern point of view the time for physical resistance to Lincoln in the North had come; it was the Confederacy's best chance to avoid what was now recognized as an otherwise inevitable defeat.

The Confederate contingent in Canada led the way, staging raids on Calais, Maine, Johnson's Island in Lake Erie, and St. Albans, Vermont. Robert C. Kennedy, an escaped prisoner of war from Johnson's Island, made his way to Canada and joined a small expedition of men who went to New York City to burn it to the ground in retaliation for unprecedented Yankee depredations in the South. On the night of November 25, 1864, Kennedy set fire to Barnum's Museum and three hotels; the others fired only their own lodgings and fled. Had they fulfilled their assignments, there would have been thirty-two fires raging simultaneously, and New York might have experienced the fate of Chicago in 1871.[42] The fire in the Lafarge Hotel interrupted a performance of *Julius Caesar* in the Winter Garden Theater, located in the same building, starring the famous Booth brothers, Junius Brutus, Jr., Edwin, and John Wilkes. (John Wilkes played not Brutus, but Marc Antony.)[43] Plans to destroy New York's water supply by blowing up the dam at the Croton reservoir and to spread epidemics of disease by means of infected clothing were also attempted or considered.[44] A Confederate officer, in and out of Canada with the apparent ease of a commuter, planned to kidnap Vice-President-elect Andrew Johnson from his hotel in Louisville, Kentucky, and believed he would have succeeded had not Johnson changed his plans and left unexpectedly.[45] These were extreme measures, but easily justified, for they belonged in the new, revolutionary kind of war the United States was waging against southern civilization. Besides, nothing came of most of them, a matter of chagrin to Confederates outraged by Yankee excesses.

There was an even more promising way to hurt the North from within. In northern prisoner-of-war camps in 1864 there were approximately 200,000 Confederate soldiers whom the United States refused to exchange for its own soldiers in southern prisons because it could afford to lose the manpower and the Confederacy could not. If any significant number of these prisoners could be freed, they might—with the help of Copperheads—be able to arm themselves at lightly guarded federal arsenals, release other prisoners, and capture and destroy northern cities. Such operations might well touch off the popular uprising the Confederate leaders so desperately wanted and force the North out of the war. For months Thompson shipped arms and ammunition to trusted Copperheads in boxes labelled "Pick Axes," "Nails," "Household Goods," and "Sunday School Books," and plans were made for attacks on Camp Douglas, Illinois, where over 8,000 prisoners were guarded by only 700 Veteran Reserve Corps soldiers, and on prison camps in Missouri, Indiana, Ohio, and New York.[46]

Promising and feasible as some of these projects were, they failed because of exposure by government agents who had infiltrated the Sons of Liberty. Perhaps equally important, they failed because the Copperhead leaders did not know how far they could trust their own presumed followers and therefore hesitated to take them into their confidence. To do so ran the risk of being exposed as traitors.[47]

In late 1864, the well-publicized treason trial in Indiana of Lambdin P. Milligan and others also undermined Copperhead zeal. Milligan was found guilty by a military commission of spying, organizing resistance to the United States, conspiring to release Confederate prisoners, and other Copperhead activities, and he was sentenced to be hanged.[48] The leadership of the Sons of Liberty was further demoralized by Lincoln's reelection, and Thompson regretfully informed authorities in Richmond that a new organization of the South's friends in the North was needed.[49]

But Confederate leaders like Thompson and Clay did not give up on the Copperheads. Back in Richmond from Canada at the end of 1864, Holcombe reported that discontent with Lincoln's leadership was still general in the Old Northwest. He recommended that "we should employ money and talent without stint" to give the dissatisfaction "the proportions of anarchy and strife."

It was important, too, that communications be maintained with the Copperheads. "Warned by our past experience, let us introduce arms more gradually and cautiously . . . , and through the ordinary channel of newspapers, as well as of campaign documents, enlighten and inflame the public mind. . . . With arms, leaders, and an opportunity," said Holcombe, "we could strike a deadly blow."[50]

There had scarcely been a time since his first election in 1860 that those who hated Lincoln had not threatened or planned to strike "a deadly blow" against him. The hate mail and the threats that he would never live to be inaugurated began arriving in Springfield immediately, together with well-meant warnings to be on guard against rumored attacks.

In February 1861 Lincoln had favored taking a southerly route to Washington to demonstrate his confidence in the people of the border slave states and to cultivate their confidence in him. But his advisers laid out a northerly route, partly for security purposes and partly to present him to a larger number of the people of the North whose support he had to have. He well knew that his life was in danger wherever he was, but he refused to worry about it. On February 11, saying good-by to the people of Springfield, among whom he had lived for a quarter of a century, he stated matter-of-factly, "I now leave, not knowing when, or whether, I may return."[51]

Along the way crowds were larger and more enthusiastic than anyone had anticipated, and the consciousness of danger was greater, too. Just before the train crossed into Indiana a condition was discovered in the track ahead that might have resulted in derailment. Nobody could be sure whether it was coincidence or conspiracy, so a pilot engine preceded the presidential train thereafter.[52] In Ohio the press reported that a small bomb timed to explode in fifteen minutes was discovered in a carpetbag in Lincoln's car.[53] It could have been a reporter's fanciful invention, but certainly there could be a fanatic Lincoln-hater— or lots of them—in any of the crowds that gathered at the watering stops and at the railroad stations where the train stopped so that Lincoln could show himself and say a few words.

Members of the presidential party included, among several Army officers, Major David Hunter, who soon became a general and was influential in arousing southern emotions against the Lincoln administration. In October 1860 Hunter had warned Lincoln from Fort Leavenworth, Kansas, that a group of young men had sworn to assassinate him if he should be elected.[54] The most formidable of the bodyguards was Ward Hill Lamon, an old Lincoln friend and legal associate from Danville, Illinois. Almost as tall as Lincoln and much huskier, Lamon was constantly at his friend's side, two revolvers and a bowie knife in his belt, his eyes ever searching the pushing throngs.[55]

In Philadelphia Lincoln learned from two separate and reliable sources of a plot to assassinate him as he passed through the ardently pro-secessionist city of Baltimore and, at the urging of General Scott, Secretary of State–designate Seward, and others, agreed to alter his schedule, passing through the city at night and unannounced. But first he visited Independence Hall and, on Washington's birthday, 1861, raised the flag above it and made a short speech on the Declaration of Independence. The Declaration, he said, involved "giving liberty, not alone to the people of this country, but hope to the world for all future time. It . . . gave promise that in due time the weights should be lifted from the shoulders of all men, and that *all* should have an equal chance." He would be the happiest man in the world, he said, if he could save the country and with it this fundamental principle. But if saving the country meant giving up the principle, "I would rather be assassinated on this spot."[56]

Lincoln arrived in Washington on a special train safe but not unscathed, for throughout the country his opponents denied the existence of any "Baltimore plot" and ridiculed him as a coward. The story of his secret entrance into the capital that most embarrassed Lincoln was published in a sympathetic newspaper, the New York *Times*, and written by a reporter, Joseph Howard, Jr., who believed in the reality of the plot. Lacking factual information, Howard simply made up details and described Lincoln as disguising himself in "a Scotch plaid cap and a very long military cloak, so that he was entirely unrecognizable."[57] The fabrication proved an inspiration to cartoonists. Lincoln was variously shown as a Scotsman in kilts dancing a highland fling; as a poltroon fleeing for his life, the ribbon of his cap streaming in the wind behind him; as a faceless figure topped by a cap whose ground-length coat made him look very much like the trunk of a tree; and as a fugitive stealing into the city in a freight car. In the New York *Leader*, a Democratic newspaper, Charles G. Halpine published a poem, "The Night Ride of Ancient Abe," with picturesque elaborations on Howard's story.[58] Nobody appreciated a joke more than Lincoln, but he was the butt of this one, and it was not really funny.

According to Lamon, Lincoln always regretted the way he had "sneaked" into Washington and never again paid much attention to advisers concerned for his safety.[59] "I cannot be shut up in an iron cage and guarded," he snapped at his friend Leonard Swett, who warned him so often against the dangers of exposing himself to potential assassins that it became a sore subject between them.[60] He had no fear of political assassins, Lincoln told Halpine, because the man who would succeed him, Vice-President Hannibal Hamlin of Maine, was at least as objectionable as Lincoln himself to Confederates and Copperheads, and, as far as homicidal maniacs were concerned, well, there was no protection against them anyway.[61]

Threatening letters arrived continuously and in large numbers; Greeley guessed that if he had received 100, Lincoln must have received 10,000.[62] Many of them were vicious in the extreme. One day a gentleman waiting to see Lincoln at the White House observed the secretary, whose duty it was to open the mail, discarding some of it after a quick reading. The visitor objected; Lincoln ought to read the letters addressed to him. The secretary handed him the hate-filled discards. After a few moments, the man threw them on the table and sank back in his chair, speechless with shame and indignation. Finally he caught his breath. "You are right, young man!" he gasped. "You are right! He ought not to see a line of that stuff! Burn it, sir! Burn it! What devils there are!"[63]

Lincoln knew of the letters, of course, but he did not take them seriously. Anyone who really had murderous designs against him, he said, would not inform him of them in advance. If he were in constant fear of his life, he could not hold public receptions or confer with officials at various government offices and Army headquarters; he could not escape the pressures of the White House by afternoon drives about town, or by visits to his cottage on the grounds of the Soldiers' Home just outside of Washington, or by occasional attendance at the theater. He could only die once, he told Secretary of the Navy Gideon Welles, and he was determined "not to suffer from continual apprehension."[64]

During the summer months Lincoln frequently resorted to the Soldiers' Home that General Scott had founded for his Mexican War veterans. The home was high enough to catch a breeze if one was blowing, and there were tall shade trees about the cottage. Though the institution was only three miles beyond the city proper, part of the distance was through open countryside, and there was a dense wood at the edge of the grounds, an ideal spot for sharpshooters or kidnappers to lie in wait. The danger was not imaginary. On one August evening near the home, Lincoln was riding along at a slow gait, deep in thought, when he was suddenly aroused by the firing of a rifle no more than 150 yards away. The shot came so close he could hear the bullet whizzing past him. He spurred his horse and dashed for his cottage, telling Lamon when he arrived breathless and hatless that the firing was probably accidental. Neither he nor Lamon believed it.[65]

By late 1863 the danger from frustrated Lincoln-haters became so intense that Lincoln was forced to accept a military escort on his drives to and from the Soldiers' Home. Accordingly, barracks for a company of Ohio Volunteer Cavalry were built near the White House, and henceforth both of the president's residences were patrolled by armed guards. But since Lincoln often simply slipped away in his carriage without telling anyone, the protection was by no means complete.[66]

For most of the war he had no protection at all during his nighttime walks to the military telegraph office, located in the War Department immediately west of the White House. Just before bedtime, he would come out the front door of the White House, pause for a moment or two in the portico, his tall figure unmistakable under the gas jets, and then slowly proceed alone down a path through the White House grounds to learn the latest news of his troops.[67] Secretary of War Stanton repeatedly scolded the president for this and other acts of foolhardiness, and during the 1864 reelection campaign he finally persuaded Lincoln to accept an official civilian bodyguard on these walks and on other excursions in Washington. Four members of the

Washington Metropolitan Police Force were assigned to this duty.[68]

It is impossible to learn very much about the various anti-Lincoln conspiracies—except the one that succeeded—because they were by nature secret; the conspirators made no public announcements of their plans, postponements, cancellations, and failures. It is also difficult to distinguish real conspiracies from empty boasting and from mere rumors growing out of barroom confidentialities—a problem historians have shared with the men who were close to Lincoln at the time. Warnings of danger were as common as threats of it, and those that seemed worthy of investigation always received it from Lincoln's secretaries, John G. Nicolay and John Hay, or the War Department, but always without result. "Warnings that appeared to be most definite," wrote Nicolay and Hay, "when they came to be examined proved too vague and confused for further attention."[69]

After the war, newspapers and magazines carried innumerable articles about conspiracies against Lincoln by men and women who claimed to have been involved in them or to have known someone who was. It was easy to believe that these plots had existed, for had not one of them, seemingly no different from the others, succeeded? But during the war there was practically nothing in the press to suggest to the public that Lincoln's life was in jeopardy, it being easy to dismiss the diatribes of the most aggressively anti-Lincoln papers as merely extreme examples of a kind of partisanship already familiar in American politics. Furthermore, political kidnappings and murders were such rare crimes in modern history that most people could not imagine that they were truly possibilities. When informed by the U.S. minister in France of plots being formed by Confederates in Europe against the lives of Lincoln and other officials, Secretary of State Seward replied that, while there had been such conspiracies prior to the outbreak of hostilities, he felt there was no longer cause for anxiety. "Assassination," he wrote on July 15, 1864, "is not an American practice or habit, and one so vicious and so desperate cannot be engrafted into our political system. This conviction of mine has steadily gained strength since the civil war begun [sic]. Every day's experience confirms it."[70]

One of the few newspaper stories published during the war about the danger to the president from kidnappers and assassins appeared in Greeley's New York *Tribune,* as part of a series of lengthy dispatches from Washington that the *Tribune* carried beginning in January 1864. The writer's name was withheld (though after Lincoln's death it became familiar enough), but the correspondent identified himself as a Northerner who had been in South Carolina at the beginning of the war. Conscripted into the Confederate service, he was wounded at the battle of South Mountain, Maryland, in mid-September 1862, and was then detailed as a clerk in the War Department in Richmond. While on temporary assignment in November 1863, he altered his travel pass to enable him to reach Gordonsville, Virginia. From there he made his way after dark to a U.S. military unit, and thence to Washington.

Written in an intimate and lively style and full of the details of firsthand observation, the correspondent's letters provided readers with a fascinating look at life and politics within the Confederacy. Among the subjects discussed were the persecution and imprisonment of southern supporters of the Union. Public and private intolerance of those who opposed the Confederate government was so strong, the correspondent reported (perhaps in part to explain his own two-and-one-half-year collaboration), that most men and women still loyal to the United States guarded the secret with their lives.

Another subject discussed in the correspondent's letters was the large number of Confederate spies and agents in the North and the ease with which they travelled back and forth. Often they did it with the unwitting cooperation of the U.S. Army, presenting themselves as refugees at a military outpost, taking oaths of loyalty, and then proceeding about their business unimpeded. To return, they simply travelled to some Union stronghold like Harpers Ferry, took another oath of allegiance under an assumed name, and received a pass from an accommodating provost marshal to go to Berryville or Winchester, Virginia, or another city within reach of Rebel lines, and then waited for an opportunity to cross back into the Confederacy.

By far the most startling of the correspondent's letters, appearing in the *Tribune* on March 19, 1864, described a conspiracy to kidnap Lincoln that was said to have originated in the

Confederate War Department. The key figure was identified as one of the South's leading secret agents, a soldier of fortune who went by the name of Colonel George W. Margrave (or Margrove) but who was reputed to be a member of the Rhett family of South Carolina. According to the correspondent, Margrave spent the early months of 1863 in the North consulting with Copperheads and peace advocates about their prospects and about the possibility of killing or kidnapping Lincoln. Described as "one of the most cool and reckless villains in the Confederacy," Margrave reputedly boasted that he had so many friends in Baltimore he could walk the streets of that city and put up at the best hotels without fear of betrayal.

Late in 1863, the *Tribune* story continued, Margrave submitted a detailed kidnapping plan to Confederate Secretary of War James A. Seddon. Margrave and 150 picked men would go secretly to Washington, Georgetown, Baltimore, and Alexandria and take quarters enabling them to be in touch with each other every day. When Margrave gave the order, they would meet in Washington, seize the president some quiet Sunday, either at the White House or en route to church, thrust him into a closed carriage, and, with fresh horses picked up in relays, dash for a boat on the Potomac. The bulk of Margrave's force would prevent pursuit by blowing up bridges and felling trees across the road.

Though believing the plan might be successful, Secretary Seddon feared it would be against the laws of war and said he would discuss it with President Davis and Secretary of State Judah P. Benjamin. On the day of Margrave's departure for the North, the *Tribune* correspondent said he had asked another clerk, Beverly R. Wellford, Jr., a man who was "familiar with all the secrets of the Department," whether the plan had been adopted. "You will see Old Abe here in the Spring as sure as God," he said Wellford had replied.[71]

Soon after this conversation, the *Tribune's* correspondent made his escape to the North, and he heard no more of Colonel Margrave.

The Democratic press angrily challenged the truth of the *Tribune's* story and denied that Lincoln was in danger from either public or private individuals anywhere. In response, the correspondent published a letter he claimed to have brought with him from Richmond. Addressed to Wellford, and dated September 30, 1863, it was from a young man who signed himself "Cullom." His father had recently been in Richmond, Cullom wrote, and had talked with the president, secretary of war, and other officials. "I inquired of him if he had heard anything of the *ruse de guerre* to capture 'Honest Abe,' and he said he had, but that the affair would probably be managed rather by individual enterprise than by the Government." His father told him the names of the men working on the project—most of them, Cullom was sure, well known to Wellford. "Speak a good word for me at once," Cullom pleaded. "As I told you, I would willingly sell my soul to the devil for the honor of playing a conspicuous part in the destruction of the *great hydra*." As prima facie evidence of the letter's genuineness, the correspondent presented it to Greeley in its original envelope, bearing a ten-cent Confederate stamp and the postmark of the city in which it had been mailed. The editor assured his readers that the document was in his possession as described.[72]

He had lived among the Rebels long enough, the correspondent declared, to know that "there is no atrocity conceivable that they would not unhesitatingly commit, if it promised to aid, in the slightest degree, the infernal work of the Rebellion." They believed their cause to be just, and it was only natural that there should be men who felt justified in serving it in any way.[73] In Richmond, the correspondent continued, some wealthy citizens had formed an organization to raise money for the kidnappers of Lincoln. They had sent out circulars to individuals throughout the Confederacy and had raised "an immense sum." The plan was to obtain a furlough for the guerrilla cavalry leader, John S. Mosby, and let him carry out the capture unofficially. "Whether these schemes have been abandoned," wrote the correspondent, "or whether the kidnappers are only awaiting a favorable opportunity to execute them, remains to be seen; but certain it is that too much caution cannot be observed by the President, or the military commanders stationed at the Capital."

To observe and report on affairs in Canada, the correspondent went to Montreal in October 1864. It was easy for him to pass himself off as a Rebel, for he undeniably knew much about things in Richmond, and he soon gained the confidence of some of the southern agents. In one of the dispatches he sent secretly to the *Tribune,* he warned that every town from Quebec to Windsor was crowded with hot-headed Confederates and that additional St. Albans–type raids across the border could be expected. This warning—and others—was promptly transmitted to authorities in Washington.[74]

In 1866 the correspondent was exposed as a perjuror and sentenced to prison. Everything he wrote and said is therefore suspect. Yet his descriptions of conditions in the South and in Canada were not only credible but convincing, and his warnings about the danger to Lincoln only too well justified. If there is little doubt that Colonel Margrave and volunteer Cullom were fictional characters, there is none at all about the existence of kidnapping conspiracies remarkably like the one attributed to Margrave. Whatever the correspondent's past and future crimes, his wartime letters to the *Tribune* have the ring of truth.

The northern public was only dimly aware of it, but Lincoln was in grave danger throughout the war from partisans of the Confederacy. Rebel soldiers, seeing him as the major obstacle to the South's achievement of independence, volunteered to serve their country by killing him. Confederate Secretary of War Seddon told one volunteer that his department discouraged such proposals, clearly indicating that he had received others. At least two soldiers, one of whom was said to be a Yankee serving in a Georgia regiment, wrote to Davis directly to offer their services in disposing of Lincoln and other northern leaders. Davis referred both letters to the secretary of war. One of them, with its presidential endorsement, was discovered among Confederate records after the war and was thought to prove that Davis sanctioned political assassinations. Davis denied it.[75]

As the dispatches of the New York *Tribune's* correspondent revealed, southern civilians also sought to bring about Lincoln's death. In Selma, Alabama, in December 1864, one George Washington Gayle placed an advertisement in the local newspaper. If the people of the Confederacy would raise $1,000,000 for him, Gayle stated, he would agree to kill Lincoln, Seward, and Vice-President-elect Johnson by the following March 1. "This will give us peace and satisfy the world that cruel tyrants cannot live in a 'land of liberty.'" For starters, Gayle pledged $1,000 to the fund himself. Other southern newspapers also carried advertisements placing a price on Lincoln's head.[76]

Some Confederate military commanders, as well as individual soldiers and civilians, were interested in the possibilities of action against the political leadership of the United States. Shortly after Lincoln's first inauguration, the Texas Ranger Ben McCulloch considered making a sweep into Washington—still only lightly defended—with five hundred men, to carry off the president and members of his cabinet.[77] Such a raid would have had a good chance of success in March 1861, but it was not attempted; hostilities between the sections had not yet broken out, and such an extreme action would have been unjustifiable.

Circumstances were very different by 1863. During the winter months of 1863–64 Colonel Bradley T. Johnson, a Confederate partisan from Maryland, worked out a plan to load his battalion of Maryland cavalry across the Potomac above Georgetown (where the South had many friends), circle both Georgetown and Washington from the north, capture Lincoln at the Soldiers' Home, and continue in an arc to the east and south through Maryland to Virginia, avoiding Washington and its major defenses altogether. After the war, it was said that this plan had had the enthusiastic approval of Johnson's commanding officer, General Wade Hampton, who had been tempted to lead the operation himself at the head of a much larger force. Neither officer had been able to undertake the mission, however, for in June 1864, when Johnson had hoped to execute his plan, their forces were required to assist Jubal Early in the defense of Lynchburg, and another opportunity did not arise.[78]

Thomas N. Conrad, a southern spy who operated a signal station on the Potomac and frequently ventured into Washington to pick up information, developed a plan to kidnap Lincoln en route to the Soldiers' Home, rush him above the city into lower Maryland, and deliver him to Mosby in Virginia. In two postwar books and a newspaper article, Conrad claimed not only to have had the official approval of Secretary Seddon, but to have received a letter from him, dated September 15, 1864, ordering Mosby to give Conrad his fullest cooperation. In the second book, however, a few pages after quoting Seddon's letter, Conrad inexplicably stated, "Neither President Davis nor his Secretary of War had any knowledge of my contemplated attempt to capture Mr. Lincoln." Whether they did or not, it seems unlikely that Conrad, a valued southern officer with important contacts in Richmond, would have gathered a group of men about him and alerted Rebel agents along his expected route of flight—as he said he had—without some kind of encouragement from someone in authority.[79] Conrad abandoned his plan when the cavalry unit began to accompany Lincoln to the Soldiers' Home.

Although these and other kidnapping schemes appear to have been seriously conceived and to have had at least the possibility of success, many plans for capturing Lincoln and taking him to Richmond as a hostage must have been childishly unrealistic or proposed in a spirit of empty braggadocio. Davis later stated that during the war he had talked to only one would-be kidnapper who he believed really intended to do what he said. The man was a kinsman, Walker Taylor of Kentucky, a cousin of Davis's first wife. A specialist in undercover operations on the staff of General Simon Buckner, another Confederate Kentuckian, Taylor was wounded in the face and neck at Fort Donelson in February 1862. Recovering, he made his way in civilian clothes through Union lines to his home outside Louisville. He then boldly took a train to Washington, where he had relatives in the service of the U.S. government, including an uncle, General Joseph Taylor, with whom he stayed. The general was decidedly nervous while his reckless nephew was in town, but he was ignorant of the younger man's true purpose: the kidnapping of Lincoln, an idea that had occurred to him during his convalescence. Walker Taylor not only attended a public reception at the White House but also introduced himself to the president as "Mr. Taylor, of Kentucky." Observing that he had been wounded, Lincoln asked him at what battle and then proceeded to compliment the performance of the Union troops at Fort Donelson. Taylor remained in town for some days, watching the president's comings and goings, and then early in the summer of 1862 he quietly left for Richmond to see Davis.

He could bring Lincoln to Richmond, Taylor told the Confederate president over breakfast, "just as easily as I can walk over your doorstep." He would collect some of the Kentuckians he had seen in town, Taylor explained, capture Lincoln en route to the Soldiers' Home, and carry him to the Potomac at the point where he himself had recently crossed. Davis turned him down. Lincoln was a western man, he reminded Taylor, and would resist being captured. "In that case you would kill him. I could not stand the imputation of having consented to let Mr. Lincoln be assassinated. Our cause could not stand it." Besides, what good would Lincoln be as a prisoner? He was not the same as the government of the United States. If brought to Richmond, he would have to be treated as a head of state, and Davis had neither the time nor the facilities to entertain him as such. "No sir, I will not give my authority to abduct Lincoln."[80]

Davis recalled this incident after the war, when he could hardly have said anything but that he had rejected the idea of kidnapping Lincoln. But it is probable he was reporting truly his wartime attitude. As a war leader Davis was conservative and conventional, unlikely to have been attracted to so daring and radical an enterprise. He would have recognized, too, that the abduction of the president of the United States—even if it could be accomplished without injury to his person—would be strongly disapproved by the European heads of state whose active support the Confederacy hoped desperately to receive. Political leaders do not look kindly upon acts of violence against political leaders.

Still, strong suspicions that top Confederate leaders were involved in a kidnapping conspiracy have been raised by recent investigations, and in at least one matter Davis did break away from the conventional laws and practices of war. On August 21, 1862, he authorized a Confederate War Department order specifying that U.S. General David Hunter and all other officers who drilled, organized, or instructed slaves with a view to using them as soldiers were to be considered outlaws. If captured, they were not to be treated like prisoners-of-war but held for execution as felons.[81]

Denounced as an outrage in the North, Davis's order was a reflection of the near-hysterical reaction of southern whites to the intentions of the U.S. government—foretold by General Hunter—to recruit slaves for the Army. To white Southerners, the use of slave soldiers was an unconscionable violation of the laws of warfare and was seen as a deliberate attempt to bring about what the South most feared—a massive slave rebellion that would cause the slaughter of thousands of women and children. As Lincoln had been warned by Democrats and conservative Republicans, his racial policies did unite many Southerners in an unwavering determination to resist.

No policy of the Confederate government—not even the "outlaw" order—was capable of arousing in the North so extreme an emotional reaction as Lincoln's program of freeing and arming the slaves produced in the South. One must believe, therefore, that there were many more potential assassins and kidnappers of Lincoln among supporters of the Confederacy than there were of Davis among supporters of the Union. Certainly there is little evidence of serious anti-Davis conspiracies. But one incident that may have indicated the existence of such a conspiracy and that had serious repercussions was the Kilpatrick-Dahlgren raid on Richmond in early March 1864.

With Robert E. Lee's army still in winter camp, the city of Richmond was a tempting target for a Yankee cavalry raid that could destroy railroads and other facilities and liberate Union prisoners-of-war. Accordingly, an expedition under the command of General Hugh Judson Kilpatrick departed for the Rebel capital on February 28. Although it reached the outskirts of the city, the expedition was beaten back. One of the U.S. casualties was Colonel Ulric Dahlgren, leader of a detached force that was supposed to enter Richmond from the south at the same time that Kilpatrick entered it from the north. Among the papers found on Dahlgren's body were notes for a speech he had prepared for delivery to the cavalrymen he expected to lead through the streets of the city. "Jeff. Davis and Cabinet must be killed on the spot," Dahlgren had written. "The men must keep together and well in hand, and once in the city it must be destroyed and Jeff. Davis and Cabinet killed."[82]

When he heard of the Yankee effrontery, Davis laughed; "easier said than done," he seemed to have felt. But Lee took the matter more seriously and recommended publication of the Dahlgren document so "that our people & the world may know the character of the war our enemies wage against us, & the unchristian & atrocious acts they plot & perpetrate."[83]

Dahlgren's notes caused a sensation in the South. General George Meade, under whose command Kilpatrick and Dahlgren had served, forwarded to Lee a note from Kilpatrick repudiating what Dahlgren had written, and Meade himself assured

Confederate authorities that neither he nor the U.S. government sanctioned the kind of warfare indicated in the speech. If the document was authentic, the intention to kill Davis and the others had originated with the dead colonel. Privately to his wife, however, Meade admitted, "I regret to say Kilpatrick's reputation and collateral evidence in my possession, rather go against this theory."[84] Meade apparently suspected that Kilpatrick and Dahlgren had intended all along to burn the capital and murder the leaders of the Confederacy.

Few friends of the South doubted it, and many were certain that the already much-hated president of the United States was himself responsible. There must have been more than one angry Confederate who resolved that if the opportunity arose he would dispose of the man who had taken so many lives and caused so much misery. Why should not Lincoln himself become a victim of the war he had chosen to wage against the South, a total war, a war without rules or mercy? .

2

"Sic Semper Tyrannis!"

Mᴀʀᴄʜ 4, 1865, Iɴᴀᴜɢᴜʀᴀᴛɪᴏɴ Dᴀʏ, was damp and un-
pleasant in Washington, but the political atmosphere was not as
menacing as it had been four years before. Then the capital had
been full of the enemies of the new Republican administration—and surrounded by them, too—and only a few hundred
regular Army soldiers and a few more hundred volunteers were
on hand to provide protection. Now there were so many soldiers within and around the city that it had the appearance of an
armed camp. Still, there were the predictable rumors that Lincoln would not live to retake his oath of office, that the ceremonies at the Capitol would mark an end, not a beginning.

The danger was real, for only the previous month Lincoln had
once again outraged Copperheads and peace advocates by scut-
tling a peace conference—this one at Hampton Roads, Virginia,
attended by a delegation of Confederate officials led by Vice-
President Alexander H. Stephens. As he had the previous July
when the Confederates at Niagara Falls had sought to end the
war by peaceful negotiation, Lincoln refused to consider peace
or even a temporary armistice except on his own terms: Union
and the abolition of slavery. Lincoln's refusal to abandon these
terms came as no surprise to Jefferson Davis, but it provided
the Confederate president with another opportunity to tell his
people that the only alternative to submission to Lincoln's will
was rededication to the goal of independence through military
victory.[1]

The obvious security precautions were taken during the inaugural ceremonies conducted at the crowded east front of the
Capitol. In addition to the president's military escort, members
of the Metropolitan Police held off the crowds along Pennsyl-

vania Avenue, and soldiers, mounted and afoot, paraded up the muddy streets along with the official carriages and floats. Other soldiers mingled in the crowd looking for suspicious individuals, and the military forces guarding the bridges leading into the city were reinforced.[2] A ruckus occurred in the Capitol rotunda when a man attempted to follow the president's party out the east door to the inaugural platform. The man was intercepted and held back by a policeman after a severe struggle. Later, when John Wilkes Booth's picture was widely disseminated, the policeman claimed that the man had been Booth; he was thereupon promoted for having saved Lincoln's life at the inauguration.[3] Booth was indeed present at the inaugural ceremonies, but it is unlikely that he was involved in this incident.

In his Inaugural Address Lincoln recalled the situation four years before. Neither section had wanted war in 1861, he said, "but one of them would make war rather than let the nation survive; and the other would accept war rather than let it perish." That was how things looked to the Unionists. To Confederates and to northern opponents of military action, it was the North that made war and the South that accepted it.

Toward the end of his speech, Lincoln prayed "that this mighty scourge of war may speedily pass away."

His prayer was soon answered. On March 23 he boarded the steam yacht *River Queen*, sailed down the Potomac to Chesapeake Bay, and up the James River to City Point, Virginia, some ten miles from Petersburg. For months General Ulysses S. Grant had been besieging Petersburg, essential to the defense of Richmond, and now he expected General Robert E. Lee to evacuate it at any time. Lee did so on April 3, and the same day Lincoln followed the U.S. soldiers in.[4]

Secretary of War Edwin M. Stanton was dismayed at such recklessness. "Allow me respectfully to ask you," he telegraphed, upon learning of the president's intentions, "to consider whether you ought to expose the nation to the consequences of any disaster to yourself in the pursuit of a treacherous and dangerous enemy like the rebel army. . . . Commanding generals are in the line of their duty in running such risks; but is the political head of a nation in the same condition?" Lincoln thanked him for his concern and said he expected to visit Richmond the next day. "I will take care of myself," he added.[5]

On April 4, just one month after his second inauguration, Lincoln entered Richmond. Towering above his tiny escort of six sailors in front and six behind, and accompanied only by two officers, his son Tad, and William H. Crook, one of his police bodyguards, the president of the United States walked through the streets of the Rebel capital to the Confederate White House. Most of the whites who watched him pass, uncertain what fate would befall them, were silent, but the blacks, now free—though slaves the day before—beheld their deliverer and greeted him with cheers and tears. Some of those closest knelt before him. "Don't kneel to me," Lincoln told them, somewhat testily. "You must kneel to God only and thank him for your freedom." He shook some of the outstretched black hands and then disappeared into the home that had been Davis's.[6] "Never in the history of the world," wrote his secretaries John G. Nicolay and John Hay, "did the head of a mighty nation and the conquerer of a great rebellion enter the captured chief city of the insurgents in such humbleness and simplicity."[7]

But Lincoln's entrance into Richmond did not seem humble to everyone. Those who hated Lincoln were infuriated by the spectacle of his being received like a god in the capital of the country he had ruined. Asia Booth Clarke believed that her younger brother, John Wilkes Booth, had been reconciled to the South's impending defeat, but that Lincoln's "triumphant entry into the fallen city (which was not magnanimous), breathed fresh air upon the fire which consumed him."[8]

A week later, on April 11, Booth became further inflamed. Standing in a crowd at the White House listening to Lincoln speak on Reconstruction, he heard the president state that he favored enfranchising intelligent (i.e., literate) southern black men and those who were serving in the Union armies. Booth turned to one of his two companions, a man of several aliases then being called Lewis Paine, and urged him to shoot Lincoln on the spot. Naturally, Paine declined. "That means nigger citizenship," Booth said in disgust to his other companion, David Herold. "Now, by God, I'll put him through." As the three men walked away, Booth muttered, "That is the last speech he will ever make."[9]

The fifth of the six children of Junius Brutus Booth and Mary

Ann Holmes who survived to maturity, John Wilkes Booth was born May 10, 1838, on the family farm near Bel Air, Maryland, twenty miles from Baltimore. He was named for a man much admired by his father, John Wilkes, the eighteenth-century English political agitator and reformer. Wilkes championed the cause of the American colonies against the rule of George III and acted as English representative of a revolutionary society formed in Boston, the Sons of Liberty. Young John Wilkes Booth was raised to respect the ideals of liberty and opposition to tyranny with which his namesake was identified.[10] It cannot be definitely stated that he became a member of the Copperhead organization, the Sons of Liberty, but he certainly felt an affinity for its objectives and may have taken pride in his namesake's association with its name.

Booth grew up with the tastes of a southern aristocrat on the farm, where a substantial house known as "Tudor Hall" was eventually built, and where there were barns, stables, slave quarters, even a pond for swimming, and in Baltimore, where the family customarily spent the winters in a comfortable two-story dwelling on Exeter Street.[11] He maintained the proper condescension toward slaves and was reluctant to eat at the same table even with white hired hands. He looked down upon foreigners, too, especially ignorant Irishmen, and attended secret meetings of the nativist American (or Know-Nothing) party.[12] Future generations of Americans would have difficulty reconciling such attitudes with Booth's commitment to liberty, but in the mid-nineteenth century liberty had not yet melded with equality, except in the abstract.

Booth's father, born in London, had come to the United States in 1821 and, by the time of his death, was one of the country's best known actors and its leading tragedian. John Wilkes, unlike his older brothers, Junius Brutus, Jr., and Edwin, had been too young to receive professional guidance from his father and never appeared on the stage with him. But from the senior Booth he inherited a rare dramatic talent. Edwin, who went on to a career that surpassed even his father's in distinction, believed that his younger brother could have made "a brilliant mark in the theatrical world."[13]

Booth's first theatrical tour as a star took him through the South to Montgomery, Alabama, during the fall of 1860. Packed theaters and favorable notices followed him from town to town, encouraging him in the hope that he was indeed his father's son and reaffirming his attachment to Southerners and Southern institutions.[14] The tour ended in time for him to join several members of his family for Christmas in Philadelphia. His sister Asia lived there in an old mansion with her husband, John Sleeper Clarke, an actor who specialized in comedy and who was then both the manager of the Arch Street Theater and one of its stars. His mother and another sister, the reclusive Rosalie, were staying nearby in a house rented by Edwin. Already nationally recognized as an actor, Edwin was in Philadelphia for performances in *Macbeth* and *Henry VIII* at the Academy of Music.[15]

It could not have been a very merry Christmas season for the Booths, for like other families they were divided on political matters, and during that secession winter political matters were difficult to repress. Edwin and John later opposed each other's views so strongly that Edwin forbade political discussions when John visited his home in New York. But it is likely that at this time they were still exchanging opinions, and it is safe to assume that John expressed his with the same extravagant fervency that characterized his appearances on the stage. Edwin later recalled that the family used to laugh at John's "patriotic froth" on the subject of secession,[16] but he was probably speaking only of himself, for John was the darling of his mother and sisters. They might have disagreed with him, as Asia did, but they would not have laughed at him.

Booth's "patriotic froth" might have been amusing to an older brother, but there was nothing funny about his political views, which, it will be seen, were shared by millions of Americans in both sections. Sometime between the secession of the first state, South Carolina, on December 20, 1860, and the secession of the second, Mississippi, on January 7, 1861, Booth wrote down his political beliefs in the form of an address to Philadelphians unfriendly to the South, though he probably had Edwin in mind. A rambling first draft, the speech runs to fourteen closely written manuscript pages, with four additional pages of material to be inserted at marked places within the text. In addition, there are three extra pages of fragments and paragraphs that he may or may not have wished to use. It is unlikely that the speech was ever publicly presented, but writing it must have helped him in his arguments with his brother.[17] More important to readers of our day, the speech, even briefly summarized, shows how completely Booth fit into the southern side of the tragic and irreconcilable division in America that caused well-meaning patriots in both sections to consider their adversaries to be traitors.

For Booth the crisis was a struggle between those who would uphold the Constitution and those who would overthrow it. South Carolina's rights under the Constitution were being swept away, and its secession was therefore justified. Any attempt by the abolitionists who controlled the government at Washington to use force against it would be an act of tyranny worse than any committed by George III and would unite the South in a patriotic defense of states' rights. It was not slavery that threatened the Union, for the fathers of the country, better Christians and men of sounder judgment than any leaders presently in power, had approved of the institution and had considered it a blessing for everyone, slave and free. What threatened the Union was the prolonged and abusive attack on slavery by the abolitionist traitors, who sought to achieve their objective by creating a centralized despotism in place of the union of equal states established by the Constitution. The disunion being forced upon the South in defense of sacred principles would not be peaceful; Daniel Webster himself had said so. It would be accompanied by misery and desolation for the whole country, and, even if it were possible for the North to force the South back into the Union, would that be a cause worth the sacrifice of equal rights, of justice, of the Constitution? Booth could not believe that the people would permit it. Surely they would rally to the support of the Union as it was, the Union the fathers had made, the Union God had blessed![18]

At one point in his speech, Booth, speaking as a loyal citizen cautioning Philadelphians against supporting the unconstitutional policies of the abolitionists, referred to himself as "of the North." Sometime later, perhaps when Lincoln's call to arms after Fort Sumter heralded war, he came to think of himself as "of the South." It was not a switch of loyalty or allegiance, for Booth remained steadfast in his devotion to what he believed were the true principles of the American Union. As he and others "of the South" saw it, the abolitionist-consolidationists who had forced the southern states to secede to protect their constitutional rights were the real disunionists and traitors. The only way to preserve the Union established by the Founding Fathers was to stop the Republicans from destroying it.

Between 1861 and 1864 Booth's dramatic career was meteoric. He travelled extensively and almost continuously throughout the North, and to New Orleans and Canada as well, appearing in most of the major cities and in many minor ones and achieving a reputation and popularity to rival Edwin's. "It was the harvest time for theaters," wrote Asia,[19] for the public craved entertainment and could afford to pay for it, and Booth enjoyed an income of over $20,000 a year. Despite his success in the North, he continued to be outspoken in his defense of the South. When asked why he did not fight for it, he often answered that he had promised his mother he would not.[20]

But there is evidence to suggest that he did fight for it, though not in uniform. Early in the war, in an effort to prevent or impede the passage of northern soldiers through their state to Washington, Maryland partisans of the Confederacy destroyed railroad bridges and engaged in other acts of sabotage. With the writ of habeas corpus suspended, U.S. military authorities imprisoned hundreds of Marylanders, possibly including Booth. In October 1861 a newspaper listed the names of ten prisoners who had been released upon taking loyalty oaths, among them one John Wilkes.[21]

In late April or early May 1862 Booth was arrested in St. Louis for having said, according to the provost marshal before whom he was taken, "he wished the whole damned Government would go to hell, or something to that effect." A great many people were saying far worse about the government without being arrested, and in this instance it is likely that Booth was under special surveillance because of his relationship to the actress Blanche DeBar Booth, daughter of Junius Brutus Booth, Jr., and her maternal uncle Ben DeBar, who managed theaters in St. Louis and New Orleans in which Booth played. The DeBars (Blanche did not use the name Booth on stage) were known as "enthusiastic" and "violent" in their pro-Confederate views; the provost marshal stated that he himself had heard Blanche DeBar declare it would be right to kill Lincoln. It therefore seems likely that the military watched the DeBars closely and that officials were especially sensitive to the comments of their friends and relatives.[22]

Sometime later, while talking to Asia in her Philadelphia home, Booth exclaimed, "So help me holy God! my soul, life, and possessions are for the South." When Asia asked him why, then, he did not fight for it, Booth made no reference to having promised his mother he would not. Instead, according to his sister, he told her that he was fighting for it with his money, his knowledge of drugs, and his ability to move freely throughout the North making important contacts. He was, he confided in her, a spy, a smuggler of information and medicine into the South. Quinine was in particular demand, and Booth was proud that he knew where to get higher quality batches of it than were being used in northern hospitals. He was so successful in smuggling quinine, he said, that his Rebel friends sometimes called him "Doctor."[23] After the hasty evacuation of Richmond in April 1865, a book containing a record of letters received by the Confederate War Department was discovered. An entry for November 9, 1864, listed receipt of a letter from "Doctor J. W. Booth."[24]

Booth called frequently at Asia's home during the war, often sleeping in his clothing on a couch downstairs. Men called at late hours. From upstairs, Asia thought she could recognize the voices of some of them, but they would not reply when she called. Others she was sure were complete strangers, and all spoke quietly or in whispers. Once when Asia commented upon how rough her brother's hands were, he muttered something about nights of rowing.[25]

In June 1864 Booth's oldest brother, Junius Brutus Booth, Jr., returned to the East from California, where he had spent most of his time since 1852 as an actor and impresario. He was shocked to find John Wilkes so sympathetic to the South and talked to him at great length about it. The younger Booth was grateful for the attention, for his brother Edwin and brother-in-law John Sleeper Clarke considered him a monomaniac on this sensitive subject and not worth talking to. But Junius was unable to bring political peace to the Booth family, which gathered occasionally at Edwin's home on East 19th Street, New York, and in August 1864 a particularly severe quarrel took place.[26]

The argument may have begun over the failure of the Niagara Peace Conference in July. A document later found in Booth's handwriting proved that he was one of the many people who blamed that failure on Lincoln's obstinacy and bad faith. Perhaps the brothers fought over the forthcoming presidential election, in which Edwin was supporting Lincoln. John, on the other hand, believed Lincoln's appearance, his coarse jokes and vulgar similes, and his frivolous character were a disgrace to his office, and that he was a mere tool of the abolitionist fanatics who were trying to destroy slavery by "robbery, rapine, slaughter and bought armies." If reelected, John told Asia, Lincoln would overthrow the Constitution and become king of America. "You'll see—you'll see," he cried, "that *reelection* means *succession*."[27]

It was probably about the time of this quarrel, and possibly as a direct result of it, that Booth decided whatever he was doing for the Confederacy as an occasional spy and smuggler of quinine was not enough. The North was strangling the South, he believed, not because of superior pluck or devotion, but because of the advantage derived from its armies of foreign mercenaries, chiefly Irish.[28] If a way could be found to release the Confederate soldiers languishing in northern prisoner-of-war camps, it would cancel out the North's superiority of manpower and be tantamount to assuring victory and independence for the Confederacy. Like other Confederates and Copperheads who played with the idea, Booth decided he would attempt to kidnap the president of the United States, demanding for ransom the release of the prisoners. With assistance, he could intercept Lincoln on one of his trips to the Soldiers' Home and rush him across the Eastern Branch Bridge and through southern Maryland to the lower Potomac, where a boat would be waiting, and on to Richmond.

Over wine and cigars in a room at Barnum's Hotel in Baltimore, in late August or early September 1864, Booth convinced two boyhood friends, Samuel B. Arnold and Michael O'Laughlin—both of whom had served a time in the Confederate Army before making their ways behind Union lines—that the plan was not only easily executed but also that it was humane and patriotic in its object, devoid of selfish personal ambition, and legitimate as an act of war. Solemnly, the three men shook hands, and Arnold and O'Laughlin swore never to speak of the project to a living soul.[29]

It was no idle fancy for Booth. Late in September he disposed of the Pennsylvania oil leases in which he had speculated, dividing them among Junius, one of his sisters, and Joseph H. Simonds, his business agent. He found them distracting, Booth told Simonds, and he wanted to be able to concentrate on his profession.[30] The next month he went to Montreal, taking most of his theatrical wardrobe with him, though he did not intend to give a performance.[31]

Booth spent the night of October 18, 1864, at St. Lawrence Hall, Montreal, headquarters for Jacob Thompson and others of the Confederate representatives in Canada, and then took a room on a back street nearby.[32] Testimony that he was seen in intimate conversation with the Rebel agents is not altogether reliable,[33] but it would have been strange indeed had he not contacted these men. After all, he had a plan to kidnap Lincoln and take him to Richmond, a coup that might win the war for the Confederacy. It seems unlikely that he would have failed to acquaint them, perhaps in guarded terms, with what he intended to do, and to ask their approval and help. It seems equally unlikely that these leaders, who were perhaps less sensitive than their president to infractions upon the laws of war and whose mission in Canada was to stir up trouble within the United States, would have refused to listen to Booth. Of course, it does not follow that they agreed to help him. It cannot be proved that they gave him the names of people in southern Maryland and northern Virginia who would be sympathetic. But somebody did, for Booth knew exactly where to go and whom to meet in the region through which he hoped to escort Lincoln.

Before returning to the United States, Booth opened an account at the Ontario Bank of Montreal—the bank in which Thompson's money was deposited—and bought a bill of exchange for a little over sixty-one pounds. He also made arrangements to have his theatrical wardrobe shipped to Nassau; from there it would be run through the Union blockade and be waiting for him at Richmond when he himself arrived.[34] The trunk never made it, and neither did he.

Back in New York about November 1, Booth purchased carbines, revolvers, cartridges, belts and caps, canteens, and handcuffs, and took them to Baltimore. There he turned most of them over to Arnold and O'Laughlin to be taken to Washington.[35]

In late November 1864, three or four weeks after his return from Canada, Booth stopped at Asia's home in Philadelphia and left her a packet to be locked away in her safe. He had done this several times in the past before setting out on trips, explaining the envelope contained stock and other personal papers. On this particular visit he attempted to show her a cipher, by which she understood him to mean the official Confederate code; but she refused to look at it. She did not want that kind of information, she told him. As he handed her the packet, he told her that if anything should happen to him, she should open it alone. He watched her put it in the safe, kissed her tenderly, and left.[36]

When the time came, Asia followed her brother's instructions. Inside the packet she found bonds, stocks, and coupons designated for different members of the family, and, among other letters, one apparently intended for her husband and another addressed to her mother.

The long letter for Clarke, dated only "1864," was a defense of the southern cause and of what Booth was now planning to do to serve it. Although he told his brother-in-law he could do whatever he thought best with the letter, Booth obviously intended it for publication. He therefore addressed it "(in the words of your master) 'To Whom It May Concern,'" the phrase Lincoln had used in his letter to the Confederate commissioners at Niagara Falls the previous July—the letter that had so abruptly terminated that Confederate effort to win peace and independence.

"The very nomination of Abraham Lincoln four years ago," Booth's letter began, "spoke plainly war—war upon Southern rights and institutions. His election proved it. . . . In a *foreign* war, I, too, could say, 'Country, right or wrong.' But in a struggle *such as ours* (where the brother tries to pierce the brother's heart), for God's sake choose the right. When a country like this spurns *justice* from her side she forfeits the allegiance of every honest freeman and should leave him, untrammelled by any fealty soever, to act as his conscience may approve. People of the North, to hate tyranny, to love liberty and justice, to strike at wrong and oppression, was the teaching of our fathers. The study of our early history will not let me forget it, and may it never.

"This country was formed for the *white*, not for the black man," the letter went on. "And looking upon *African* slavery from the same standpoint held by the noble framers of our Constitution, I, for one, have ever considered it one of the greatest blessings (both for themselves and for us) that God ever bestowed upon a favored nation. Witness heretofore our wealth and power; witness their elevation and enlightenment above their race elsewhere."

In the next paragraph Booth referred to John Brown, at whose execution in 1859 he was present (though he was not present at Brown's capture, as he later claimed). "I thought then, *as now*, that the Abolitionists were the *only traitors* in the land and that the entire party deserved the same fate as poor old Brown, not because they wished to abolish slavery, but on account of the means they have ever endeavored to use to effect that abolition. . . . The South can make no choice. It is either extermination or slavery for *themselves* (worse than death) to draw from. I know *my* choice. I have also studied hard to know upon what grounds the right of a State to secede has been denied, when our very name, United States, and the Declaration of Independence, *both* provide for secession.

"But there is no time for words. . . . My love (as things stand today) is for the South alone. Nor do I deem it a dishonor in attempting to make for her a prisoner of this man, to whom she owes so much of misery."

Booth signed the letter, "A Confederate, At present doing duty *upon his own responsibility*," but then crossed out the words "At present," perhaps because he expected never to seek or receive official authorization, perhaps simply because he wanted to give the impression he would never seek or receive it.[37]

In the letter to his mother enclosed in the same packet, Booth assured her of his deep love for her. Though he wanted to be a dutiful son, he told her, he had another duty, "a noble duty for the sake of liberty and humanity due to my country." For four years he had suffered the torment and frustration of keeping his thoughts to himself, and "even in my own home constantly hearing every principle dear to my heart denounced as treasonable." He had cursed his idleness, Booth wrote in a passage that suggests Asia may have exaggerated his services to the Confederacy as a spy and smuggler, and had begun "to deem myself a coward and to despise my own existence. . . . I have borne it mostly for your dear sake," he told his mother, "and for you alone have I also struggled to fight off this desire to be gone [from the North]." But a fate over which he had no control now "takes me from you dear mother, to do what I can for a poor oppressed downtrodden people. . . . I care not for the censure of the north. [Just] So I have your forgiveness, and [I] feel I may hope it, even though you differ with me in opinion."[38]

Booth was in and out of Washington during the winter. There was a shooting gallery on Pennsylvania at 11th Street, and he went there frequently. "He shot well," the proprietor remembered, and "practiced to shoot with accuracy in every possible position." He was often accompanied by two men, but he was always "*the* man." An actor friend said he was "a dead shot."[39] He made several trips into southern Maryland, ostensibly to buy horses and land, but in reality to scout out the area and to establish his contacts.

Most of the people of lower Maryland were, in fact, devoted Confederates trapped within the United States by the fact that the Potomac flowed to the south of them instead of to the north. They were left largely to themselves, for the area was without strategic importance. They were thus free to maintain contact with their southern countrymen and to conspire against the United States. It was later revealed that many people in the region had heard of a plot to kidnap Lincoln—Booth's plot or someone else's—and that a number of citizens kept boats in readiness along the river and its tributaries for the possible use of the kidnappers.[40]

One of Booth's contacts in lower Maryland was Dr. Samuel A. Mudd, the thirty-one-year-old son of a wealthy landowner in Charles County. Mudd drove Booth about the countryside, introduced him to a neighbor from whom the actor bought a one-eyed horse, and entertained him in his home overnight.[41] The two men met again in Washington on December 23, when Mudd introduced Booth to John Harrison Surratt, who became Booth's closest associate in the abduction conspiracy.[42]

Only the month before, Surratt had moved to the capital with his sister, Anna, and his widowed mother, Mary E. Surratt, from the little crossroads community ten miles south known as Surrattsville. There, in the early 1850s, Surratt's father had built a tavern and hostelry, and there he served as U.S. postmaster until his death in 1862. The senior Surratt was "an impetuous Southerner," wrote Confederate spy Thomas N. Conrad, "full of intense prejudice and hate toward the Yankees—as was almost everybody in lower Maryland—outspoken in his convictions, and proud of every Southern victory."[43]

Conrad stopped often at the Surratt tavern on his trips between Washington and his signal station on the Potomac, and so did many other Rebel spies, agents, scouts, and blockade runners. For the tavern was designated by the Signal Corps of the Confederate Army as an official station on one of the secret lines of communication established between Richmond and Washington.[44] Following her husband's death, Mary E. Surratt operated the establishment. In the fall of 1864 she leased the tavern to John M. Lloyd, and on November 1 moved into a house she owned on H Street in Washington and took in boarders. Her elder son, Isaac, was a soldier in the Confederate Army, and twenty-one-year-old John had had three years' experience as a Confederate dispatch carrier by the time he met Booth. He embraced Booth's kidnapping scheme with the double enthusiasm of youth and southern patriotism. "It seemed," he later remembered, "as if I could not do too much or run too great a risk."[45]

Booth called frequently at the Surratt boardinghouse to consult privately with Surratt and, at times, with Mrs. Surratt as well. Anna and a young woman boarder were excited by their acquaintance with the handsome actor and bought pictures of him at a downtown gallery. "When my brother saw them," Anna said later, "he told me to tear them up and throw them in the fire, and that, if I did not, he would take them from me." But Anna did not dispose of the portraits; instead, she hid them behind an innocuous picture that had been given her as a present by another of the boarders, Louis J. Weichmann. An Army officer found them there. Although Surratt's instructions to his sister showed that he was aware of the danger involved in his association with Booth, he continued to expose his family to it by receiving Booth often and warmly in his mother's home.[46] Also received were Confederate spies, smugglers, and dispatch carriers, who found the Surratt boardinghouse to be much the same kind of "safe house" within Washington as the Surratt tavern had been outside it.[47]

It was not difficult for Booth and Surratt to find men to help them carry out their kidnapping conspiracy. George A. Atzerodt was a German-born carriage painter who kept at least one boat at Port Tobacco, Maryland, on the Potomac; David E. Herold, unemployed, knew equally well the streets and alleys of Washington and the roads of southern Maryland; and Lewis Paine (real name Lewis Powell), was a Confederate veteran who had been serving with Mosby's Rangers. He called Booth "Captain," and would follow him anywhere.[48] No doubt other individuals knew all or something about Booth's plans—two actor friends, John Mathews and Samuel K. Chester, whom Booth had sought unsuccessfully to recruit; Mrs. Surratt; Weichmann, who worked as a clerk in the War Department's Commissary of Prisoners office; and others known and unknown. But only Booth, Arnold, O'Laughlin, Surratt, Atzerodt, Herold, and Paine can be said with certainty to have been active members of the abduction plot.

Although all of the conspirators with the exception of Arnold and O'Laughlin were occasional or frequent visitors at the Surratt boardinghouse, the only time they met together as a group was in mid-March 1865, when Booth entertained them at a midnight oyster dinner in a private room at Gautier's, a fashionable restaurant on Pennsylvania Avenue. At this meeting Booth presented the absurd idea of seizing Lincoln in his box at Ford's Theater, handcuffing him, lowering him to the darkened stage, and spiriting him out the back door. Faced with the unanimous and vociferous opposition of his friends, he had no choice but to back down and return to the original plan of capturing the president on the open road.[49]

Soon afterward, in the afternoon of March 17, Booth was told that the president was going to attend a matinee performance of *Still Waters Run Deep*, which the cast was putting on for the soldiers at Campbell Hospital, on the road to the Soldiers' Home but two miles closer in. It seemed to be the opportunity for which Booth had waited, and quickly the specifics of the operation flashed through his mind. They would intercept the president's carriage near the hospital on its return trip and escort it—not through the center of the city to the Navy Yard Bridge as originally planned—but along Boundary Street (now Florida Avenue) to Benning's Bridge. Once across the Eastern Branch, they would abandon the carriage, mount their prisoner on a fast horse, and flee through the friendly countryside of southern Maryland to their boats on the Potomac.

Booth gave the order for action, and within minutes he and his men—except Herold, who drove Booth's buggy, a box of ammunition, and some coils of rope down the road toward Surrattsville—were mounted and on their way out the Seventh Street road to a rendezvous at a tavern near the hospital. Excited by their boldness, they went over the plan and toasted success. Booth then left to make inquiries at the hospital about when the performance would be over and the president likely to leave. His face was pale when he returned; Lincoln was not there.[50]

What were the reactions of the men when they heard this news? Frustration? Relief? Fear that the government had learned of their conspiracy? Surratt, Paine, and Booth made their separate ways back to the Surratt house, and, greatly agitated, held a private conversation and departed. Paine, Arnold, and O'Laughlin took the train to Baltimore; of the entire group only Surratt and Booth again appeared regularly at the boardinghouse.[51] The kidnapping conspiracy had ended in fiasco.

But Booth had not yet given up. On Friday, March 24, returning to Washington from a short trip to New York, he stopped at the home of Arnold's parents in Baltimore. Since Arnold was at a brother's farm, Booth left a message that he wanted to see him at Barnum's Hotel. By the time Arnold arrived, Booth had departed for Washington, but he left a letter telling his friend he wished to give their enterprise another try the next week. If it failed again, he said, they would abandon it forever.[52] The following Monday, March 27, Booth telegraphed O'Laughlin in Baltimore, "Get word to Sam. Come on, with or without him, Wednesday morning. We sell that day sure. Don't fail."[53]

O'Laughlin did fail to come to Washington that Wednesday, and so did Arnold. It was just as well, for nearly a week before, on March 23, Lincoln had left aboard the steamer *River Queen* on the voyage that was climaxed by his visits to Petersburg and Richmond.

If Booth had ever been a mature, resourceful, and determined leader of a daring conspiracy to save the Confederacy by kidnapping the president of the United States, he was by March

1865 only a frantic and impulsive zealot. He had spent himself poor on horses, equipment, and the partial support of his men and had even had to borrow $500 from O'Laughlin. In the middle of the month—the only time he ever assembled his men all at once—he had provoked them to near-mutiny by seriously proposing the kidnapping of Lincoln in a crowded theater. On March 17 he had led them into action, only to learn what he could have read in that day's Washington *National Intelligencer:* that Lincoln was not attending the performance at the Campbell Hospital but was presenting a battle flag to the governor of Indiana and speaking to an Indiana regiment at the National Hotel— Booth's own hotel.[54] On March 27 he had attempted to summon O'Laughlin and Arnold to Washington and presumably had alerted Paine, Herold, and Atzerodt as well (Surratt had left for Richmond), for a "sure" capture on March 29, only to learn again what he should have known all along, that Lincoln was out of town.

In the letter to his mother that he left at Asia's the preceding fall, Booth had cursed his four-year idleness and said he had begun "to deem myself a coward and to despise my own existence." How, then, must he have felt about himself at the end of March, when his six months' conspiracy to kidnap the president had collapsed so ignominiously and left him looking so ridiculous before his friends? Now personal failure and humiliation had been added to his anger at the terrible wrong he felt was being committed against the South, to his hatred for the man chiefly responsible for it, and to the frustration he had so long felt at having his deeply held political views greeted with derision by members of his own family.

It is no wonder that he suffered from severe depression. When asked by a friend when he planned to go to Richmond, where he had been popular, he replied in a melancholy tone, "I never shall go to Richmond again." And then he repeated himself. "I never shall go to Richmond again." It would be too much for him to see the Confederate capital occupied by Yankee soldiers.[55] At a time when most Washingtonians were celebrating the surrender at Appomattox by setting off fireworks and gathering in the downtown streets to see the illuminations of public buildings, another friend asked him out for a drink. "Yes," said Booth accepting, "anything to drive away the blues."[56]

He was drinking a great deal these days, often at John Deery's billiard parlor and saloon near Grover's Theater; more than once Deery saw him drink a quart of brandy within two hours.[57] He brooded over Appomattox, reminding Henry Clay Ford, treasurer of Ford's Theater, that back in 1861 when Lee had accepted his sword before the Confederate Senate, he had sworn that he would never surrender it. When Ford responded that Lee was a good general and a brave southern gentleman and that he must have known what he was doing at Appomattox, Booth mumbled that he himself was as good and brave as Lee. "Well," Ford responded, "you have not got three stars yet to show it."[58]

If Booth had difficulty in accepting the necessity of Lee's surrender, it was due in part to the suddenness and unexpectedness of the Confederate collapse. Even as late as March 20, 1865, Lincoln told the Russian chargé d'affaires in Washington that he had hoped the war would be over by the end of the year,[59] and in Richmond people went to church on Sunday, April 2, never dreaming that Davis and his cabinet and the Confederate Congress would flee the city before the end of the day.[60]

To most Yankees the war seemed as good as over after Appomattox; but many Southerners, like Davis himself, expected the struggle to continue. The day before Richmond's evacuation, John H. Surratt left the city for Montreal with dispatches from Secretary of State Judah P. Benjamin (which he carried inside a biography of John Brown) for General Edwin G. Lee, who had only a few days before replaced Jacob Thompson and Clement C. Clay as chief Confederate representative in Canada. Of the surrender at Appomattox of his second cousin, General Edwin Lee wrote, "I cannot and *will* not believe that because General Lee was compelled to surrender 22,000 men, we therefore have no more armies, and can wage war no more."[61] Of course, the surrender did mean that the Confederacy needed soldiers more than ever. Therefore, when Surratt arrived from Richmond, Lee sent him to Elmira, New York, to study the layout of the prison there with a view to assisting in the breakout of its thousands of southern prisoners-of-war.[62] Booth himself had no idea that the war was over. Had he not believed that the South would continue to fight, he told a Confederate officer who helped him across the Rappahannock River on April 24 and escorted him to a temporary refuge at Richard Garrett's tobacco farm near Port Royal, Virginia, "he would not have struck the blow as he did."[63]

Whatever was going through Booth's mind those last unhappy days in Washington, he had no fixed purpose to kill Lincoln in Ford's Theater on the night of April 14. Out late as usual on the night of April 13, he returned to his room at the National Hotel and, at 2:00 A.M. on the 14th wrote a letter that could not have come from the pen of a man planning to murder the president of the United States later in the day.[64]

Dearest Mother:

I know you expect a letter from me, and am sure you will hardly forgive me. But indeed I have nothing to write about. Everything is dull—that is, has been till last night [the illumination].
Everything was bright and splendid. More so in my eyes if it had been a display in a nobler cause. But so goes the world. Might makes right. I only drop you these few lines to let you know I am well, and to say I have not heard from you. Excuse brevity; am in haste. Had one from Rose. With best love to you all, I am your affectionate son, ever,

John

At about noon that day, Booth stopped for his mail at Ford's Theater on 10th Street and learned that Lincoln and Grant and their wives planned to occupy the presidential box that evening for a performance of the popular comedy, *Our American Cousin*, starring Laura Keene.

Lincoln and Grant together! The commander-in-chief and the general-in-chief!

Perhaps Booth had already decided to assassinate Lincoln if he got the chance. Perhaps the decision came to him only now when he discovered he had an opportunity to kill at the same time the two men chiefly responsible for the South's impending defeat. Perhaps the prospect of this twin killing led his despairing mind to imagine the effect upon the Union of the killing of still more of its leaders, and that this vision, in turn, caused him to experience a thrilling resurgence of hope for his beloved Confederacy. So many men had been sacrificed, why not the officials who were responsible for all the killing and for the merciless destruction of southern rights and institutions? They were the guilty ones, and their deaths would end the war!

Early in the afternoon, Booth arranged to meet Atzerodt, Paine, and, in all probability, Herold, at the Herndon House, a hotel not far from Ford's Theater, at 8:00 P.M. Then he spent the rest of the day hurrying about the city on errands preparatory to the assassination of Lincoln, Grant, Vice-President Andrew Johnson, Secretary of State William Seward, and possibly Secretary of War Stanton. He would save the South by bringing down the government of the United States, leaving the country leaderless and bewildered.[65]

And he would redeem himself.

Meanwhile, among the people around Lincoln there was, in addition to gratitude that the long war was at last as good as over, a sense that the danger of assassination was as good as over, too. The president had walked unharmed through the streets of Richmond. Grant's terms to Lee at Appomattox had reflected the spirit of the Second Inaugural Address, and Lincoln was clearly planning to preside over a peace of "malice toward none, charity for all." How could there still be danger? William Crook, the police bodyguard who had been with Lincoln in Richmond, said he had drawn "a full breath of relief" when that visit was over, "and had forgotten to be anxious since."[66]

Of course, there were still rumors in circulation, but there always had been and none of them had ever amounted to anything. There was less reason now than ever to take them seriously. Afterward, when it was too late, Seward—who had fractured his jaw and broken an arm in a carriage accident on April 5—told Secretary of the Interior John P. Usher that if it had not been for his accident, Lincoln would not have exposed himself at the theater on April 14. "It seems," Usher recalled, "that he knew of or anticipated some design or plot against the President."[67] Perhaps Seward's information came from the letter he had received early in the month stating that a group of rebels in Canada was plotting the assassination of the leading members of the government. After Lincoln's death, it was reported in the press that Seward had informed a member of the cabinet of this danger, but that his accident had intervened and prevented the taking of action.[68] But if Seward had attached any special significance to the warning, he could easily have told Lincoln not to appear unnecessarily in public, for the president visited him at his sickbed on April 9. In any case, this alleged plot was not the one that took Lincoln's life.

On April 11, Ward Hill Lamon, who had always been so concerned for his friend Lincoln's safety, left for Richmond on a presidential mission. He later stated that before departing he had asked Lincoln to promise not to go out after dark while he was away, "particularly to the theatre." "Well," Lamon said Lincoln had replied, "I promise to do the best I can towards it." In his *Recollections* Lamon published a letter he said he had written to Lincoln on December 10, 1864, also warning him about attendance at the theater.[69] But, like many other writers of reminiscences, Lamon was not above padding the record in his own favor, and this letter seems suspiciously prescient. The manuscript is not among the Library of Congress's collection of letters Lincoln received, but, identified as an "author's copy," is in Lamon's own papers at the Huntington Library. The April 11 warning against attending the theater also seems to be wisdom after the fact, for Lincoln was in much less danger inside a theater crowded with soldiers and civilians than he was in his carriage anywhere on the streets of Washington.

Early in the afternoon of April 14, James P. Ferguson, who operated a restaurant next to Ford's Theater, heard that Grant would be attending the performance that night. In order to have a good view of his favorite general, he bought himself a ticket in the front of the dress circle, or balcony, on the extreme left side, directly opposite the presidential box. He was disappointed, for at the last minute the Grants changed their plans and took the late afternoon train for Philadelphia. In their place, Mary Lincoln invited Major Henry R. Rathbone and his fiancée, Clara Harris, as guests. The play had already begun when the party arrived, but the actors stopped in the middle of their lines, the orchestra played "Hail to the Chief," and the audience rose to its feet to cheer and applaud the president. Lincoln stood briefly in the front of his box, smiling and bowing, then sat down. The play resumed.

Shortly after 10:00 P.M., during the second scene of the third act, Ferguson saw John Wilkes Booth, whom he knew well, walk behind the dress circle to the right, as the presidential party had done not long before, and then lean casually against the wall near a door that led to a small anteroom in the rear of the president's box. After a moment, Booth stepped down one step, opened the anteroom door, and disappeared inside. Ferguson then saw the flash of a pistol shot, the gleam of a knife, and Booth jumping over the railing of the box to the stage below.[70]

Thrown off balance by Major Rathbone's attempt to grab his clothing, Booth caught the spur on his right heel in the folds of a flag draped beneath the railing and hit the stage hard, his back mostly to the audience. But, a true professional, he turned around before hastily delivering the line he believed would seal his honored place in history. "*Sic Semper Tyrannis!*" he cried. It was the well-known motto of the state of Virginia, and Booth had no doubt seen it on the masthead of the Richmond *Daily Whig* and on a card emblazoned with Confederate flags and the arms of Virginia found at the Surratts.'[71] "Thus always to tyrants!" Then, brandishing his knife, he hobbled quickly backstage left, out a door in the rear of the theater leading into an alley, leapt upon a waiting horse, and vanished into the night.

Eyewitnesses, not all of them as alert to the sudden and astonishing action they saw and heard as they afterward claimed to have been, have differed about what Booth shouted and when. But that is only natural. Upon thinking it over, they might easily have transposed Booth's Latin into "The South is Avenged" and similar expressions. "I heard that shot every night for many weeks," wrote a member of the audience, one Dr. Samuel R. Ward, who climbed on the stage and saw Lincoln's inert body being removed from the box. "Nothing ever left so deep an impression on my mind." He had read statements by people claiming to have been present that Booth did not cry "*Sic Semper Tyrannis!*," "but I am sure that he did," Dr. Ward declared.[72] Booth himself wrote that he had said it, but his assertion that he said it before he fired his derringer is hardly credible. Still, he did say something while in the box; Major Rathbone thought it sounded like "Freedom."[73]

At about the same time Booth entered Lincoln's box, Lewis Paine talked himself into Seward's home in Lafayette Park— across the Avenue from the White House—where the secretary was in bed recovering from his accident. He was a messenger from Dr. S. F. Verdi, Paine said, with medicine that must be given to Seward personally. Despite the protestations of a servant, Paine went upstairs and repeated his story to Frederick Seward, who opened the door to his father's room, saw that he was asleep, and told Paine simply to leave the medicine.

Paine started down the stairs, then suddenly turned upon Frederick and beat him violently about the head with his pistol until he was unconscious. Then he rushed into Seward's room, pushed aside a male nurse, jumped on the sickbed, and began to slash Seward about his face and neck with a large knife. When the nurse and another of Seward's sons attempted to pull him away, he stabbed them with his knife, broke away and ran downstairs, wounding a State Department messenger who was on his way up as he passed.

His horse was found near the Capitol early the next morning, still saddled and bridled, and sweating so profusely there was a puddle beneath it. Investigation proved it to be the one-eyed horse Booth had bought from Dr. Mudd's neighbor.[74]

Earlier in the evening, Secretary of War Stanton had visited Seward, returning home in time to greet some serenaders who had announced they would call upon him. Afterward, he dismissed his servants, locked up the house, and started to prepare for bed. While he was undressing, his wife responded to an insistent knocking at the front door. She hurried upstairs. "Mr. Seward is murdered," she gasped. "Humbug!" Stanton replied. "I left him only an hour ago." But, of course, he went downstairs. By this time the entryway was filling up with alarmed citizens, one of whom held Stanton back as he started out the door. "You mustn't go out," the man said. "They are waiting for you. As I came up to the house I saw a man behind the treebox, but he ran away, and I did not follow him." Stanton said he would risk it and took a waiting hack to Seward's, where he found that the doctors and soldiers were in control. Then, in company with Secretary of the Navy Gideon Welles, he rushed to the William Petersen house across the street from Ford's Theater, to which the unconscious Lincoln had been carried.[75]

Booth had learned of Grant's change of plans during the afternoon of April 14, and it is possible that he sent a man after the general on his train. Between Baltimore and Philadelphia someone tried to force his way into the locked car in which Grant was travelling, but the train crew restrained him, and he disappeared. Later Grant received an anonymous letter from a writer who claimed to have been this man, thanking God that his effort to kill the general had failed.[76]

Who these potential assassins of Stanton and Grant were—if, indeed, they were potential assassins—is unknown.

Atzerodt's assignment was to kill Johnson. Like Paine, he said Booth did not tell him what he was supposed to do until the 8:00 P.M. meeting at the Herndon House. The unfortunate German made no effort to approach the vice-president and insisted that he had never intended to. He was probably telling the truth.[77]

Seward recovered from his wounds, so Booth's effort to save the Confederacy by incapacitating the government of the United States, conceived and organized on the spur of the moment, resulted in the death of Lincoln alone.

In a memorandum written during his attempt to escape, the assassin blamed his failure on "others, who did not strike for their country with a heart."[78]

In reality, Booth himself was to blame. His pistol went off half-cocked.

The Assassination as a
Confederate Grand Conspiracy

THE PEOPLE IN DOWNTOWN WASHINGTON were the first to hear. They emptied the theaters, hotels, and restaurants where they had been celebrating and gathered in frightened crowds, craving information, at the major intersections, and in front of William H. Seward's home and the house across the street from Ford's Theater. Mounted patrols galloped noisily to unknown destinations and contributed to the sense of imminent danger. Rumors spread. All the cabinet members were dead. Ulysses S. Grant was dead. The city was surrounded. The surrender at Appomattox had been repudiated, and the war would go on. With daybreak the terror subsided, but even a week later a vague fear that the conspiracy had not yet run its course mingled with the more conspicuous emotions of grief and anger.[1]

"Damn the rebels," swore Secretary of the Navy Gideon Welles when he heard the news, "this is their work."[2] It was the most common and the most natural reaction. Like many people throughout the land, Edward Bates, former attorney general, was certain that John Wilkes Booth's "*Sic Semper Tyrannis!*" was a clue to the unravelling of a grand conspiracy, "for this assassination is not the work of *one man*."[3] "Damned—eternally damned—be the assassin!" exclaimed a federal judge in Indiana. "Doubly damned be the instigators to the crime. May the infernal gods sweep them all to hell in a hurricane of fire!"[4]

For fear that it would cause angry reprisals against Southerners, the news was withheld a few days from most military units in the South, though not from their commanders. On April 17, under a flag of truce, General William Tecumseh Sherman met

Confederate General Joseph E. Johnston, commander of the Rebel army resisting his march northward through the Carolinas, and handed him a telegram from Secretary of War Edwin M. Stanton announcing the assassination. Sherman watched him carefully as he read it. "The perspiration came out in large drops on his forehead, and he did not attempt to conceal his distress. He denounced the act as a disgrace to the age, and hoped I did not charge it to the Confederate Government." Sherman told Johnston that he did not believe Robert E. Lee or other Confederate Army officers were involved, "but I would not say as much for Jeff. Davis, George Sanders, and men of that stripe."[5] A Connecticut soldier heard of Lincoln's murder while at the morning pump with his friends. "We all became angry," he said, "and hated the South worse than ever. Thought all the leaders should be condemned to death."[6]

Northern Democrats who had denounced Lincoln and his policies hoped desperately that Booth had acted on his own, without the sponsorship of either Rebels or Copperheads, but it seemed most likely that the moving spirits behind the assassination conspiracy "were of the North and South, in combination."[7] The New York *Herald* believed that the real source of the crime was "to be found in the fiendish and malignant spirit developed and fostered by the rebel press North and South. That press has, in the most devilish manner, urged men to the commission of this very deed."[8] Throughout the war, wrote Adam Gurowski, a Polish nobleman who worked in the State Department, Copperhead newspapers had pointed to Lincoln as a tyrant and to Seward as his henchman. "Murder and slaughter by infuriated wretches are now the fruits of those stimulating teachings."[9]

Apparent confirmation of the prompt assumption that the assassination was the result of a grand conspiracy of Confederates and Copperheads appeared almost immediately. Before daybreak on April 15 officers from the War Department entered and searched Booth's room at the National Hotel. There they found a letter from Samuel B. Arnold (though it was signed simply "Sam") dated March 27, advising Booth to postpone their enterprise because the government "suspicions something is going on," and recommending that he "go and see how it will be taken at R——d." In addition, they found a Confederate secret cipher, which proved to be keyed to a deciphering device recently taken from the office of Confederate Secretary of State Judah P. Benjamin in Richmond.[10]

Stanton spent the grim assassination night in the back parlor of the house in which Lincoln lay dying, supremely in charge of affairs. He interrogated eyewitnesses, took precautionary measures against possible attacks on other government leaders, and notified all of his commanders whom he could reach by telegraph in a wide circle around Washington of what had happened, ordering them to seize and hold all suspicious individuals. After witnessing Lincoln's death at 7:22 A.M., April 15, his tear-strewn face buried in the bedclothes,[11] he returned to the War Department to organize the pursuit, capture, trial, and punishment of all who were involved with Booth in the president's murder. Just before noon he sent a letter to Charles Francis Adams, U.S. minister to England, about the horrors of the night before. "The murderer of the President has been discovered [i.e., identified]," he wrote, "and evidence obtained that these horrible crimes were committed in execution of a conspiracy deliberately planned and set on foot by rebels under pretense of avenging the South and aiding the rebel cause."[12] But he waited until later before making the charge public, and his letter to Adams was nearly two weeks in transit.

From more than one source it was learned that John H. Surratt had been involved in something or other with Booth, and before dawn on April 15 officers of the Metropolitan Police called at the boardinghouse on H Street in search of him. He was in Canada, they were told. On April 17 Mrs. Mary Surratt and her whole household, including Lewis Paine, who had blundered upon the scene, were arrested by the War Department and held for questioning; and Arnold and Michael O'Laughlin were taken into custody the same day at Fort Monroe, Virginia, and Baltimore, respectively. Of the known members of the kidnapping conspiracy, only Surratt, Booth, and David Herold, the actor's companion in flight, were still at large. On April 20, Stanton offered rewards totalling $100,000 for their capture. "All good citizens are exhorted to aid public justice on this occasion," the secretary stated.[13]

Responsibility for the investigation of the assassination fell to Joseph Holt, judge advocate general of the U.S. Army and head of the Bureau of Military Justice. Born in 1807 to one of Kentucky's leading families, Holt made a fortune at the bar in Kentucky and Mississippi and retired from the active practice of law while he was still in his forties. After leisurely travel abroad with his second wife, a daughter of U.S. Representative Charles A. Wickcliffe of Kentucky, Holt purchased a comfortable home on New Jersey Avenue in Washington and settled down to a position of social leadership in the capital. A southern Democrat who had denounced the passage by northern states of "personal liberty" laws designed to impede the recovery of fugitive slaves, Holt had supported the compromise of 1850. As President James Buchanan's postmaster general in 1859, he sanctioned the non-delivery of abolitionist literature in the mails, and during 1860 he spoke against Republican threats to prevent the secession of southern states by force. But when secession became a reality, he changed his position and came out vigorously for preserving the Union at whatever cost. After the secessionists in Buchanan's cabinet were finally removed, he became secretary of war and, along with then Attorney General Edwin M. Stanton and Secretary of the Treasury John A. Dix, helped to strengthen the will and the policies of the faltering president.[14]

A cultured southern gentleman, Holt was noted for graciousness among friends; but during the Civil War many of his friends became enemies and his attitude toward them was vindictive and unforgiving. Alienated from the South and from Southerners, he embraced the Union cause, writes Mary B. Allen, "with something of the fury of the scorned added to the zeal of the convert." During 1861 he was helpful to Lincoln in keeping their native state loyal. In one public letter he declared that any Kentuckian who did not support the Union was "either a maniac or a monster," a stricture that included, among other members of his family, his mother and a brother, and he insisted that "rebels and traitors" should be severely punished.[15]

Holt was in Charleston, South Carolina, on April 14, 1865, participating in the ceremonies at Fort Sumter that were designed to bring the Civil War to a symbolic close. In a speech delivered afterward in a Charleston hotel, he advocated mercy for the "deluded masses" of the South but not for their leaders, many of them former friends. For "these miscreants, the Iscariots of the human race," he exclaimed, "may God in His eternal justice forbid that there should ever be shown mercy or forbearance."[16]

At about the time he was speaking these grim words, Booth entered Lincoln's box and pulled the trigger, an act that redoubled the determination of many men besides Holt to see that those responsible for the war and for its last despicable atrocity should receive the retribution they deserved.

As judge advocate general of the Army—a civilian position to which Lincoln appointed him in September 1862 with the nominal military rank of colonel (later brigadier general)—Holt was responsible for seeing that the administration of military law in courts-martial, courts of inquiry, and military commissions was uniform and just.[17] More important, Holt possessed the discretionary power to determine if any given offense was one of the "disloyal practices" referred to in Lincoln's famous proclamation of September 24, 1862, which subjected the offender to trial by a court-martial or a military commission. Holt interpreted this authority very broadly and made extensive use of military commissions in the cases of civilians not subject to trial by courts-martial. He was thus the principal agent by which Lincoln extended military control over political prisoners—the practice that was so widely condemned as unconstitutional and despotic and that was one of the factors leading Booth to believe that he was killing a tyrant.[18]

Now, after the assassination, Holt's Bureau of Military Justice was in charge of the collection of evidence that would bring to trial before another military commission the "maniacs and monsters," the "rebels and traitors," who were responsible for Lincoln's death.

From War Department agents, from private detectives, and from the public at large, evidence poured into the Bureau, where it was evaluated by Holt and Henry L. Burnett, the successful prosecutor before military commissions of the Copperhead leaders Clement L. Vallandigham and Lambdin P. Milligan. Much of it was worthless, originating with cranks or reward-seekers, much of it was earnest but mistaken, and much of it deserved and received further investigation. Within a week Holt found what he expected to find, and on April 24, just ten days after the assassination, Stanton made it public: "This Department has information that the President's murder was organized in Canada and approved at Richmond."[19]

The announcement was Stanton's, but the conclusion was Holt's, for Stanton, preoccupied with the search for the missing conspirators, with the controversy over Sherman's surrender terms to Johnston, and with other department business, did not personally examine the mass of evidence collected by the Bureau.[20] When President Andrew Johnson asked Stanton on May 2 for the names of the Confederates against whom there was evidence of complicity, the secretary was as ignorant of their identities as the president and asked Holt to supply him with the names that very morning. Holt complied; the names were those of Jefferson Davis and, of the Confederacy's Canadian representatives, Jacob Thompson, Clement C. Clay (once among Holt's closest friends), Beverly Tucker, George Sanders, and William C. Cleary.[21]

At a cabinet meeting the same afternoon, Stanton submitted a paper written by Holt summarizing the case against each of the men and followed it with a proclamation for the president's signature. "Whereas it appears from evidence in the Bureau of Military Justice that the atrocious murder of the late President, Abraham Lincoln, and the attempted assassination of the Hon. William H. Seward, Secretary of State, were incited, concerted, and procured" by the individuals listed by Holt, "now, therefore, to the end that justice may be done, I, Andrew Johnson, President of the United States, do offer and promise for the arrest of said persons, or either of them, within the limits of the United States, so that they can be brought to trial" rewards of $100,000 for Davis, $25,000 for Clay, Thompson, Sanders, and Tucker, and $10,000 for Cleary.[22]

Johnson looked around the table for advice. Stanton, confident of Holt's judgment, told him he ought to sign, and so did Secretary of the Treasury Hugh McCulloch and Acting Secretary of State William Hunter. With some misgivings, Secretary of the Navy Welles favored signing if there was really proof of guilt. Johnson signed, making official and explicit Holt's avowal that the assassination was the result of a grand conspiracy involving the Confederate leadership and the Copperhead Booth and his associates. [23]

By the time of the president's sensational proclamation, Booth had been captured and killed. For nearly two weeks, though badly crippled by the leg he had fractured in his jump to the stage, he and Herold were able to elude the hundreds of soldiers and civilians hunting them in lower Maryland and northern Virginia. They travelled along one of the regular Rebel communication routes, and it could have been no coincidence that they went for help only to individuals who, despite the fortune in reward money that could have been theirs, did not betray them. At the end, in Bowling Green, Virginia, U.S. officers, certain that they were closing in on their prey, forced out of an eighteen-year-old soldier formerly of Mosby's command the information that the men they wanted were at Garrett's farm near Port Royal, a few miles away. [24]

Early in the morning of April 26, Herold surrendered to the troops that had surrounded the tobacco barn in which he and Booth were sleeping, but Booth announced that he would fight his way out. The barn was set on fire, and, as Booth made his way to the door one of the soldiers, Boston Corbett, shot him in the neck through an opening in the side wall. He lived for two or three hours. Among his last words were, "Tell mother I die for my country." [25]

Before Davis and the other leaders of Booth's "country" could be tried for having "incited, concerted, and procured" Lincoln's murder, they had to be captured. However, the government could proceed without loss of time in the prosecution of those individuals already arrested who were known or believed to have been associated with Booth in the conspiracy. There were hundreds of prisoners, most of them Washingtonians, Marylanders, and Virginians, to choose from, [26] for Holt was determined that no guilty party should escape even if it meant the temporary imprisonment of many innocent ones. Afterward, many of the latter angrily denounced the War Department for its wholesale denial of due process and for its alleged intimidation of witnesses—charges to which Democratic politicians and writers found the public increasingly responsive. But at the time the public demanded thoroughness and would have been far more critical of the department had it done too little to investigate and avenge Lincoln's murder. Only later was it possible to condemn it for having done too much.

A courtroom was prepared on the third floor of the Old Penitentiary on the grounds of the Washington Arsenal (now Fort Lesley McNair).[27] On May 10, Booth's twenty-seventh birthday, eight civilian prisoners were formally charged before a military commission with having combined in the assassination plot with Booth, Surratt, and the men named in the president's May 2 proclamation. The prisoners were Samuel B. Arnold, Michael O'Laughlin, David Herold, George Atzerodt, Lewis Paine, and, in addition, Edman (sometimes Edward) Spangler, a stagehand at Ford's Theater, Mary E. Surratt, whose son John was still missing, and Dr. Samuel A. Mudd, upon whom Booth called early on the morning of April 15 for treatment of his leg.[28]

Although they were given far less time to prepare their cases than they would have been allowed by a civil court, the accused were able to acquire the services of attorneys who were not only courageous (under the circumstances), but qualified and capable. Arnold and O'Laughlin were represented by Walter S. Cox, a graduate of Harvard Law School who had successfully practiced in Washington for many years. Spangler's counsel was Thomas Ewing, Jr., a Union general and former chief justice of the Supreme Court of Kansas, whose father had been a U.S. Senator and a member of the cabinets of three presidents. Ewing also participated in the defense of Mudd and Arnold. Herold had the services of Frederick Stone, an attorney of prominence in Port Tobacco, and for years a family friend. The cases of Paine and Atzerodt were assumed by William E. Doster, former provost marshal of the District of Columbia. Mrs. Surratt's attorney was the most distinguished of all. He was Reverdy Johnson, U.S. Senator from Maryland, who was recognized as one of the nation's leading constitutional lawyers and was renowned for his impressive courtroom presence.[29] Unfortunately for her, Mrs. Surratt did not receive the full benefit of his services.

Among the rules of procedure adopted by the commission was one that provided that each defense counsel should file evidence of having taken the oath of loyalty prescribed by Congress, or swear to such an oath before the commission. A member of the commission, Brigadier General Thomas M. Harris of West Virginia, raised a question about whether Senator Johnson recognized such oaths as binding. It was a dispute growing ostensibly out of a comment made by Johnson in 1864 following Maryland's state constitutional convention; but in reality it reflected the tensions existing between leaders of opposing political parties in border states during the Civil War. Indignantly, Johnson showed that Harris had misinterpreted his comment and proceeded to criticize the commission for, in effect, questioning his loyalty. He was entitled to practice before the Supreme Court of the United States, he reminded the judges, and he pointedly observed that he was also a member of the Congress that created armies, generals, and military commissions. The president of the commission, the "outlawed" General David Hunter, pounded the green-covered table at which the commission members sat and angrily retorted that he had hoped the day was over when the people of the North would be bullied and insulted by the "humbug chivalry" of the South. It was a characterization the Marylander could never forgive. Whether out of personal pique or a belief that his standing with the court was such that he could not help his client, Johnson never again appeared before the commission, although the commission voted to allow him to do so. Instead, the defense of Mrs. Surratt was entrusted to two junior attorneys, Frederick W. Aiken and John W. Clampitt.[30]

The incident may have proved fatal to Mrs. Surratt, who very nearly escaped the gallows as it was, and might have done so in the opinion of Ewing and Doster had she had the benefit of Johnson's appearance in court.[31] If so, the consequences for the commission were also momentous, for more than anything else the hanging of Mrs. Surratt soon turned public opinion against it and gave substance to charges that it was a "kangaroo court." Doster later wrote that the commission had concluded from the first that the defendants were guilty and that it had acted as if its function was simply to decide the degree of guilt in each case and to fix the sentences accordingly.[32] A twentieth-century writer referred to the commission members as "epauletted assassins."[33] In offending the sensitive honor of defense attorney Johnson, the commission may thus have contributed to the eventual erosion of its own.

And yet the commission was not the vindictive, closed-minded body its critics have called it. The seven generals and two colonels who composed it were described by Lincoln's secretaries, John G. Nicolay and John Hay, as "officers not only of high rank and distinction, but of unusual weight of character."[34] General Harris, a physician before the war, even suggested to Doster that the best defense for Paine would be to establish that he was insane, which Doster tried, unsuccessfully, to do.[35] Toward the end of the trial another commission member, General Lew Wallace, later famous as the author of the novel *Ben Hur*, wrote his wife that he believed the commission would be able to arrive at its verdicts after no more than two hours of deliberation and that three or four of the defendants would be acquitted. At least, he added, "they would be, if we voted today." Special Judge Advocate John A. Bingham was to begin his closing argument for the prosecution the next day, and Wallace was uncertain of the effect his speech might have.[36] The effect of Bingham's speech was devastating for the defendants, but it cannot be said that the commission had decided from the first that all were guilty.

Throughout the trial, according to Doster, the conduct of Judge Advocate General Holt and Special Judge Advocate Burnett was "courteous and moderate." But Bingham's "mind seemed to be frenzied and his conduct violent."[37] First elected to the House of Representatives from Ohio in 1854, Bingham served four consecutive terms before being defeated for reelection by a Democrat in 1862. He was at that time appointed a judge advocate by Lincoln and worked closely with Holt until his reelection to the House in 1864. A slender man with a high forehead and deep-set eyes, Bingham gave the impression of feeling not simply a desire but a moral need to expose the errors and flabby thinking of others. Not given to doubt himself, he was able to influence less dogmatic men by the very force of his convictions and by the depth of his learning and his easy command of language.[38] He was a formidable, even a fearsome prosecutor, and his closing statement, delivered on June 28 and 29, determined the outcome of the trial.

Bingham's major assumption was that there never had been a conspiracy to kidnap the president; that, instead, assassination had been the object of Booth and his friends from the beginning. Of the eight defendants, only Arnold had said anything about an abduction plot at the time of his arrest, and, although Atzerodt later amended his confession to include participation in a kidnapping scheme, that he had not mentioned it at first lessened the possibility that the military judges would believe him. Doster and Cox made passing references to kidnapping in their defenses of Paine and O'Laughlin, but neither Herold, Mudd, Spangler, and Mrs. Surratt nor their attorneys said anything at all about kidnapping. That their silence might have meant they knew nothing about it is immaterial, for the prisoners were well known to be more or less intimately involved with Booth, and it was easy to believe that if they said nothing about a conspiracy to kidnap it was because there had been no such thing.[39] Talk about capturing Lincoln and holding him for ransom, Bingham insisted, was simply a "silly device" to fool the government.[40]

Besides the disbelieved statements of Arnold and Atzerodt, the only information about an alleged kidnapping conspiracy that was presented at the trial came from the testimony of the actor Samuel K. Chester. Booth had told him, Chester testified, that he was part of a conspiracy involving between fifty and one hundred men "to capture the heads of the Government, including the President, and to take them to Richmond." Lincoln was to be taken prisoner in Ford's Theater, and all Booth asked of Chester was, upon signal, to open the door at the rear of the stage. In exchange for this easy assistance, Chester said Booth had promised him he would never want for money as long as he lived.[41]

The idea of kidnapping not only Lincoln but also various other government officials and escorting them all to Richmond was as fantastic and incredible as the idea of capturing Lincoln inside a crowded theater. Once again Bingham explained that it had all been a ruse, this time to trick Chester into joining the conspiracy, because Booth had known that his friend would have "recoiled with abhorrence from the foul work of assassination and murder."[42]

So convincingly did Bingham describe the Confederate grand conspiracy and the alleged role played by each of the defendants, and so forcefully did he argue that in a conspiracy the act of one was the act of all, that far from acquitting three or four of the accused—as Wallace had believed likely—the commission on June 30 found all eight defendants guilty. Mrs. Surratt, Paine, Atzerodt, and Herold were sentenced to be hanged; Arnold, O'Laughlin, and Mudd to life imprisonment; and Spangler, believed to have played the role in Booth's escape from the theater that Chester had declined, was sentenced to imprisonment for six years.[43]

Because of President Johnson's illness, Judge Advocate General Holt did not present the record of the court's findings to the president until July 5. In a private meeting in the White House Holt also submitted a short report on the trial. An immense mass of evidence had been presented by between three and four hundred witnesses, the report noted, and Holt assured the president that "the rights of the accused were watched and zealously guarded by seven able counsel of their own selection." The proceedings were regular and the findings of the commission were, in Holt's opinion, justified by the evidence. The judge advocate general then made the recommendation upon which the president acted: "It is thought that the highest considerations of public justice, as well as the future security of the lives of the officers of the Government, demand that the sentences based on these findings should be carried into execution."[44] The president signed the document and ordered that the executions be carried out on July 7. Holt then gathered up the papers and returned to the War Department.

Although it was rumored that the commission had recommended that Mrs. Surratt's sentence be commuted to life imprisonment because of her sex and age, no presidential commutation was forthcoming. On the morning of July 7, therefore, the doomed woman's attorneys applied for and received a writ of habeas corpus from the Supreme Court of the District of Columbia. At noon Major General Winfield Scott Hancock, military commander of the District of Columbia, and Attorney General James Speed appeared in court to state that the writ had been suspended by the president. Early the same afternoon, Mrs. Surratt and the three men were hanged.[45] They had not been given much time to prepare for death, but, as the Washington *Chronicle* observed, Lincoln had not been given much time either.[46]

Observing the execution from a second floor window at the Arsenal, attorney Doster was sickened by the sight of two sol-

diers politely removing Mrs. Surratt's bonnet and then respectfully fixing the noose about her neck. It was a revulsion soon
shared by many others.[47]

During the course of his powerful summation speech, Bingham
had exclaimed that "Jefferson Davis is as clearly proven guilty of
this conspiracy as is John Wilkes Booth."[48] And, indeed, it followed that since Booth's friends had been convicted of having
plotted the assassination with Davis and the Confederate representatives in Canada, these latter were guilty of having plotted it with them. The testimony of witness after witness appeared
to establish the fact beyond reasonable doubt. One witness was
Dr. James B. Merritt, a physician who had taken over a practice
in the village of Ayr, in southern Canada West (now Ontario) in
December 1864.

A member of the sizable and highly mobile southern colony
in Canada, Merritt testified that the assassination of Lincoln and
other U.S. officials had been freely talked about by Southerners
with whom he came in contact. At a meeting in Montreal in
February 1865, he said he had heard Confederate agent Sanders describe an assassination plot involving Booth and Surratt,
which had the approval of Davis. Later, in Toronto, Merritt said
he asked Clay, Holt's old friend, what he thought of it. "He said,"
Merritt reported, "he thought the end justified the means." Early
in April 1865, Merritt said he had encountered a man named
Harper who told him he was about to lead a group of fifteen to
twenty men to Washington. With associates already there—
Merritt believed Harper had mentioned Booth as being one of
them—they planned to "kick up the damndest row that had ever
been heard of." In alarm, Merritt said he had hurried to the
office of one Squire J. Davidson, a justice of the peace in Galt,
to seek an order for the arrest of Harper and his men. Davidson
declined to issue the order, Merritt testified, because he considered the whole matter absurd.[49]

Another witness was Richard Montgomery, a U.S. spy who
had performed such valuable services for the government that
Lincoln had taken a personal interest in his welfare.[50] Montgomery testified that Thompson had told him the South had so
many friends in the North that Lincoln could be disposed of at
any time. In January Thompson had told him that a group of

bold and daring men had approached him with a plan for the assassination of Lincoln, Stanton, Grant, and others, and that he was in favor of it. However, Thompson had stated he would not give it his approval until he had heard from the authorities in Richmond.[51]

By far the most convincing and incriminating witness was the persuasive Sandford Conover. He was none other than the New York *Tribune*'s anonymous correspondent who had fled from his position in the Confederate War Department late in 1863 and whose articles about life in the wartime South and about various plots against Lincoln had so fascinated readers in 1864. An agreeable man with a remarkable talent for self-promotion, he had adopted the alias of James Watson Wallace and gone to Canada in October 1864. Quickly ingratiating himself with some of the southern representatives, he had combined the careers of journalist, adventurer, and self-proclaimed spy.[52]

At the trial Conover claimed to have been on intimate terms with all of the southern leaders named in the president's May 2 proclamation, and many others besides. He testified that Thompson had not only told him about a plan for the assassination of Lincoln and other officials but also had asked him to join the operation, which was to be led by Booth. He further stated that some time between April 6 and April 9, 1865, he was in Thompson's office when Surratt arrived from Richmond with letters from Davis and Confederate Secretary of State Benjamin. After reading them, Thompson had tapped them with his hand and said, "This makes the thing all right."

Conover further stated that in one of the letters he continued secretly to send to the *Tribune* he had told about this assassination conspiracy, but the paper had not published his warning. He feared Horace Greeley had withheld it, Conover said, because his newspaper had too often been accused of sensationalism.[53] Officials of the *Tribune*, however, declared they had never received the dispatch and two others Conover said he had sent and announced they had reason to believe the letters had been intercepted by Rebel agents.[54]

The testimony of Merritt, Montgomery, and Conover was given under oath before closed sessions of the military commission, and the witnesses were believed to be unknown to each other. "It is either overwhelmingly conclusive of the complicity of the

Confederate leaders in the assassination conspiracy," observed the New York *Times*, "or it is an unmitigated lie from beginning to end."[55] The testimony of half a dozen other witnesses appeared to establish beyond any doubt the truth of what Merritt, Montgomery, and Conover had sworn.[56]

Additional testimony was presented to remind the members of the commission—and the public—that Confederates and Copperheads had plotted an uprising in Chicago at the time of the 1864 presidential election, had tried to burn the city of New York, had engaged in raids across the Canadian border, and had sought to spread infectious diseases in the North.[57] The effect of such testimony was to make the assassination of Lincoln appear to be just one more incident in the Confederacy's massive conspiracy against the United States.

While it is unlikely that Holt doubted for a moment that Davis and the others were guilty as charged, he and Stanton were far too able and experienced to fail to recognize that the evidence presented at the conspiracy trial was not proof of guilt but only hearsay and that it was only as credible as the witnesses who gave it.

How credible were the witnesses? Even while the trial was in progress a flood of letters and affidavits denouncing Merritt, Montgomery, and Conover as liars and imposters was published in Canadian newspapers and reprinted in the United States. Sanders was said to have been hundreds of miles away from Montreal at the time Merritt claimed to have heard him describing Booth's assassination conspiracy, and Justice of the Peace Davidson declared that Merritt's story about visiting him to seek an order arresting the man Harper and his associates "is a miserable fabrication containing not one particle of truth."[58] It was claimed that Montgomery had been recognized as a Union spy at the time of the Niagara Falls conference and that he had not been taken into the confidence of the Rebel leaders thereafter. Conover's testimony was dismissed as almost entirely perjured, and his claim to have been on intimate terms with Thompson was confuted by publication of a letter that, under the alias of James Watson Wallace, he had sent to Thompson on March 20, 1865. The letter began, "Although I have not had the pleasure of your acquaintance."[59]

Disturbing as these early attacks on the government's chief witnesses must have been, they were only to be expected from Rebels and their sympathizers in Canada, and many of the alleged perjuries and discrepancies could be explained or rationalized away. Still, they must have shaken Holt's confidence—especially his confidence in Conover—for when Conover wrote in July that since the trial he had continued to investigate the assassination conspiracy and had located men of "unimpeachable character" who had been given funds by the Confederate government to dispose of Lincoln, Johnson, and members of the cabinet, Holt did not reply. In August Conover wrote again; if Holt was not interested in seeing his new evidence, he said, he would leave for Mexico. The judge advocate general soon wished he had let him go. But if Conover really could secure new evidence about the conspiracy, Holt and Stanton both agreed he ought to be given a chance to do it.[60]

Conover travelled through the South and to Montreal and Toronto—still dangerous cities for a spy who had blown his cover—and reported to Holt in a series of marvelously convincing letters. Reading them today, it is easy to believe that Conover had not only located new witnesses but also that he was close on the trail of startling new evidence that would cinch the case against Davis and redeem his own tarnished reputation. Nobody wanted more desperately to believe in Conover's success than Holt. In one note enclosing a check for $150, which he supposed Conover would need "from the number of witnesses you seem to have on hand," Holt instructed his agent to do his work as quickly as possible, but to do it thoroughly and not to miss any important witnesses.[61]

Conover's performance seemed to be as good as his promise, for by spring 1866 he had produced a total of eight witnesses who had left their sworn depositions in the office of the Bureau of Military Justice. To Holt, the case for the assassination as a Confederate conspiracy appeared stronger than ever.[62]

In the meantime, Davis, captured by federal troops in Georgia on May 10, 1865, and Clay, who had voluntarily surrendered to authorities after the issuance of Johnson's May 2nd proclamation, were imprisoned in Fort Monroe, Virginia, awaiting trial. On July 21—two weeks to the day after the hanging of the four conspirators condemned to death by the military commission for having conspired Lincoln's assassination with Davis and Clay— the cabinet voted to try Davis for treason, not assassination, and in a civil rather than a military court. Even Stanton voted for the motion, an indication that he recognized the case against the Confederate leaders as the planners of Lincoln's assassination was not so strong as Holt represented it.[63]

Other Republicans had reached the same conclusion. Early in her efforts to bring about a speedy trial for her husband, Varina Davis learned that such influential leaders as Greeley, Henry Wilson, John A. Andrews, Gerrit Smith, and Thaddeus Stevens were all convinced that Davis had not been involved in the assassination.[64]

On November 24, 1865, Stanton revoked the rewards that had been offered for the capture of Thompson, Tucker, Sanders, Cleary, and Surratt. He later explained he had done it because he was convinced that the men were out of the country; if they were arrested it would be by government representatives who had no right to claim rewards.[65] Perhaps so, but it is certain the secretary hoped the fugitives never would be arrested and brought back for trial. It was going to be hard enough to dispose of the cases of Davis and Clay.

There is further evidence that Stanton early lost faith in the idea of the assassination as a grand conspiracy of Confederate leaders. When Virginia Tunstall Clay's appeals for a prompt trial for her husband were ignored by Holt, once so close to them, the determined woman called upon Stanton. She believed her husband would receive a fair trial, she told the secretary in November 1865, unless it was handled by Holt's Bureau of Military Justice, with which Stanton was associated. "'Madam,' he answered, 'I am not your husband's judge—[.]' 'I know it!' I interrupted. 'And I am thankful for it; and I would not have you for his accuser!' 'Neither am I his accuser!' he replied. I could scarcely believe I had heard him aright. His manner was gravely polite. I remember thinking at that moment, 'Can this be the rude man of whom I have heard? Can I have been misinformed about him?'"[66]

At about the same time Virginia Clay learned Stanton was not her husband's accuser, she learned that Johnson was not either. In several interviews the president told her he believed her husband to be innocent and gave her the impression that only the power of men he dared not antagonize prevented him from releasing Clay from prison. But he assured her he would not allow Clay to be tried by a military commission and asked her to trust him. When, at the president's request, Holt submitted a lengthy report of the evidence against Clay, Johnson allowed her to copy it.[67]

In protesting his innocence of the charges against him, Clay had written the president that at the time of the May 2nd proclamation he had been absent from Canada for nearly six months and therefore could not have attended the meetings described by government witnesses at the conspiracy trial.[68] Clay was lying, Holt told Johnson in his report: four of Conover's new witnesses had sworn that they had seen Clay in Canada in January and February "and also within a few days of the assassination."

If Stanton and Johnson were uncertain about who was lying— Clay or the new witnesses—they soon found out, for Clay easily proved he was not in Canada "a few days" before the assassination. Despite Holt's positive assurances to Stanton in March 1866 that the new depositions against Davis and Clay were true and despite his strong recommendation that both prisoners be speedily tried by a military commission, Clay was paroled in April and returned to his home in Alabama.[69]

There proved to be more difficulties involved in trying Davis for treason in a civil court than the cabinet had anticipated, for during the war Confederate soldiers had been treated as belligerents and been given the protection of the laws of war. Could their leaders now be tried as traitors? Among the Republicans who thought not was Thaddeus Stevens, who offered to defend them if they were.[70] Furthermore, the Constitution required that any treason trial be conducted before a jury in the state in which the crime was committed. In the opinion of Attorney General Speed, that meant Davis would have to be tried in the federal circuit court of Virginia, where any jury impaneled would be so biased in his favor as to make conviction an impossibility. It is no wonder the administration did not actively pursue its decision to try Davis for treason and, instead, looked for a way by which he could be released from prison with a minimum of embarrassment.[71]

The administration was no more eager to seize and try Surratt, who had been located in England in September 1865. Only Holt refused to recognize that a military trial for a civilian in time of peace was out of the question—and that a civil trial would serve to emphasize the fact that the other conspirators had not had one. As with Davis, it also seemed impossible that Surratt could be found guilty in a civil court of conspiring to assassinate; and an acquittal would be looked upon as an indication that his mother and some of the other conspirators had been unfairly tried and punished by the military commission. After two months of meaningless correspondence with its representatives in England, the State Department therefore permitted Surratt to lose himself on the continent.[72]

The first Congress to meet after the end of the war convened in December 1865. Curious about why Davis had not been brought to trial for his role in the assassination conspiracy—despite the fact that, months before, eight individuals with whom he was supposed to have conspired had been tried, convicted, and executed or imprisoned—the House of Representatives in January 1866 asked the president for a report of the case against the Confederate leader.

As a result of this request Holt doggedly reviewed for the president the charges that had been made against Davis by witnesses at the conspiracy trial, his faith in their integrity apparently still unshaken. In addition he referred to the depositions of the new witnesses so far brought to his office by Conover—depositions that he said confirmed and extended what had previously been learned about the complicity of the Confederate leaders. The new witnesses, he declared, were "without any motive whatever to misrepresent," and what they stated could be "accepted as strictly true." He believed more strongly than ever that Davis should be tried before a military commission "such as during the past summer tried and condemned his alleged confederates in guilt."[73]

Stanton could not go along. He was not as impressed as the judge advocate general with the testimony of either the old or the new witnesses. Jointly with Attorney General Speed he advised the president that it would not be in the public interest to release the evidence against Davis to the House of Representatives.[74]

The refusal of the administration to release the evidence it had collected against Davis as an assassination conspirator, together with the recognized futility of trying him for treason in a civil court in Virginia, confirmed the suspicions of many members of Congress that Johnson had no intention of trying him anywhere for anything. Unaware that not only Johnson but Stanton and Speed and other members of the cabinet as well now believed the government could prove nothing against Davis, some Radical Republicans became angry. Johnson appeared to be protecting the ex-Confederate president in exactly the same way his Reconstruction policies were protecting the ex-Confederate states.

On April 9, 1866, Congress for the first time overrode a Johnson veto (of the Civil Rights Act) and on the same day the House instructed its Committee on the Judiciary to inquire whether there was probable cause that any person named in the president's May 2nd proclamation was guilty as charged—and, if so, whether legislation was needed to bring him promptly to trial. [75] The two actions signified the seizure by Congress of the initiative in Reconstruction policy. It would enact its laws over the president's vetoes, and if Johnson would take no action against Davis the House of Representatives would.

Holt appeared before the Judiciary Committee in April and confidently restated his case against Davis, supplementing it with the depositions of the eight new witnesses now supplied by Conover. He had complete confidence in the integrity of these witnesses, he told the committee; and he urged it to bring the most important of them to Washington so that it could cross-examine them and judge their reliability for itself. [76]

In the same month Varina Davis called upon the president, assured him that the case against her husband was perjured, and asked him to revoke his May 2nd proclamation. She was as much surprised by his reaction as Virginia Clay had been earlier: Johnson believed her husband to be innocent but explained that "he was in the hands of wildly excited people, and must . . . show he was willing to sift the facts." [77] His meaning was clear. The Judiciary Committee's investigation must be allowed to proceed before the president could take any action in behalf of Davis.

It did not take much sifting of facts to demolish the new evidence against Davis that had been sworn to by Conover's witnesses. The Judiciary Committee agreeing to Holt's suggestion that it cross-examine these witnesses, Holt sent a member of his staff, Colonel L. C. Turner, to New York to locate Conover and the five of his eight witnesses who lived in the vicinity and bring them to Washington. After some vaguely disturbing difficulties, Turner located two of them, William Campbell and Joseph Snevel, who promised to bring Conover to Turner's hotel room. But at the appointed time, Campbell appeared alone. "I talked to him," Turner related, "and asked questions and he was a good deal embarrassed. He finally asserted, 'This is all false: I must make a clean breast of it; I can't stand it any longer.'"

Campbell was a fraud. His real name was Joseph A. Hoare, and his testimony and that of the other seven witnesses—whose names, identities, and stories were also false—had been fabricated by Conover. Not only had Conover written Campbell's story for him word by word, but also he had rehearsed him in its delivery in a room in the National Hotel. Then Conover had escorted him down the Avenue to Holt's office to recite his lines under oath. Later, Snevel made similar revelations to Turner.[78]

Back in Washington, Campbell repeated his confession to the thunderstruck judge advocate general. Conover was promptly summoned to appear before the Judiciary Committee, where he was unexpectedly confronted with Campbell. The contrite witness repeated what he had told Turner and Holt. But Conover, always quick and resourceful, swore in reply that Campbell was now lying. He suggested to the committee that Campbell had been bribed by friends of Davis, and that he now saw he could profit more from denying his deposition than from sticking to it.

After the hearing, Holt told Conover he was "utterly astounded" by Campbell's testimony, to which Conover cooly replied, "You cannot be more so than I am." The two men agreed that the only way for Conover to restore his credibility was to bring before the committee the other witnesses whose depositions had been taken and to have them reaffirm their statements. For this purpose, an officer of the committee escorted Conover to New York, where the perjurer promptly disappeared. He had not been heard from since, Holt informed Stanton in July. "Conover has been guilty of a most atrocious crime, committed under what promptings I am wholly unable to determine." Holt immediately withdrew from the Judiciary Committee the depositions of all eight of Conover's witnesses and admitted that Conover had deceived him.[79]

The House Judiciary Committee did not allow the exposure of Conover and the absence of any credible evidence against Davis to moderate its conviction—or its hope—that the Confederate leader was involved in the assassination. After reviewing the 1865 conspiracy trial testimony of those government witnesses whose integrity had not been completely destroyed, it concluded that Davis probably "was privy to the measures" that led to Lincoln's death, recommended that the War Department's investigation of the assassination be continued, and urged that Davis and the others named in the May 2nd proclamation be put on trial without unnecessary delay.[80]

In a well-publicized minority report the Democratic member of the committee, Andrew J. Rogers of New Jersey, made the extraordinary revelation that the other members had denied him the opportunity to study the documents upon which the report was based. He had been put off week after week with one excuse or another, said Rogers, and was finally told that in the interests of national security only Representative George S. Boutwell of Massachusetts, author of the report, should see the papers. But Boutwell relented, and Rogers was allowed to look at the documents at "twelve o'clock yesterday." The charges against the Confederate leaders, Rogers declared, were false, perjured. Far from participating in the conspiracy against Lincoln, Davis and the others were themselves the victims of a conspiracy designed to save the reputations of "certain officers of the government" who had made reckless accusations after the assassination and who then had proceeded to manufacture evidence to support their charges.[81]

Rogers was not the only one who stated that Davis had been framed by false evidence suborned by Holt and Stanton. In August 1866 the anti-Republican New York *Herald* published letters purporting to have been exchanged among Holt, Conover, and Campbell, which appeared to prove collusion, and also, clumsily, to implicate the Radical leaders Stevens and Ben Wade, neither of whom had taken a stand against Davis.[82]

Holt angrily responded that the letters were fabrications designed, like Rogers's report, to defame his character and thus help to free Davis.[83] He also requested a court of inquiry to investigate the charges raised by the *Herald*'s letters. But his request was denied by recommendation of the cabinet (where he no longer had much support) on the grounds that public officials should take no notice of newspaper attacks.[84] He had to be content with a letter from Stanton. "The President is entirely satisfied with the honesty and fidelity of the Judge Advocate General," wrote the secretary, and believes "that there is no ground to impeach his personal or official honor and integrity, and that his conduct requires no inquiry or vindication. . . . In this view the Secretary of War fully concurs."[85]

The controversy over the *Herald*'s letters dragged on for several months, but in the end the letters proved to be another of Conover's hoaxes. This one may have been inspired by the *Herald* and been intended to discredit Radical leaders in Congress as well as Holt.[86]

In fall 1866 Conover was discovered and arrested and brought to Washington to stand trial under his real name, Charles A. Dunham, for perjury and the suborning of perjury. Sentenced to prison for ten years, he confessed that he had coached the lying witnesses in their stories in order to take revenge against Confederate President Davis, by whose order he had been imprisoned for six months in 1863 in Castle Thunder prison, Richmond. But he continued to insist that his testimony against Davis and the Confederate agents in Canada given at the 1865 conspiracy trial was strictly true, and on this point Holt supported him for the rest of his life.[87]

In a December 1866 letter to the president, Holt once again urged a military trial for Davis, despite the Supreme Court's recent ruling in *Ex parte Milligan* that such trials were illegal in areas where the civil courts were open and functioning. No part of the May 2nd proclamation, Holt assured Johnson, had been based on information supplied by Conover, whom he had not even known at that time. The proclamation had been based chiefly upon the testimony of Merritt and Montgomery, as corroborated by many other witnesses. Its validity, he reminded the president, had been confirmed by the military commission, which, "after a long and patient investigation," arrived at verdicts of guilty for each of the eight defendants. The guilt of Davis had "thus become [a] matter of solemn record, and this record stands unimpeached."[88]

If Holt really believed that the record of the military commission stood unimpeached and that the Confederate leaders had been proved guilty as charged, he was doubtless the only member of the administration who did. In May 1867 Davis was released from prison on bail. He was never brought to trial.[89]

The first session of the Republican-dominated 39th Congress—December 1865 to July 1866—was vitally concerned with trying and punishing Jefferson Davis. The second session—December 1866 to March 1867—had lost all interest in Davis and was vitally concerned, instead, with getting rid of Andrew Johnson.

During the war Johnson had talked very much like a Radical Republican. But as president he permitted the former leaders of the Confederacy to continue in political power in their states, and he sanctioned passage by the southern legislatures of the "Black Codes," laws that made a mockery of the Emancipation Proclamation and the Thirteenth Amendment, abolishing slavery throughout the United States (ratified in December 1865). He was so partial to the ex-Rebels that some Republicans wondered if he had not had some kind of nefarious understanding with them.

As the only citizen who could be said to have profited from Lincoln's death, Johnson had been included from the first on some lists of assassination conspiracy suspects. Booth himself had put him there by calling either on him or on his private secretary at their hotel the afternoon of April 14, and leaving his card. "Don't wish to disturb you; are you at home?" Booth had written.[90]

When Stanton's letter of April 15 to Charles Francis Adams stating that the assassination had been planned and executed by Rebels to aid the southern cause was published in the English press, James Mason of Virginia, Confederate representative in England, angrily denied the charge. Lincoln's death, he said, could not benefit the South. "But I can well understand that it may have material influence in aiding the cause of that overpowering party in the United States of which Mr. Stanton is the type, and Andrew Johnson, who succeeds as President, with ["Beast"] Butler of the notorious prefix, are the exponents and leaders."[91] Beverly Tucker, indignant at finding his name included in the president's May 2nd proclamation, issued from Montreal an "Address to the People of the United States." Johnson, he observed, had had a strong motive to plot the assassination with Booth, but Confederates could have had no reason to want to remove the generous-hearted Lincoln in order to make Johnson president. "Where," asked Tucker, "is the record of *his* humanity, magnanimity and mercy?"[92]

By 1866, however, Johnson's southern enemies had changed their tune, and it was the Radical Republicans—some of them, at least—who speculated about whether the president could have been involved in the assassination. Upon hearing of one pamphlet that argued that he had been, Mary Lincoln wrote, "My own intense misery, has been augmented by the *same thought*—that, *that* miserable inebriate Johnson, had cognizance of my husband's death—Why, was *that card* of Booth's, found in his box[?] . . . I have been deeply impressed, with the harrowing thought, that *he* had an understanding with the conspirators & *they*, knew *their man*. . . . As sure, as you & I live, Johnson, had some hand, in all this. . . ."[93] Radical Congressmen looking for an impeachable offense hoped she was right.

In January 1867 the House Judiciary Committee, investigating the president's conduct, heard testimony from the notorious Lafayette C. Baker, a former Army officer once chief of the War Department's National Detective Police, which was all Johnson's most extreme antagonists could have hoped for. Baker swore that he had seen and could obtain wartime correspondence between the president and Davis and other Confederates that proved Johnson had been a Rebel spy. Johnson's well-publicized Unionist sentiments, his radical denunciations of Rebel leaders, and his call for their severe punishment had all been part of his cover and, of course, had helped him to secure the nomination as Lincoln's vice-presidential running mate in 1864.[94]

But Baker was unable to produce these sensational letters or any evidence that they had ever existed, and in the end it was he, not Johnson, who was exposed. As two exasperated members of the committee exclaimed, "It is doubtful whether he has in any one thing told the truth, even by accident."[95]

In one thing, however, Baker did tell the truth to the Judiciary Committee. He revealed that at the time of his death Booth was carrying a pocket diary—actually an 1864 diary that the actor used in 1865 for memoranda. Although the diary had been reported in some newspapers in April 1865, its existence was overlooked or forgotten, and no questions were asked at the conspiracy trial when the government failed to present it as evidence along with the other items taken from Booth's body. The omission of so important a document was surprising enough in itself; but Baker caused a sensation by stating, when the diary was submitted to the committee, that pages had been torn from it during the two years it had been in the custody of the executive branch. "Who spoliated that Book?" asked Representative Ben Butler of Massachusetts, with a gesture toward the White House. "Who suppressed that evidence?"[96]

While fleeing for his life in company with Herold, Booth had written two passages in the diary to explain and justify his killing of Lincoln. In one of them he said, "Tonight I will once more try the river with intent to cross, though I have a greater desire and almost a mind to return to Washington and in a measure clear my name which I feel I can do."[97]

"How clear himself?" cried Butler. "By disclosing his accomplices? Who were they?" If all the evidence, including the missing pages, had been presented in 1865, the irascible congressman continued, training his sights upon the former vice-president, it might have been possible to learn "who it was that changed Booth's purpose from capture to assassination; who it was that could profit by assassination who could not profit by capture and abduction of the President; who it was expected by Booth would succeed to Lincoln if the knife made a vacancy."[98]

In response to Butler's request, a special Assassination Committee was established by the 40th Congress—which convened immediately after the expiration of the 39th—to see if evidence could be found linking Johnson to the assassination. The committee sent an agent to Fort Jefferson, the military prison on the Dry Tortugas off the coast of Florida, to interview Arnold, Mudd, and Spangler (O'Laughlin had died of yellow fever), received an obliging offer to incriminate the president from the indomitable Conover, and pursued every possible lead. But it did not even bother to report. "Speaking for myself," Butler later conceded, "I think I ought to say that there was no reliable evidence at all to convince a prudent and responsible man that there was any ground for the suspicions entertained against Johnson."[99]

Nevertheless, the belief that Johnson was somehow involved in Lincoln's death persisted into the next century.[100]

Baker's testimony before the Judiciary Committee that pages had been removed from Booth's diary by someone in the executive department—seized upon by Butler in an attempt to incriminate Johnson—caused no damage to the president or anyone else. It was contradicted by the two War Department representatives (one of them a cousin of Baker) who took the diary from Booth, by Assistant Secretary of War Thomas T. Eckert, and by Stanton and Holt, all of whom swore that the pages—whose absence was conspicuous because of the jagged stubs that remained—had been missing when they first saw the little book. Booth was known to have cut or torn sheets from the diary to send as notes, and other uses for the pages by someone hiding in the woods are easily imagined. Under cross-examination, Baker retreated from his original testimony and admitted he had "never examined that diary sufficient[ly] to recollect anything in it."[101]

Nevertheless, Baker's revelation that Booth had carried a diary did cause lasting damage to the reputations of Stanton, Holt, and Special Judge Advocate Bingham, for it helped to establish the facts—so scornfully rejected and ridiculed at the 1865 conspiracy trial—that there really had been a plot to kidnap Lincoln, and that Booth's decision to kill was made at the last moment.

Toward the beginning of the first of the diary's two passages, Booth had written (probably on April 17, 1865), "For six months we had worked to capture. But our cause being almost lost, something decisive and great must be done." This statement and the diary as a whole, Bingham explained in the House of Representatives in 1867, was not evidence of the kind the government was obliged to introduce at the trial; it was the declaration of a murderer made after the fact, and could not be used in his behalf or in behalf of any co-conspirator.[102]

Perhaps so. But in the letter he had left for his brother-in-law in November 1864—the "To Whom It May Concern" letter—Booth had stated his intention to try to make "a prisoner of this man" who had caused the South so much misery. Added to the confessions of Arnold and Atzerodt and to the testimony of Chester, Booth's statements made a strong prima facie case for the reality of the abduction conspiracy. Both statements—the one in the letter and the one in the diary—were known to the government, but neither was mentioned at the trial. Instead, Bingham had insisted positively and with deadly effectiveness that assassination had been Booth's object from the beginning.

If the prosecutors may be reproached for an overzealous determination to convict, defense counsel may be reproved for failure to track down Booth's statements. The diary had been mentioned in the press and the "To Whom It May Concern" letter had been widely reprinted in the press, yet apparently none of the distinguished attorneys was aware of the existence of either document. Perhaps the oversight occurred because they had been given insufficient time to prepare their cases. Perhaps it occurred because, overwhelmed by the government's vigorous assurances that their clients were guilty as charged, they believed it futile to search for sources to prove otherwise. But had the members of the military commission been given these additional reasons to suspect that there might have been a kidnapping scheme after all, they would have wished to know which members of the conspiracy knew of Booth's decision to assassinate. Of the four defendants who were hanged, Atzerodt, Herold, and Paine would probably have been doomed by their knowledge of Booth's plans for the night of April 14, even though they had not learned what the plans were till that very evening. But Mrs. Surratt, in whose favor there was already sympathy on the commission, could not have been so easily tied to Booth's new purpose and would likely have escaped with her life.

Still another blow to Holt's grand conspiracy theory—and to the secretary who had endorsed it—came in the summer of 1867 when John H. Surratt was finally brought to trial. Surratt was serving as a private in the Papal guard at the Vatican when, in April 1866, he was found and reported by a Canadian reward seeker. The head of the U.S. delegation to the Papal States promptly notified the State Department, which was now even less interested in recovering the fugitive than it had been the previous September, when he had been located in England. Once again the department consumed months in superfluous correspondence with its representatives. At last, just before Surratt was to be turned over to U.S. authorities by the Vatican, he escaped under suspicious circumstances, only to be tracked down again by zealous consular officials in Naples, Malta, and Alexandria, who did not understand how desperately their superiors in Washington wanted him to disappear for good. Captured in Egypt in November 1866, Surratt was brought home under heavy guard and indicted for murder in the criminal court of the District of Columbia.[103]

During his trial, which lasted from June 10 to August 10, 1867, Surratt's attorneys were able to show convincingly that their client had been in Elmira, New York, at the time of the assassination. Whatever his previous relations with Booth had been, he could not have participated in Lincoln's murder. Indeed, Surratt was a less prominent figure at his own trial than the ghost of his mother, which was invoked over and over again to embarrass the government and impress the jury with how unfair the 1865 military trial had been. Mrs. Surratt was portrayed as the innocent victim of wartime hatreds and the desire for revenge, wicked emotions that the Republicans were alleged to be perpetuating by trying Surratt for murder and also by relentlessly attacking President Johnson.[104]

The attempt to create sympathy for the president by associating him with Mrs. Surratt as a victim of Republican extremism angered Edwards Pierrepont, a prominent New York attorney who had joined the prosecution at the request of Secretary Seward. On August 3 he sought to counteract it by introducing in court the short report on the conspiracy trial that Holt had presented to Johnson on July 5, 1865. Attached to the papers was the rumored petition for clemency for Mrs. Surratt, signed by five of the nine members of the commission. He could not understand, Pierrepont exclaimed, how the defense counsel could blame the death of Mrs. Surratt on the unfairness of the military trial. The president himself had approved the commission's findings and sentences, and, "when it was suggested by some of the members of the commission that in consequence of the age and the sex of Mrs. Surratt it might possibly be well to change her sentence to imprisonment for life, he signed the warrant for her death with the paper right before his eyes." With a flourish, Pierrepont tossed the records on the defense table.[105]

Holt retrieved the papers later in the day and allowed the text of the petition to be published in the press. On August 5, 1867, the date of publication, Johnson sent to the War Department for the records and, upon examining them, declared emphatically that he had never before seen the petition. "He was positive," according to William G. Moore, his private secretary, who took notes of the president's comments in shorthand, "that it had never before been brought to his knowledge or notice." The president said he had been reluctant to sign the death warrant for Mrs. Surratt and had asked Judge Advocate Holt many questions, but "nothing whatever was said to him respecting the recommendation of the Commission for clemency." In the press Johnson was also reported as having said the petition had never been "officially brought to his attention."[106]

Most Republicans were not at all impressed by the president's declaration, which was given wide publicity in the Democratic papers. After all, the petition had been attached to the president's order approving the findings and sentences of the commission; Johnson "could not have written the one without reading the other."[107]

Neither Johnson nor Holt offered any clarification of the matter until 1873, and public opinion—that the petition had been withheld from the president, or that Johnson had seen it and had chosen to disregard it—divided largely along lines of political partisanship. But for partisans on both sides, the knowledge that a majority of the military commission had recommended clemency for Mrs. Surratt contributed to the growing sentiment that she had been unjustly put to death.

So, too, did the failure of Surratt's jury to find him guilty of participation in the crime for which his mother and the seven other defendants had been convicted by the military commission. Standing eight to four in his favor, the jury was dismissed, and in 1868 the charges against him were dropped.[108]

Johnson's term of office ended on March 4, 1869. During his last weeks as president, he ordered the exhumation of the bodies of Mrs. Surratt, Paine, Herold, Atzerodt—and of John Wilkes Booth, the man who had led these friends to their premature deaths—from their burial places beneath the stone floor of a warehouse on the Arsenal grounds and turned them over to their families for private reinterment. The newspapers took note of the president's action only matter-of-factly. Johnson also granted full and unconditional pardons to the prisoners at Fort Jefferson—Mudd, Arnold, and Spangler—whose return to their homes was scarcely noticed at all.[109]

Contrary to what is sometimes stated, the president never did revoke his proclamation of May 2, 1865, charging Davis, Clay, Thompson, and other of the Confederate representatives in Canada with having "incited, concerted, and procured" Lincoln's assassination. But only diehards still took that charge seriously, and all of the accused were included in the sweeping presidential pardon of December 25, 1868.

There was nothing left of Holt's grand conspiracy except long-lingering bitterness.

4

The Assassination
as a Simple Conspiracy

It is not surprising that so many people should have assumed on April 15, 1865, that Lincoln's assassination was the result of a grand conspiracy involving Confederates and Copperheads, or that they should have accepted President Andrew Johnson's May 2nd proclamation to that effect as a simple confirmation of an awful truth. What is surprising is that so many people, even Republicans, rejected the grand conspiracy theory from the beginning.

In the New York *World* early in May reporter George Alfred Townsend stated he thought it was possible that the Rebel leaders in Canada had known of John Wilkes Booth's intentions and that they might have "patted his back," but he was "certain Booth's project was unknown to Richmond." Booth, said Townsend, was "the sole projector" of the assassination plot.[1] The writer of one of the earliest pamphlets on the assassination stated that Lincoln's most bitter enemies in the Confederate government "would have shrunk with horror" from the commission of such a deed.[2] In upstate New York the abolitionist and philanthropist Gerrit Smith called the president's charge "absurd" and "insane,"[3] and Thaddeus Stevens thought Johnson had made a mistake in capturing Jefferson Davis; it would have been wiser to have helped him escape! When he looked at some of the evidence upon which the May 2nd proclamation had been based, Stevens called it "insufficient in itself, and incredible." Later, in May 1866, he said, "Those men are no friends of mine. They are public enemies. . . . But I know these men, sir. They are gentlemen, and incapable of being assassins."[4]

Many people who rejected the grand conspiracy charge could not have been quite so confident as they sounded. But they remembered the War Department's wartime arrests of individuals guilty of no crime, and assumed—or hoped—that the department was up to its old tricks. So, in the end, it proved to be, because of the readiness of Joseph Holt to believe the worst of the "maniacs and monsters" who had rebelled against the United States.

Long before the mistake was formally acknowledged by Davis's release from prison, prominent Republicans began to qualify or repudiate the government's charge. Before the end of 1865, Henry J. Raymond, chairman of the National Union Committee as well as editor of the New York *Times*, published a revised and expanded edition of his 1864 campaign biography of Lincoln. He could not believe, Raymond stated, that the assassination had been procured by Rebel authorities. But, like Townsend, he, too, thought it possible that the Confederate agents in Canada had known of Booth's plans and had given them their sanction. Nevertheless, it seemed to Raymond that the assassination conspiracy had originated chiefly, if not exclusively, "with the man who played the leading part in its execution."[5] In his history of the war, *The American Conflict* (1866), Horace Greeley stated that the government had proved Lincoln was the victim of a conspiracy involving Confederates but not "that the chiefs and master-spirits of the Confederacy were implicated in the crime. Booth himself was, so far as has been shown, the projector and animating soul of the monstrous plot."[6]

As increasing numbers of people came to accept the probability that Lincoln's assassination was the product of a simple conspiracy involving only Booth and a small group of his friends, there was a vigorous reaction among Democrats against the Republican leadership that had committed itself and the government to the theory of the grand conspiracy. To be sure, the May 2nd proclamation had been issued in the name of Democrat Andrew Johnson. But Johnson's impeachment and near-conviction by the Republican Congress, and the inept effort of some Republicans to involve him in the assassination conspiracy, had exonerated the president and established him as another victim of Radical vindictiveness.

It was Secretary of War Edwin M. Stanton—not Johnson, not

Holt—who had to shoulder most of the blame for the charge that there had been a Confederate grand conspiracy and for the denial at the conspiracy trial that there had ever been a kidnapping plot. In the minds of those people who believed that the military commission's petition for clemency had been deliberately withheld from the president, Stanton also stood condemned as the murderer of Mary E. Surratt, for it was assumed that Holt had withheld the petition under orders. When the secretary died of pulmonary complications in 1869 at the age of fifty-five, rumors began almost immediately that he had slit his throat in remorse over having executed an innocent woman. His physician and friends (and subsequent biographers) all denied it emphatically, but the accusation was too gratifying to his enemies to be put to rest.[7]

At the end of the century, Stanton was accused of offenses more grievous than suicide, and in the next century of a crime far worse.

For a generation after 1865 Americans tended to view Lincoln's assassination from partisan points of view. Democrats blamed Stanton for the unfounded charges against Davis and the other Confederate leaders, for railroading the conspirators to prison and the gallows in a military court, and for the judicial murder of Mrs. Surratt. Many Republicans defended the military trial on the grounds that the commander-in-chief of the Army and Navy had been killed in time of war, maintained that Mrs. Surratt was probably guilty, and recalled the incitements of the Democratic press to just such a crime as Booth's. But, despite this partisan alignment, the assassination seldom arose as an issue in national election campaigns.

In 1872 the "Liberal," as opposed to the "Radical," wing of the Republican party refused to support President Ulysses S. Grant for reelection, and, calling for an end to wartime animosities, formed an uneasy alliance with the Democrats to back Horace Greeley for president. It was time, said Greeley in his speech accepting the nomination, for Democrats and Republicans to "clasp hands over the bloody chasm" that had divided them. *Harper's Weekly,* vigorously pro-Grant, reminded potential Liberal defectors that Democrats had plotted Lincoln's assassination at Baltimore in 1861 and restated the grand conspiracy theory that the murder of the president had been planned in Richmond and Canada. The powerful weekly conceded that the assassination had not yet been traced beyond its active agents, but when the conspirators still at large were discovered, the magazine asked, did anyone doubt that they would prove to be southern slave owners and northern Democrats? The front page of the issue of September 14, 1872, was a cartoon by Thomas Nast that pictured Greeley reaching across the "bloody chasm" of Lincoln's grave to clasp hands with the ghost of Booth.[8]

Perhaps no Republican waved "the Bloody Shirt" more joyously than Robert G. Ingersoll, "the great agnostic," whose political speeches won him friends even among voters who were shocked by his religious views. During the presidential campaign of 1876, Ingersoll reminded an audience of Union veterans in Indianapolis that every state that had seceded had been Democratic, that every soldier who had shot at the flag had been a Democrat, and that "the man that assassinated Abraham Lincoln was a Democrat. Every man that sympathized with the assassin—every man glad that the noblest President ever elected was assassinated, was a Democrat."[9] In most of the rest of the campaigns of the nineteenth century Ingersoll continued to denounce the Democrats and to hold them responsible for whatever he believed to be wrong with the country. But in no other of his published speeches did he blame them for Lincoln's assassination. Nor did Nast or *Harper's Weekly* again link the Democratic party to Booth.

It was not Lincolnian compassion that caused the Republicans to stop blaming Democrats for Lincoln's death. The truth was that they had more to lose than to gain by treating the assassination as political. For Lincoln's martyrdom raised him above politics and gave the Grand Old Party itself the elevation necessary to support its claim that it was the only true representative of American nationalism. As the Saviour of the Union, as the American national god, Lincoln was the greatest asset the party possessed, and it simply would not do to admit that he had ever done anything for which a Democrat might rationally want to kill him. His murder could be attributed to Booth's madness and fanaticism, to the spirit of slavery and rebellion, to disloyalty, northern or southern, but not to the Democratic opposition as such. To blame the Democrats would be to give them a motive, and that would put the Republicans on the defensive.

The only time the Democrats raised an assassination-related issue in a presidential campaign was in 1880, when for the first and last time their candidate was a Civil War veteran—General Winfield Scott Hancock, a hero of Gettysburg and other battles. It was Hancock who, as commander of the Middle Military Division (which included Washington), had appeared in the Supreme Court of the District of Columbia on the morning of July 7, 1865, and officially declined to honor the writ of habeas corpus which the court had issued on behalf of Mrs. Surratt, on the grounds that the writ had been suspended by the president. In 1880, for fear that his connection with the death of Mrs. Surratt might lessen his appeal to Catholic Democrats, especially in New York, the official campaign biography stressed that at the time of the execution Hancock had only been a soldier carrying out orders. He had hoped till the end for a presidential reprieve, and Mrs. Surratt's friends in no way blamed him for her death. John W. Clampitt, Mrs. Surratt's only surviving attorney, contributed a lengthy public letter to the campaign exonerating Hancock and laying exclusive responsibility for the suspension of the writ on President Johnson and his "ill-advisers."[10]

Since the Republicans knew enough to leave the emotion-packed issue of Mrs. Surratt out of the campaign, the Democrats gained nothing by bringing it up. Indeed, they may even have lost the presidency by publicizing the fact that Hancock had had anything at all to do with the executed woman. The party had carried New York in 1876 and did again in 1884; Hancock lost it by a few thousand votes in 1880, and with it a majority in the electoral college.[11]

After 1880, there was no further significant comment on Lincoln's assassination in national political campaigns. The Republicans could not bring it up without reviving discussion of some of Lincoln's controversial policies, and the Democrats certainly could not take credit for it.

The issue of Mrs. Surratt, however, did not disappear. In 1872, when ex-President Johnson sought to revive his political career with what proved to be an unsuccessful run for Congress from his home district in eastern Tennessee, an opponent criticized him for having ordered a military trial for the conspirators and for having executed Mrs. Surratt. "In 1865 the city of Washington was an armed camp," Johnson explained in reply; "Lincoln was our commander-in-chief; he was foully murdered, and a court duly organized sat upon the case and convicted his murderers, a woman included; I was unwilling to pardon her; and that is all there is to it."[12]

But there was more to it, after all. In 1873, while campaigning for election to the U.S. Senate, Johnson was required by political exigencies to say more than that he had been "unwilling" to pardon Mrs. Surratt. He had to say, as he had said in August 1867, that he had not been shown the military commission's petition for clemency, thus shifting from himself to Holt—and the deceased Stanton—primary responsibility for the hanging of a woman widely regarded by Democrats, Catholics, and southerners as a martyr. Holt, still judge advocate general, was thus obliged to defend his honor. In doing so, he reopened a controversy that embittered the rest of his life and became the most sensitive issue of contention among students of the assassination until the 1930s.

In a lengthy report to Secretary of War William W. Belknap, which was published in the press and issued as a pamphlet under the title *Vindication*, Holt noted that had he been guilty of withholding the petition from the president, the dereliction would have been known to Johnson immediately after the execution. The petition was at the time being spoken about in Washington and in the newspapers. Johnson would therefore have known "that I had been guilty of the greatest offense possible, . . . and an imperative obligation would have rested upon him to have me tried and punished, . . . since the offense, if it existed, would have involved the enormity of treacherously misleading him in the performance of the most solemn of his duties." But Johnson had not only brought no charges and asked for no investigation, he had retained Holt as judge advocate general to the end of his administration. The president knew, Holt concluded, "that I had performed my whole duty, and that I had not only presented the petition to him, but that he had read it and commented on it in my presence."

To support his case, Holt submitted copies of letters to prove that Johnson had also discussed the petition with members of his cabinet. John A. Bingham, chief prosecutor at the conspiracy trial, declared that after the executions in July 1865 he had called upon Secretaries Stanton and William H. Seward and had heard from them both that the plea for clemency had been discussed by the cabinet and that all members present had agreed that it should not be honored. When Bingham asked if he could make this fact public, Stanton "advised me not to do so, but to rely upon the final judgment of the people." James Harlan, former secretary of the interior, remembered "distinctly" that the cabinet had discussed with the president the commutation of Mrs. Surratt's sentence. No formal vote was taken on the question, but he did not recall any differences of opinion. Harlan was not sure whether the discussion had taken place in a regular cabinet meeting, or if some of the members had just happened to meet at the White House. He was certain only of the presence of himself, Stanton, Seward, and James Speed. Former Attorney General Speed stated that he had seen the petition attached to the record of the trial in the president's office before the execution, but, he said, "I do not feel at liberty to speak of what was said at Cabinet meetings. In this I know I differ from other gentlemen, but [I] feel constrained to follow my own sense of propriety." Other letters, including two solicited earlier from employees of the Bureau of Military Justice, seemed to confirm Holt's insistence that Johnson had indeed seen and discussed the petition before the hanging of Mrs. Surratt.[13]

Holt's friends found his *Vindication* completely convincing. "I hope you will not consider it intrusive," Lincoln's secretary John Hay wrote, "for me to write a word, expressing not merely my own opinion but that of all with whom I conversed upon the subject, that there is not the shadow of a doubt in any candid mind about the prepostrous [*sic*] charges you have so absolutely refuted."[14] Holt did not consider Hay's letter intrusive.

But, of course, Johnson was yet to be heard from. In his reply, which was also widely published in the papers, the ex-president asked why Holt had waited so long to seek vindication. When his official integrity was first attacked in 1867, why did not Holt ask for a court of inquiry? "All his witnesses were then living, the circumstances attending the execution were fresh in the public mind. His reputation was at stake, and must have been as dear

to him then as now." Furthermore, Stanton had lived until December 1869 and Seward until October 1872, yet Holt had not
asked them for letters about the incident and was thus forced to
rely upon the hearsay evidence offered by Bingham. Those who
knew Stanton, said Johnson, would find it hard to believe that
he had told Bingham "to rely upon the final judgment of the
people" and had at the same time ordered all information on the
subject withheld from the people.

The informal discussion of cabinet members to which Secretary Harlan referred, Johnson continued, had taken place on the
day of the execution. The commutation of Mrs. Surratt's sentence had indeed been discussed, as it was being discussed at
the time by newspapers and by individuals throughout the
country. But "it does not therefore follow that any conversation
which may have been had respecting sex or age was caused by
the existence or presentation of the petition in question." If Speed
saw the petition attached to the court record, said Johnson, it
must have been in the War Department rather than in the White
House, for Holt had carried the papers away with him immediately after Johnson signed the order to proceed with the executions. Johnson remembered that when the papers were brought
to him for his consideration and signature, Holt had argued "with
peculiar force and solemnity" against commuting Mrs. Surratt's
sentence. To spare her and hang the three men, Holt had said,
"would be to offer a premium to the female sex to engage in
crime."

In his *Vindication*, Holt had said it would have been a crime
to withhold knowledge of the petition from the president and
had claimed that he had not done so. Why, then, Johnson asked,
had he withheld it from the record of the trial compiled and
arranged by Benn Pitman and published with the official approval of the War Department? Pitman's volume, he observed,
included an appendix with documents far less interesting and
pertinent.[15]

Like Johnson, writers who have taken his side in the dispute
with Holt have questioned Bingham's statement that Stanton
had told him not to speak of the petition but to leave the final
judgment to the people. Indeed, it would be easy to dismiss this
alleged order as an invention of Bingham designed to strengthen
Holt's case. But apparently Holt did not see it as such. Among

his papers is an undated memorandum in his handwriting in which, with seeming sincerity, he states his opinion that the man he believed his friend had betrayed him:

As illustration of the animus which presided over this careful bury-ing away of the truth out of the sight of men, it is proper to mention that from the time Mr. Stanton & myself were associated together as members of Mr. Buchanan's Cabinet, our relations had continued to be—apparently at least—those of the most cordial personal friend-ship. On my part, the cordiality had been heartfelt and I had every reason to believe that it was so on Mr. Stanton's part also[—]even at the very moment he was impressing the seal of silence upon Judge Bingham's lips—Lulled by the simple credulous trust inspired by the sincerity of my own friendship for him, suspicion of the fatal step then taken agst [against] me was of course impossible.[16]

Holt seems to have believed Bingham's story, to have be-lieved, first, that Seward and Stanton had said the petition had been discussed by the cabinet, and, second, that Stanton had ordered Bingham not to speak of that fact. Stanton's order, Holt told Speed, "was a deliberate and merciless sacrifice of me, so far as he could accomplish it."[17]

If Holt believed what he said, he must have searched for an explanation of Stanton's conduct. He would not have had to search for long, for he well knew that Stanton believed Holt and his Bureau of Military Justice had bungled the handling of the as-sassination, thus damaging Stanton's own reputation and less-ening his place in history. How much greater the secretary would seem had he ended the war with a triumph of arms and the prompt punishment of Lincoln's murderers, instead of with the false accusation against Davis and the others. If Holt felt Stan-ton had betrayed him, he must have recognized that Stanton felt Holt had betrayed *him*.

Andrew Johnson died in 1875, and the only individual left who could say anything new about whether or not the petition for clemency had been discussed by the cabinet was Speed. De-spite persistent appeals from Holt, Speed refused to his death in 1887 to say more than that when he saw the record of the trial the petition was attached to it. Thoroughly exasperated, Holt declared that Speed must have made some kind of pledge to Johnson to protect the former president's reputation by remaining silent.[18] In 1889 the former judge advocate general gathered together some letters he and Speed had exchanged earlier in the decade and published them in the *North American Review* under the title "New Facts about Mrs. Surratt." The letters contained no new facts about Mrs. Surratt, but they did perhaps arouse some sympathy for Holt as the victim of what appeared to be Speed's misplaced and old-fashioned commitment to the privacy of cabinet discussions.[19]

Two months later Speed's son John attempted to ease Holt's anguish by publishing in the same journal a short speech his father had delivered in Cincinnati a month or two before his death. In this speech the former attorney general had referred to that "maudlin sentiment" that claimed the military trial had been unjust and that held certain public officials responsible for the sentences imposed. Among the leaders being criticized, Speed had said, "is my distinguished friend, the then Judge Advocate General of the Army. Judge Holt performed his duty kindly and considerately. In every particular he was just and fair. This I know. But Judge Holt needs no vindication from me nor any one else. I only speak because I know reflections have been made, and because my position enabled me to know the facts, and because I know the perfect purity and uprightness of his conduct."[20] Speed's speech fell short of stating that the president had discussed the petition with his cabinet and was thus less than the total exoneration Holt craved. But it must have given the old man some satisfaction.

Holt's last years were lonely and bitter. A widower without children, he remained estranged from many of his Kentucky relatives, even returning their occasional letters unopened. Washingtonians often saw him sitting in the shade of the portico of his house, a massive man with shaggy eyebrows and a full head of gray-white hair. One passerby thought he looked "the personification of gloom." In his old age, wrote the historian James Schouler, Holt became increasingly "gloomy, morose and suspicious."[21]

As a Unionist from a border state and as judge advocate general of the Army and head of the Bureau of Military Justice during the war, Holt had known so much about the treachery and desperation of the enemies of the United States, North and South, that it was impossible for him to accept the idea that the men who were responsible for the death of Lincoln were not the same men who were responsible for the rebellion. As time passed, he could perhaps admit to himself that he had not been able to prove the case for the assassination as a Confederate grand conspiracy, but it is unlikely he ever wavered in his conviction that there was a case to be proved.

But who, now, would prove it? The Civil War and Lincoln's death were sinking into the past. A new generation with no memory of the war or of its concluding nightmare had been born, and the awful realities of both the war and the assassination had faded from the minds of the older generations. Reminiscences of the war years being published as books and articles did not— could not—rescue the truth of the past from oblivion; like most memoirs, they tended to be idealized and romantic. The reunited North and South were making heroes of each other's heroes, and it thus seemed almost certain that the old Confederate leaders would get away with murder, just as they had gotten away with treason and rebellion.

Thus Holt may have mused, sitting in the shade of his portico. If so, it was cause enough for gloom.

By the 1890s Lincoln's assassination had long been an event in history rather than the living trauma it had been when it occurred. But it was an historical event whose history had not been written. The collapse of the grand conspiracy theory meant general acceptance, by default, of the assumption that Lincoln had been killed by a simple conspiracy organized by Booth. Yet nothing of the sort was ever stated officially; the government issued no white paper as a corrective for the discredited grand conspiracy detailed in Pitman's officially approved volume. No president revoked the May 2nd proclamation. A few memoirs of Booth as an actor and a man were beginning to appear, but no serious attempt had been made to probe into his thinking or the true nature of his conspiracy. As part of the same sweep of public emotion that—with the encouragement of Republican leaders and hagiographic biographers—had turned Lincoln into a demigod, the assassination had been dehumanized as well as depoliticized. Lincoln was Christ-like, Booth was a fiend.

Understanding of Lincoln's assassination was thus inhibited by factors that did not beset the study of other historical events.

In 1890, when private secretaries John G. Nicolay and Hay devoted twenty-five pages of the last volume of their ten-volume biography of Lincoln to the circumstances of the president's death, it was the longest treatment of the subject published since 1865. For this reason, it seemed new and original, even though all it did was to accept the reality of the abduction plot and add to it much of the story of the assassination that had emerged at the 1865 conspiracy trial. It was a significant breakthrough, nevertheless, for it represented the beginning of the writing of the history of Lincoln's assassination.

According to Nicolay and Hay, Booth was "stung to the quick" by Lincoln's reelection in 1864, for it meant the end of the South's bid for independence. After the election, Booth went to Canada, "consorted with the rebel emissaries there, and at last—whether or not at their instigation cannot certainly be said—conceived a scheme to capture the President and take him to Richmond." During the fall and winter months, while he was inducing "a small number of loose fish of secession sympathies to join him in this fantastic enterprise," he was always well supplied with money, which did not come from the speculations in oil about which he boasted. The months passed and nothing was accomplished, though the conspirators experienced some kind of disappointment toward the end of March 1865. Samuel B. Arnold's letter of March 27, found in Booth's hotel room, showed that some of the conspirators feared the consequences of their enterprise and were willing to give it up. "But timid as they might be by nature, the whole group was so completely under the ascendency of Booth that they did not dare disobey him when in his presence." After the surrender of General Robert E. Lee, "in an access of malice and rage," Booth called them together and assigned them the roles they were to play in a new conspiracy, "the purpose of which had arisen suddenly in his mind out of the ruins of the abandoned abduction scheme." Final arrangements for the murders of Lincoln, Johnson, and Seward were hastily made, for Booth did not learn until noon on April 14 that Lincoln would be at Ford's Theater in the evening. Booth, George Atzerodt, David Herold, Lewis Paine, and (said Nicolay and Hay) John H. Surratt (!) were seen riding all over the city on last-minute preparations, while Mrs. Surratt drove to her tavern at Surrattsville and told her tenant, John M. Lloyd, that the weapons hidden there earlier would probably be called for that night.[22]

Following graphic descriptions of the murder at Ford's Theater and the attempted murder at Seward's home, Nicolay and Hay proceeded to a discussion of the military trial and the fate of the conspirators. Had he not broken his leg, Booth might have escaped capture indefinitely, for it was not difficult to hide among friends, and eventually he could have made his way to a foreign country. At the trial of Booth's fellow conspirators before the military commission it was not proved that the conspirators had been acting as agents of Davis and the Confederates in Canada, as the government had charged, though evidence did prove that Booth's group had been in frequent communication with both Richmond and Canada. There was, however, no doubt as to the guilt of the defendants themselves. In the case of Mrs. Surratt, "the repugnance which all men feel at the execution of a woman induced the commission to unite in a recommendation to mercy," but President Johnson, "then in the first flush of his zeal against traitors," disregarded it.[23]

In this brief but pioneering chapter, two of the men closest to Lincoln and most deeply affected by his death thus presented the assassination as a simple conspiracy. But they stressed the existence of suspicious contacts between Booth and his group and Confederate leaders, defended the verdicts of the military commission, and took Holt's side in the controversy over the petition of clemency for Mrs. Surratt. It was as close to an endorsement of the War Department's original case as two judicious minds, after a quarter of a century, could come. It was also a kind of codification of the Republican view of the assassination that had prevailed since the late 1860s.

But Nicolay and Hay's summary was quite unsatisfactory to General Thomas M. Harris, former member of the military commission, who was so upset that he published in 1892 the first book-length account of the assassination (except for collections of newspaper articles hastily assembled in 1865–66). In his *Assassination of Lincoln. A History of the Great Conspiracy,* Harris criticized Nicolay and Hay for a general unfamiliarity with the evidence and for two of their major assumptions: first, that Booth had originally planned to kidnap Lincoln and take him to Richmond; and, second, that the decision to assassinate was a hasty impulse emerging out of rage and disappointment at the failure of the abduction plot.[24] Harris devoted the bulk of his book to a restatement of the case for a Confederate grand conspiracy, which the government had presented in 1865, his judgments uninfluenced by second thoughts or second looks at the evidence. He was as fully convinced in 1892 as he had been in 1865 of the truth of the testimony of even such witnesses as Sandford Conover, and he arrived at the same verdict he had reached in 1865; "that the assassination of President Lincoln was the result of a deep-laid political scheme to subvert the government of the United States in aid of the rebellion; that it was not merely the rash act of Booth and his co-conspirators, to whom the work was intrusted; but that behind these stood Jefferson Davis and his Canada cabinet." If the Rebel leaders had not been proved guilty at the conspiracy trial, Harris exclaimed, "I do not see how it would be possible to prove anything."[25]

That Davis and the men listed in the May 2nd proclamation had not been tried did not mean, Harris proceeded to explain, that the government recognized it had no case against them. It meant, rather, that once the rebellion was declared to be at an end the U.S. government had adopted "the benign policy of condoning the past and only securing guarantees for the future." This policy of "tempering justice with mercy" had been written into the Constitution in the Fourteenth Amendment; no Confederate leaders were to be punished beyond being made ineligible to hold political office.[26]

As might be expected, Harris was particularly sensitive to charges that the conspiracy trial had been unfair and that Mrs. Surratt had been unjustly hanged. Such talk, he noted, originated with the same people who had supported secession and who after the war seized upon the trial as a means of continuing for political purposes their abuse of the U.S. government. This abuse had never ceased, "and the case of Mrs. Surratt continues to be worked for all that it is worth by that portion of the Northern press that inherits the old copperhead animus." Though completely satisfied as to the involvement of Mrs. Surratt in the assassination conspiracy, five of the military commissioners— Harris not one of them—had recommended clemency because of sex and age. This petition, along with the record of the court's findings, had been presented to the president by Judge Advo-

cate General Holt. It was also "carefully considered and discussed by the President and a full cabinet, when, without a
dissenting voice, the sentences of the Commission were confirmed, and the prayer of the petition was rejected."[27]

Holt and Stanton, Harris continued, had been the chief targets of the attacks made by enemies of the government. They
needed no defense before loyal citizens, for "they were never
denounced by any but rebels. . . . A purer man, a truer patriot,
a braver, more intelligent and able officer than Gen. Joseph Holt
never will grace the pages of American history." Holt was hated
and denounced only because of the faithfulness and efficiency
with which he carried out his duties. Nor could Stanton's record
be "blurred by the false and vile charges or insinuations of his
enemies, for his enemies were only found amongst the enemies
of his country."[28]

There cannot have been many people in the 1890s who were
so sure as Harris that the Confederate leadership had been responsible for Lincoln's assassination. Perhaps even Harris was
not so sure as he seemed, for in 1897 he published another book
arguing the case for a very different kind of grand conspiracy.

Joseph Holt died in 1894 and thus escaped by one year having
to read David M. Dewitt's *The Judicial Murder of Mrs. Surratt*,
an experience that certainly would have killed him. For in this
monograph and in a more comprehensive book on the assassination published in 1909, Dewitt fused some of the uncertainties about Mrs. Surratt and the War Department's conduct of
the case against her into a new consensus. With Dewitt's books,
the history of Lincoln's assassination made an abrupt turn away
from the Republican assumptions—summarized by Nicolay and
Hay—that had been dominant for a generation.

A lawyer and Democratic politician who had served in the
U.S. House of Representatives in the 1870s and in the New
York State legislature in the 1880s, Dewitt approached the subjects of Mrs. Surratt and the assassination of Lincoln with the
emotional intensity of an attorney defending a grievously wronged
client and with the fire of a political partisan exposing the crimes
of the opposition. Indeed, Dewitt was a leader of the "revisionist" movement, that pro-Democratic reaction against the Republican domination of national affairs that had prevailed since

1860—a domination that had enabled Republicans to appropriate the martyred Lincoln for themselves and to assume the heroic stature of national patriots, while stigmatizing Democrats as Rebels and Copperheads. Dewitt's books on Mrs. Surratt and the assassination and a third volume on *The Impeachment and Trial of Andrew Johnson* (1903) were scalding indictments of the Republican leadership, particularly of Stanton, and they were published just as it was becoming possible for Americans to look back upon the passions and the mistakes of the past without responding like partisans. In fact, by the turn of the century, many Republicans, anxious to cement the reunion of North and South, competed with Democrats in censuring the anti-southern "excesses" of the Radicals. The history of the United States during the Civil War and Reconstruction was being revised, and Dewitt's forcefully expressed views—even though they were based upon conjecture and the reassessment of old facts rather than upon new evidence—were so plausibly reasoned and fit so neatly into the anti-Radical Republican point of view being expressed by other historians that they quickly gained predominance. Even Dewitt's heavy sarcasm and the stridency of his prose seem to have been absorbed without difficulty by a public willing to accept negative evaluations of the old Radical leaders and of the Reconstruction policies with which they were identified.

Only one other writer on Lincoln's assassination—Otto Eisenschiml—has had an influence comparable to Dewitt's. For this reason, the views of Dewitt as stated in *The Judicial Murder of Mrs. Surratt* are summarized in the following pages at some length.

Edwin M. Stanton was not merely the blunt, abrasive secretary of war so frequently criticized by his opponents during his lifetime; he was an unstable man who lost his head during pressure and was unable to make sound judgments. Like the worst of the panic-stricken wretches who swarmed the streets of Washington the night of the assassination, Stanton assumed the existence of a widespread plot to kill the leaders of the U.S. government. "Upon this theory he began," and, closing his eyes and ears to everything which militated against it, "upon this theory he prosecuted to the end, every effort for the discovery, arrest, trial and punishment of the murderers."[29]

Under Stanton's orders, Joseph Holt's "Bureau of Military (In)Justice" scoured the country for suspects and witnesses and brought them to Washington, where, by promises and threats, it "squeezed out of them" the testimony it wanted. After just two weeks of wholesale arrests, imprisonments, and inquisitions, Holt informed the president that the Bureau could prove the existence of a grand conspiracy of the Confederate leaders, and accordingly Johnson issued his May 2nd proclamation. But the War Department was in too much of a hurry to wait for the arrests of these leaders, so a military court was organized to proceed immediately to try those prisoners "selected from the multitude undergoing confinement as the fittest victims to appease the shade of the murdered President" (19–22).

Not one of the nine military judges chosen by Stanton to try these unfortunate prisoners would have withstood the challenges allowed in the civil courts to the most depraved criminal in choosing his jury. The seven generals and two colonels had come together to avenge the death of their commander-in-chief. "They dreamt not of acquittal. They were, necessarily, from the nature of their task, *organized to convict*" (26).

At the foot of the judge's table sat the three government prosecutors. Holt had "distinguished himself on many a bloody court-martial." Bingham "was one of those fierce and fiery western criminal lawyers, gifted with that sort of vociferous oratory which tells upon jurors and on the stump." His special duty as special judge advocate was "to cross-examine and brow-beat the witnesses for the defense, a branch of his profession in which he was proudly proficient." Henry L. Burnett had recently won his laurels in the military trial and conviction of Lamdin P. Milligan, "laurels, alas! soon to be blasted by the decision of the U.S. Supreme Court pronouncing that and all other Military Commissions for the trial of citizens in places where the civil courts are open illegal, and setting free the man this zealous public servant had been instrumental in condemning to death" (26–27).

Throughout the trial the judge advocates sought to prove the guilt not only of the eight defendants but also of the Rebel agents in Canada and Davis, by introducing "every now and then during the trial—whenever most convenient to the prosecution," the testimony of spies, counterspies, and double spies from

Canada. The "head, parent and tutor" of these witnesses was Conover, who was later completely discredited, along with his testimony. But during the trial, when "the passionate desire for vengeance was at its height," any scoundrel or perjuror, attracted to Washington by the scent of reward money, was eagerly welcomed by the Bureau of Military Justice. "Any story, no matter how absurd or incredible, provided it brought Jefferson Davis within conjectural fore-knowledge of the assassination, was greedily swallowed, and, moreover, was rewarded with money and employment. These harpies flocked, like buzzards, around the doors of the old Penitentiary . . . to swear that Davis and Benjamin were the instigators of Booth and Surratt." On the other hand, the commission assumed from the beginning that the testimony of any witness for the defense who had supported the rebellion was false (64–65, 68–69).

Although the existence of the abduction plot confronted them every time they looked at the evidence they had collected, the judge advocates agreed not to see it, for it demolished the preconceived theory that the Confederate government, through its agents in Canada, had conspired the murder. If the assassination occurred to Booth only after the fall of Richmond and the surrender of Lee, "as a mere after-thought, the offspring of a spirit of impotent revenge," then the murderous conspiracy to overthrow the government of the United States by assassinating its leaders, conceived by Stanton and cherished by Holt, had never existed. Furthermore, to concede the existence of the kidnapping plot would very nearly establish the innocence of Mrs. Surratt, Arnold, Michael O'Laughlin, Samuel A. Mudd, and even John H. Surratt, by explaining why the suspicious meetings at the Surratt home should have ceased after the fall of Richmond and why Surratt then left immediately for Canada (92–95).

The judge advocates, in no mood to help establish the innocence of any of the defendants before them, therefore ridiculed or deprecated talk of kidnapping, suppressed Booth's diary, and sought to prove the reality of a long-standing conspiracy to assassinate by introducing anonymous and mysteriously discovered letters and other dubious evidence. In his concluding speech Bingham told the court that Davis had been shown to be as guilty of the assassination conspiracy as Booth, and that each of the individuals on trial, and Surratt besides, was guilty not only beyond any reasonable doubt but beyond any doubt whatever (90, 94–97).

When it was all over, when the room was cleared for the last time, the judges pulled their chairs up to the table to consider their findings. But who remained with them and participated in their deliberations? Who but Holt, Bingham, and Burnett! The prosecutors closeted with the judges and participating not only in the verdicts reached but also in the sentences meted out! "Where can we look in the history of the world for a parallel to such a spectacle?" (92)

Although only the results of the two days of deliberation between the judges and the judge advocates were made a matter of record, it was possible to imagine what had happened. There was likely no disagreement between the judges and judge advocates in the cases of Herold, Atzerodt, and Paine, either as to their guilt or the price they should pay for it. But in the cases of O'Laughlin, Arnold, Spangler, and Mudd, a majority of the judges "slipped the bloody rein" the judge advocates had hoped to harness them with, and imposed prison terms rather than hanging (102–3). Then came consideration of what to do with Mrs. Surratt. In her case, too, the judge advocates found the judges reluctant to impose the supreme penalty. A vote of two-thirds of the nine commissioners was required for the sentence of death, and only four votes were on hand. Out of fear that their "female fiend" was likely to escape the halter, the judge advocates therefore called an end to the day's discussion and hurried away to consult with the secretary of war.

Now that Booth was dead and Surratt still at liberty, Stanton's "one supreme aim" was that Mrs. Surratt be condemned to death. She was "the friend of Booth, and the entertainer of Paine," and she was to be made an example to the women of the South who "had 'unsexed' themselves by cherishing and cheering fathers, brothers, husbands and sons on the tented field" (105–6).

At the meeting between Stanton, Holt, and Bingham (no mention of Burnett), it was agreed that if six votes for hanging could not be secured, then, "as a last resort," the prosecutors would suggest to the commissioners that they condemn Mrs. Surratt to death and then petition the president to commute the sentence to life imprisonment. The three men reasoned that "with the petition in their custody and the President under their dominion," they could still send their victim to the gallows (107–9).

At the next day's meeting with the military commission, Holt and Bingham, invigorated by their talk with Stanton, unfolded their strategem. "We can almost hear their voices. . . . Holt, making a merit of yielding in the cases of Spangler, of O'Laughlin, of Arnold and of Mudd, denounces the universal disloyalty of the women of the South, and pleads the necessity of an example. Bingham, holding up both mother and son as equally deep-dyed in blood with Booth and Payne, both insinuates and threatens at the same time, that, if 'tenderness,' forsooth, is to be shown because of the age and sex of such a she-assassin, then, for the sake of the blood of their murdered Commander-in-Chief, do not his own soldiers show it, but let his successor take the fearful responsibility" (109).

Before such an onslaught, one of the judges wavers and changes his vote to hanging; one more is needed, but it is not forthcoming. With Mrs. Surratt's life trembling in the balance, "the supreme reserve is at last brought forward—an argument much in use with Judge-Advocates in cases of refractory courtsmartial, as a last resort—that the President will not allow a hair of her head to be harmed, but that *terror*, TERROR is necessary; in this instance, to force the son to quit his hiding place, the life of the mother must be the bait held out to catch the unsurrendering son." The appeal works, six votes are cast for death, and Bingham sits down and writes the petition to the president to commute the sentence. General James A. Ekin copies it on a half-sheet of paper, keeping Bingham's draft "as a memento of so gentle an executioner." The petition is signed by five of the officers and, along with a succinct statement of the verdicts and sentences in each of the eight cases, is placed in the hands of Holt (109–11).

At the July 5 meeting between Holt and President Johnson in the White House, there was a perfect meeting of minds regarding the guilt of the condemned and the desirability of a prompt execution of their sentences. Johnson was still serving his "Stanton Apprenticeship," and the idea of extending clemency to any member of the band of conspirators convicted by Stanton's court was unthinkable. Probably the two men talked about "the curious weakness" of some members of the commission and of the public at large who favored clemency for Mrs. Surratt because of her sex and age. If so, both men would have rejected the idea on legal principle and because they agreed that hanging would have a salutary effect on other female Rebels. Then it was time for the president to approve the sentences of the commission.

The record that Holt now presented to the president consisted of several pages of legal-size sheets bound together at the top by a thin yellow ribbon, with the half-sheet petition in behalf of Mrs. Surratt attached at the back. The writing on these pages was in the usual legal style; upon reaching the bottom of the page, the paper was flipped up and writing proceeded on the other side from the bottom down. The trial record ended in the middle of a new sheet, leaving the last half and the whole obverse side blank. At this place, immediately following the signature of General David Hunter, president of the commission, Holt had written the order approving the sentences, setting the hour and date of the executions, and the place of confinement for the conspirators sentenced to prison. He had reached the bottom of the sheet before finishing, but instead of flipping it over as with all the other sheets, which would have left the petition directly before the president's eye, Holt had reverted to the layman's way of writing papers. He had turned the whole record over and written on the back of the sheet from the top down. The petition, which came next, was thus either exposed upside down, or was folded under the other leaves. With his hand shaking from his recent illness, Johnson signed at the place indicated by Holt, who gathered up the papers and returned to the War Department (115–19).

The petition then disappeared from view; "ignored, suppressed or slurred over when before the President, it had served its pitiful purpose. . . . It seems to have sunk suddenly into oblivion; its very existence became the subject of dispute. It was omitted from the authorized published proceedings of the Commission. It was omitted from the annual report of the Judge-Advocate. The disloyal paper must have been laid alongside the suppressed 'Diary'" (119).

In his 1873 *Vindication*, Holt had declared he and the president had discussed the petition, and he had also submitted letters purporting to show that the president had talked about it with members of his cabinet as well. But Holt could not have been telling the truth. When the existence of the petition was revealed in 1867, Johnson would not have dared to state publicly that he had never seen it before if, in fact, he had discussed it with the cabinet. Radical Republicans who had been in the cabinet, including Stanton, Harlan, and Speed, would have been only too happy to contradict him, to expose him in a lie. Yet none of them—and no other member of the cabinet, either—had ever stated that the petition had been discussed. In his letter to Holt, Harlan had stated only that the possibility of commuting Mrs. Surratt's sentence had been discussed, not that the commission's recommendation had been. Since Johnson himself had stated as much in his reply to Holt, Harlan's letter was worthless (194–95, 208–11).

Bingham's letter, in which the special judge advocate had claimed that both Seward and Stanton had informed him that they had talked about the petition with the president but that Stanton had instructed him not to make the fact public, was also worthless. Why had Bingham waited until 1873, after the death of Seward, before disregarding Stanton's order? Why had he not done so after Stanton's death in 1869? What power could Stanton have had over Bingham in 1869 that was no longer effective in 1873 (216–11)?

And what of Speed, whose sense of propriety, he had so often said, would not permit him to divulge what had been discussed in cabinet meetings? This conscientious silence, which through the years had been the source of so much public chagrin for Holt, was in reality a protective shield behind which Holt found sanctuary. If there had been no discussion of the petition, it would have violated no confidences for Speed to say so, though it would have ruined Holt and settled the controversy over the petition in favor of Johnson. But Speed said nothing, and his silence seemed to imply that he had something to say, thus giving Holt the benefit of the doubt. Holt's pleas to Speed to speak up were thus not as sincere as they sounded (211–14).

The members of the military commission, President Johnson, General Hancock, and other individuals involved in the convic-

tions and execution of Mrs. Surratt could plead "the madness of
the time" to excuse their actions. But not Stanton, Holt, and
Bingham.

Upon their three heads should descend the full weight of criminal
turpitude involved in this most unnatural execution. They sat upon
the thrones of power. They dragged a woman from her humble roof
and thrust her into a dungeon. . . . They baited her for weeks with
their Montgomerys and Conovers, their Weichmans [sic] and Lloyds,
the spawn of their bureau, dragooned by terror or suborned by hope.
They shouted into the ears of the court appeal on appeal for her head.
And, when at last five of their chosen sons sickened at the task and
shrank from shedding a woman's blood, they procured the death-
sentence by a trick. They forged the death-warrant by another. . . .
They cheated their own court. They cheated their own President. They
cheated the very executioner. They sneaked a woman into the arms of
death by sleight-of-hand. . . . The execution of Mary E. Surratt is the
foulest blot on the history of the United States of America (252–53, 257).

Although Dewitt's stunning indictment of Stanton, Holt, and
Bingham was based largely upon conjecture, it was so power-
fully stated that it has been assumed ever since the three men
were guilty as charged. Since 1895 the only writers who have
taken Holt's side of the argument with Johnson over the petition
have ignored the reasoning found in *The Judicial Murder of Mrs.
Surratt*. Even Stanton's biographers accept Dewitt's judgment
that the petition was withheld from Johnson by trickery. Benjamin P. Thomas and Harold Hyman note that there is no evidence linking Stanton to Holt's "dissimulation" and observe that
"Holt alone may have been blameworthy." But they are quick to
acknowledge that "Holt would have been a bold man indeed to
deceive Stanton in a matter of such importance. Nor does it
seem likely that the petition could have been omitted from Pitman's published record of the trial without Stanton's knowledge
and consent. And complicity in the one implies complicity in
the other."[30]

And yet, conjecture and inference of the kind so imagina-
tively employed by Dewitt could lead to an entirely different
conclusion. Without violence to the evidence, it could be argued that the petition was suppressed, not by Stanton and Holt,
but by Johnson.

Suppose that during their private meeting Holt did show the

petition to Johnson and did discuss it with him, and that both men agreed that sex and age were insufficient grounds to justify commutation of the death penalty. Johnson, still inclined to deal harshly with Rebels (especially assassins), might then have decided—with or without Holt's concurrence or knowledge—not to speak of the petition to his advisers in the cabinet before soliciting their opinions on the subject of clemency. Finding them unanimously opposed to it, the president might easily conclude that there was no need to tell them about the petition. Since Stanton believed Mrs. Surratt to be guilty and was opposed to clemency, he might see no reason to bring it up, either, especially since the president had not. He might logically conclude, too, that, under the circumstances, it would be wise to instruct Holt (who would not have objected) to omit the petition from Pitman's published record of the trial.

When the petition was produced at the Surratt trial in 1867—by a civil attorney in private practice, not by a War Department official—and Johnson stated he had never seen it before, he could not have been contradicted by Speed or Harlan because, since he had not spoken of it to them in 1865, they would not have known whether or not he had seen it. According to Bingham's story (which Holt seemed to have believed), Stanton and Seward would have known that the president had seen and discussed the petition. But neither could have unmasked Johnson without explaining why he had remained silent in 1865, and Stanton would have had to explain why he had allowed the petition to be omitted from Pitman. Seward, still on friendly terms with the president, would have been reluctant from the first to embarrass him.

Following this scenario, why did Holt bother to insist in 1873—as he had in 1867—that he had shown the petition to the president, and why did he attempt to prove that the president had discussed it with his cabinet? Because Johnson, back in politics, was trying to shift opprobrium for the death of Mrs. Surratt from himself to Holt, just as attorney Pierrepont had attempted to place it upon Johnson when he produced the petition at Surratt's trial in 1867. It was not enough for Holt to repeat he had shown the petition to Johnson; he had to try to prove that Johnson had seen it—hence, the letters from Bingham, Harlan, Speed, and others. In this hypothetical reconstruction, it is conceivable that

Holt did not know the president had failed to speak of the petition with his cabinet and that when he beseeched Speed so earnestly to speak up he really believed Speed could save him.

It is also conceivable that the letter from Bingham was entirely honest, that Stanton did tell Bingham (in Seward's presence) that the petition had been discussed by the cabinet, and, knowing that it had not been, had therefore ordered Bingham to remain silent. Bingham did not reveal the existence of Stanton's order until 1873 because there had been no reason to speak of it before. In short, given the same facts with which Dewitt worked, it is possible to conclude that Holt's forebodings that his reputation was being sacrificed by Stanton and Speed were as real as they seemed to be, and that Johnson, not Holt, was the true dissembler, with Stanton a willing accomplice in 1865 and an unhappy one in 1867.

Conjectures, unlike facts, are easily changed, and Dewitt changed his own theory about the origin of the petition for clemency. In *Judicial Murder* he represented it as a device of the judge advocates to trick the military commission into voting for the death penalty. In *The Assassination of Abraham Lincoln* (1909), he maintained that the commission forced the petition upon the judge advocates.[31]

Whatever the true story of the petition may have been, Dewitt's case against Stanton, Holt, and Bingham was every bit as emotional and partisan as he claimed their case against Mrs. Surratt had been. To excuse the military judges and others on the grounds that they were affected by "the madness of the time," while holding that Stanton, Holt, and Bingham were not affected by the times but generated their own particular wickedness, is clearly unjustifiable.

When Dewitt showed his manuscript to Thomas Ewing, the attorney who had participated in the defenses of Mudd, Arnold, and Edman Spangler, he was surprised and disappointed to learn that Ewing was not interested. Ewing's son believed he understood his father's reaction. Dewitt, he declared, argued "with great vehemence, not to say violence," and although the senior Ewing agreed that the conspiracy trial should never have been held before a military tribunal, "he recognized [that] the hideous crime and . . . the outburst of public anger . . . [had] swept men off their feet."[32] There was no good reason for Dewitt to ignore the fact that Stanton, Holt, and Bingham were also, after all, men with feet.

By focusing his blinding spotlight exclusively on the fate of Mrs. Surratt, Dewitt distorted reality by blacking out the other individuals, problems, and uncertainties with which Stanton had to deal in the chaotic weeks following the assassination of Lincoln and the simultaneous end of the Civil War. Without any evidence, he made it seem that the secretary was obsessed with a single mad objective, "one supreme aim": how to take the life of an innocent woman. Certainly he was mistaken in asserting that the death sentence for Mrs. Surratt had been bait to lure her son out of hiding. Had that been the case, there would have been a prolonged and much-publicized delay in carrying out the sentence.

A very different kind of book was Osborn H. Oldroyd's *The Assassination of Abraham Lincoln* (1901). As a young Ohio soldier on duty in Tennessee, Oldroyd was deeply moved by Lincoln's death and began immediately to build a large and matchless collection of Lincoln memorabilia. In Springfield, Illinois, he located and secured many pieces of furniture and other personal items that the Lincolns had disposed of at the time of their move to Washington. In 1883 he moved his growing collection into the Lincoln home at 8th and Jackson streets, and, under the sponsorship of the State of Illinois, to whom Robert Todd Lincoln had presented the house, opened it to the public. In the next decade he moved his museum to Washington, where the Lincoln Memorial Association had leased the Petersen house across the street from Ford's Theater. There, in "The House Where Lincoln Died," he continued to show his collection— including thousands of documents, books, and miscellaneous items relating to the assassination, the trial, and the flight of Booth—until his own death in 1930. Not even Robert Lincoln had lived so intimately for so long in an environment that was a constant reminder of Lincoln's life and death.[33]

Oldroyd's *Assassination* is an informal and rambling volume, which reads as if it had grown out of the questions asked by visitors. Indeed, it probably did, for Oldroyd was disturbed by the public's lack of knowledge about the assassination and at the same time gratified by its interest. A staunch Republican, both politically and in his view of the assassination, Oldroyd was as uncritical as General Harris in his acceptance of the testimony presented at the conspiracy trial. He believed that "had the military court reached out a little farther in its investigations, . . . it would have implicated many persons holding positions of power and authority in the service of the Confederate Government." But Oldroyd did accept the reality of Booth's kidnapping plans and conceded that, though there was little doubt Mrs. Surratt had been involved in the abduction plot, she might not "have been privy to the murder."[34]

Far longer than Nicolay and Hay's summary, far preferable to Harris's recapitulation of the conspiracy trial, and far broader in scope than Dewitt's monograph on Mrs. Surratt (which it ignored), Oldroyd's narrative was, at the time of its publication, incomparably the best source for the people of a new generation and a new century to consult for knowledge of the murder of Lincoln. One chapter remains of interest, Oldroyd's "Narrative of a Walk of the Author, May 1901, Over the Route of Flight and Capture" of Booth, a route first discovered and explored by the writer/reporter George Alfred Townsend in the 1880s.[35] On his outing, Oldroyd conversed with men and women who had helped Booth and Herold on their way, or had known those who had, and located and photographed many of the places where the fugitives had stopped. Eisenschiml, Stanley Kimmel, and others made similar trips in the 1920s and 30s, and by the 1970s the Surratt Society—located in the restored tavern at Surrattsville (now Clinton, Maryland)—was conducting two tours a year along the John Wilkes Booth Escape Trail.[36]

In 1909, the centenary of Lincoln's birth, two important books about his death were published: Dewitt's *The Assassination of Abraham Lincoln and Its Expiation*, and Clara Laughlin's *The Death of Lincoln: The Story of Booth's Plot, His Deed and the Penalty*. The first books to present the assassination as an unqualified simple conspiracy, they remained the best statements of the theory until publication in 1940 of the classic *The Great American Myth*, by George S. Bryan.

A writer on the staff of *McClure's Magazine* during its most influential years, Laughlin was assigned in 1906 to investigate Lincoln's death by Samuel S. McClure, who had noted that Lincoln biographers paid little attention to the assassination. With the enthusiastic cooperation of one of *McClure's* readers, President Theodore Roosevelt, Laughlin was permitted to examine relics of the assassination in the custody of the War Department; in the judge advocate general's office she saw Booth's diary, clothes, "and sundry things relating to his capture." The latter may have referred to the voluminous collection of documents gathered by Holt's Bureau of Military Justice, but, if so, she made no use of the papers.[37] She did, however, turn up obscure and forgotten documents in the files of old newspapers and magazines and reproduced many of them as appendices in the final third of her book. *The Death of Lincoln* thus became a kind of source book as well as a narrative of the assassination.

Laughlin used her sources—including Pitman's record of the trial and interviews with men and women, now elderly, who had firsthand knowledge of some phase of the assassination—with discrimination. "I learned how possible it is," she later wrote, "for persons who are making their best effort to tell the truth to be completely mistaken about what they saw or heard."[38]

One reminiscence in which Laughlin had confidence was that of William H. Crook, Lincoln's policeman guard. In an article for which Laughlin may have been responsible, Crook revealed in *Harper's Monthly* in September 1907 that John F. Parker, another of the guards provided for the president by the Washington Metropolitan Police, had left his post outside Lincoln's box on April 14 in order to take a seat where he could watch the play. It was the first the public had ever heard of the incident, but, repeated by Laughlin and later by Crook himself in two books of reminiscences, it quickly became a familiar feature of the assassination story.[39]

The most celebrated individual to whom Laughlin talked was John H. Surratt, living in Baltimore and working as an auditor for a shipping firm. Although she was introduced to him in his home by his daughter, she asked him no questions, for she found that "the pall of tragedy still lay heavy, stifling," over the household. Besides, according to Laughlin, Surratt never granted interviews. Occasionally alleged interviews were published in the press, but, she stated authoritatively, they were all fabrications. Surratt wanted to bury the past and never spoke of the death of his mother, nor did his children in his presence. But Laughlin did have a copy, dug from the files of the Washington *Star*, of the lecture Surratt had given in Rockville, Maryland, in 1870, describing his association with Booth in the kidnapping conspiracy and was thus able to write the fullest account yet published of that plot. Deeply moved by the Surratt tragedy, Laughlin grieved that for his boyish participation in the kidnapping scheme Surratt had had to pay "a penalty not much less hideous than some of the worst Russian horrors we read about."[40] The comparison was excessive, but it must have pleased Surratt, who lived until 1916.

Although by the time she was writing the 1865 conspiracy trial seemed "hideously unfair," Laughlin made an effort to see it in its historical setting and concluded that it "was probably as fair as a trial could be in those circumstances, in those times." Like Dewitt, she detested "Stanton, the relentless," whom she accused of feeding the public's appetite for vengeance with his own overpowering hatreds. Stanton "hated anything that defied his iron rule, hated the 'treacherous and dangerous enemy' he had worked so ceaselessly to subdue; he hated Southern women in particular, and he hated all Catholics in general."[41] The charge that Stanton hated southern women and Roman Catholics—already an old one in 1909—continues to be made. Apparently it is based on nothing more substantial than the fact that Mrs. Surratt was a southern woman and a Catholic.

Another of Laughlin's villains was Johnson. Basing her account on William M. Stewart's notoriously hostile *Reminiscences*,[42] she described the vice-president at the moment of Lincoln's death in his hotel "sleeping in a drunken stupor, . . . unshaven, unkempt, unheeding." Johnson was eager for the conspirators to be prosecuted and punished, Laughlin wrote, so that he could "show himself righteously incensed by the crime that made him President, and . . . put down the feeling that his hands were not quite clean."[43] Her dislike of Johnson (and possibly the hospitality she had been shown in the office of the judge advocate general) led Laughlin to take Holt's side in the controversy over the petition for clemency. The simple truth of the matter, she wrote, "seems to be that Judge Holt did indeed present the petition . . . and that Johnson's disclaimer and the silence of the Cabinet were a rank injustice to a man who, though narrow and bigoted, did not merit the charge of dishonour."[44]

On the other hand, she held Holt guilty of "coaching perjurors to swear to the complicity of Jefferson Davis and the Southern leaders," a crime of which he was innocent.[45]

Although marred by such hasty judgments and by the emotional excesses of the portraits of Stanton, Johnson, and Booth (to be discussed in the next chapter), Laughlin's *The Death of Lincoln* was the first book on the assassination in which any attempt at all was made to be objective.

If Laughlin acted like a journalist investigating and reporting a big story, in *The Assassination of Abraham Lincoln* Dewitt continued to play the role of the defense attorney out to discredit the morals and motives of the prosecution. Surratt's 1870 lecture had been reprinted in the Washington *Star* in April 1908, so both authors were able to treat the kidnapping conspiracy at greater length than previous writers. Laughlin did so because it was central to her depiction of Booth as a dashing youth who wanted passionately to serve the South. Dewitt stressed the plan to kidnap in order to shame the government officials who had insisted at the conspiracy trial that there had been no such thing. To strengthen his point, Dewitt even committed an offense to which special pleaders are prone: he allowed his imagination to run away from the evidence. First, he described elaborate preparations allegedly made by the conspirators in January 1865 to capture Lincoln inside Ford's Theater during a performance of *Jack Cade*, starring Edwin Forrest, preparations that went for naught because Lincoln failed to attend. Second, he described—for dramatic effect in the present tense—the interception of Lincoln's carriage on the Seventh Street road that day in March 1865: "The noise of wheels indicates that the decisive hour has come, and every rider straightens himself for the fray. The carriage drives by, but lo! the President is not inside; as if some warning had been given, another officer sits placid in his stead. Filled with chagrin and apprehension of betrayal, the horsemen scatter in all directions."[46]

Whatever Booth and his friends were up to in January, there is no real evidence that they planned seriously to capture Lincoln inside the theater, and, though they intended in March to intercept the presidential carriage on the highway, they called off the attempt at the last moment upon discovering that Lincoln's plans had changed. The interception scene in particular has been so often and so picturesquely described by writers on the assassination that Dewitt's fiction is believed in by practically everyone.

Both Laughlin and Dewitt called attention to injustices and cruelties in War Department procedures. But while Laughlin explained many of them away as products of the circumstances of the time, Dewitt held Stanton responsible for the circumstances. On assassination night the powers of the U.S. government devolved upon the secretary of war, and Dewitt was sure that "a pilot more unfit to ride the whirlwind and direct the storm" could not have been found. Stanton was energetic, but "in moments of storm and stress he was apt to lose his head." His first job was "to calm the terrors of the people" of Washington, who were quick to believe every rumor they heard, but he "could not calm his own" terrors. "Instead of endeavoring to mollify the prevailing madness, every movement he made seemed designed to keep it up to the highest pitch." He immediately jumped to the conclusion that the attacks on Lincoln and Seward were parts of a massive Confederate conspiracy and that more assassinations were to be expected. "This conclusion he fastened in the minds of the inhabitants of the District by placing guards around the residences of his colleagues and his own, and declaring the capital in a state of siege; and he spread it broadcast over the country and across the ocean by telegraph."[47]

Stanton then proceeded to organize the machinery to bring Booth and his associates, who, he believed, "were without number and scattered all over the continent," to justice. The machinery included the Washington police force, the military police attached to the provost marshal's office, men assigned to military camps in and about the capital, his own secret service agents, and the detectives and spies attached to Holt's Bureau of Military Justice. "Of these forces—more or less emulous of each other in the ordinary discharge of their duties—every man had caught in its worst form the epidemic of credulity and suspicion and, being stimulated by the hope of promotion and the large rewards placarded in all directions, plunged into a furious competition—multiplying arrests, extorting confessions, ferreting out witnesses and haling them before the nearest tribunal."[48] In short, Dewitt's Stanton assumed that the assassination was part of a grand conspiracy against the government of the United States—

and acted accordingly. Dewitt seems to have believed that the secretary should have known from the first that only a simple conspiracy was involved.

The intemperance and partisanship of Dewitt's *Assassination* did not escape its early readers. Henry Thurston Peck of Columbia University said that Dewitt had "become infected with the hysteria of the period of which he writes. His rhetoric is that of a stump speaker." Yet Peck was strongly influenced by what Dewitt had to say about Stanton. "Before long," the professor predicted, "all Americans who are interested in the period of the Civil War will cease describing him as 'the great War Secretary,' and will fully measure his meanness, his arrogance, his unscrupulous deceit, and his utter cowardice."[49] Thus do extreme partisans like Dewitt impose their views—even upon those who recognize the partisanship—and distort history.

The ominous prediction that Americans would cease to regard Stanton as "the great War Secretary" and would come, instead, to take the measure of alleged negative aspects of his character reached its ultimate fulfillment in the works of Eisenschiml, beginning in 1937. A transitional step between Dewitt and Eisenschiml in the literary destruction of Stanton's reputation was Lloyd Lewis's *Myths After Lincoln* (1929), one of the most widely read of all books dealing with the assassination.

A Chicago newspaperman whose interests turned increasingly in the 1920s and 1930s to the study of the Civil War, Lewis was caught up in the excitement of the still flourishing revisionist movement. The Stanton he described, far from being great, was even more contemptible than the Stanton described by Dewitt. On assassination night, when he learned from a friend who had come to tell him of the attacks on Lincoln and Seward that a mysterious figure had been seen skulking about his house, Stanton assumed that he, too, was an intended assassination victim. As a result, says Lewis, he was "in a panic." During subsequent days, he was "mad with fear," "almost hysterical," and sat in his office "quivering with vengeance—or was it partly fear?"[50]

In addition to being a coward whose mind became unbalanced in the presence of danger and death, Stanton was power mad. Throughout the war he had "believed himself to be the real ruler of the nation, guiding with his superior brain the weaker, softer will of Lincoln." Now, at the dying president's bedside, "his hour had come. He was dictator." When the doctors proclaimed Lincoln dead, Lewis says "Stanton did a curious thing. As though he were alone, he slowly, formally raised his hand, put his hat upon his head, then, as majestically, took it off, like an emperor crowning himself."[51]

Observed and described by an officer serving in the War Department, Stanton's action was noted without comment in a footnote in Frank A. Flower's admiring biography published in 1905. Lewis was the first writer to attach significance to it. His interpretation of a gesture that—if it had any meaning at all—was likely to have been a kind of farewell salute to a man and a president Stanton had learned to love and respect has since proved irresistible to writers seeking to arouse their readers' emotions against the secretary of war.[52] For Lewis to suggest that Stanton, was, in fact, crowning himself was as uncalled for as his suggestion that Mrs. Surratt had been infatuated with Booth. "She was fascinated by the actor," Lewis wrote, "whose moustache was so bold and whose manners were so grand. He was gallant and handsome. . . . She was charmed, and probably in love—poor woman, at the dangerous age in her sex, probably reveling in amorous fancies with this Apollo, twenty years her junior."[53] It is disappointing to find reputable writers passing off such flights of imagination as history.

Lewis's hatred for the "fanatically anti-Catholic" Stanton, unlike Dewitt's, was not produced by sympathy for Mrs. Surratt, who, he says positively and without qualification, "knew of the [kidnapping] plot and approved."[54] In an article in *Liberty Magazine* he stated that the unfortunate "widow-woman" was not only an active member of the kidnapping conspiracy but also that she was of more value to it than her "chatterbox" son. "Mrs. Surratt it was," he wrote, "who furnished the rendezvous for the plotters, who hid equipment for Booth to pick up on his flight, [and] who shut her lips in the face of inquisitors."[55] He stopped short of saying Mrs. Surratt was involved in the assassination, but he left the impression that she must have been, for he treated Louis J. Weichmann, the boarder whose testimony helped to convict her, with great partiality.

The favorable treatment of Weichmann, so much at odds with the revisionist habit of being decidedly pro–Mrs. Surratt, was no doubt influenced by Lewis's personal experiences. As a boy, Lewis saw Weichmann himself on the streets of Anderson, Indiana, where the government's star witness operated a business college, and in the 1920s he heard from the lips of Weichmann's two elderly sisters the story of their brother's involvement with the Surratts and the misery it had cost him. He had done his duty at the conspiracy trial, the sisters insisted, but he was denounced by friends of Mrs. Surratt as a liar, and ever after he felt his life was in danger from some of them. On his deathbed he dictated a statement to his sisters that Lewis was the first to see and reproduce. "This is to certify," Weichmann had declared on June 2, 1902, "that every word I gave in evidence at the assassination trial was absolutely true; and now I am about to die and with love I recommend myself to all truth-loving people."[56] Lewis was much impressed with this document, "for death-bed statements are better than sworn testimony, the legal men say, arguing that no man will send his soul climbing up through the stars to God weighted down with a lie." In another magazine article Lewis even said the statement "solves the case of Mrs. Surratt," but he omitted the claim from his book.[57]

Like all revisionists, Lewis was aggressively hostile toward the Radicals, whom he called "a little group of willful Republicans" (borrowing the phrase from Woodrow Wilson's characterization of the U.S. Senators who opposed his League of Nations), and he assumed they had acted from the most devious and reprehensible of motives. He reproached Stanton for announcing that a grand conspiracy of Confederate leaders was behind Lincoln's assassination instead of telling the public "that there was no evidence that the murder was anything but the fool exploit of a disgruntled actor performing, as he said, on his own initiative." The implication was that Stanton knew his charge was false and that he made it solely to win public support for what revisionists said was the Radical program of making the South pay for its crimes.

The "judicial murder" of Mrs. Surratt aside, one might suppose that Lewis's suggestion that Stanton knew the assassination was a simple conspiracy but for political purposes proclaimed it was a grand conspiracy would be the most despicable outrage imaginable against him. But Eisenschiml, another Chicagoan and a friend of Lewis, imagined something worse.

By all odds, the best and most comprehensive book on the assassination as a simple conspiracy is Bryan's *The Great American Myth* (1940). As Bryan observed in his foreword, the assassination had from the first become "involved in a tangle of disorder and error, of falsehood and credulity, from which it has not yet been set free."[58] If he had had the influence he deserved, Bryan might have gone a long way toward setting it free, for his research was undertaken in the scholarly tradition of seeking the truth, and the tone of his writing was judicious and unemotional. The great irony of *The Great American Myth* is that it was published just after Eisenschiml revolutionized the subject of Lincoln's murder with an entirely new grand conspiracy theory, entangling the assassination in new "disorders and errors, falsehoods and credulities" and reducing Booth, once again, to the secondary role of hired gunman. The public was far more interested in the sensational new Eisenschiml thesis and in the elaborations that immediately followed it than in Bryan's sober analysis of Booth's simple conspiracy. The result was that instead of beginning a new era of scholarship by freeing the assassination from the myths, misconceptions, and deliberate distortions of the past, *The Great American Myth* had very little impact at all.

Abraham Lincoln, Monday, April 10, 1865.

John Wilkes Booth.

John Wilkes Booth, pistol and knife in hand, being urged into Lincoln's box at Ford's Theater by the Devil. In the Lincoln murder conspiracies, many different individuals have been cast in the Devil's role.

SURRAT.   BOOTH.   HAROLD.

War Department, Washington, April 20, 1865,

☞ $100,000 REWARD!

THE MURDERER

Of our late beloved President, Abraham Lincoln,

IS STILL AT LARGE.

$50,000 REWARD

Will be paid by this Department for his apprehension, in addition to any reward offered by Municipal Authorities or State Executives.

$25,000 REWARD

Will be paid for the apprehension of JOHN H. SURRATT, one of Booth's Accomplices.

$25,000 REWARD

Will be paid for the apprehension of David C. Harold, another of Booth's accomplices.

LIBERAL REWARDS will be paid for any information that shall conduce to the arrest of either of the above-named criminals, or their accomplices.

All persons harboring or secreting the said persons, or either of them, or aiding or assisting their concealment or escape, will be treated as accomplices in the murder of the President and the attempted assassination of the Secretary of State, and shall be subject to trial before a Military Commission and the punishment of DEATH.

Let the stain of innocent blood be removed from the land by the arrest and punishment of the murderers.

All good citizens are exhorted to aid public justice on this occasion. Every man should consider his own conscience charged with this solemn duty, and rest neither night nor day until it be accomplished.

EDWIN M. STANTON, Secretary of War.

DESCRIPTIONS.—BOOTH is Five Feet 7 or 8 inches high, slender build, high forehead, black hair, black eyes, and wears a heavy black moustache.

JOHN H. SURRAT is about 5 feet, 9 inches. Hair rather thin and dark; eyes rather light; no beard. Would weigh 145 or 150 pounds. Complexion rather pale and clear, with color in his cheeks. Wore light clothes of fine quality. Shoulders square; cheek bones rather prominent; chin narrow; ears projecting at the top; forehead rather low and square, but broad. Parts his hair on the right side; neck rather long. His lips are firmly set. A slim man.

DAVID C. HAROLD is five feet six inches high, hair dark, eyes dark, eyebrows rather heavy, full face, nose short, hand short and fleshy, feet small, instep high, round bodied, naturally quick and active, slightly closes his eyes when looking at a person.

NOTICE.—In addition to the above, State and other authorities have offered rewards amounting to almost one hundred thousand dollars, making an aggregate of about TWO HUNDRED THOUSAND DOLLARS.

Reward poster for the assassins of Lincoln, showing John Surratt, John Wilkes Booth, and David Herold.

Secretary of War Edwin M. Stanton, 1862. Stanton has been portrayed as both villain and hero in the Lincoln murder conspiracies.

A circlet of conspirators.

Judge Advocate General Joseph Holt.

The nine members of the 1865 military commission, the two special judge advocates, and the judge advocate general. Left to right: David R. Clendenin, C. H. Tomkins, Thomas M. Harris, Albion P. Howe, James A. Ekin, Lew Wallace, David Hunter, August V. Kautz, Robert S. Foster, John A. Bingham, Henry L. Burnett, and Joseph Holt.

Clara E. Laughlin

Lloyd Lewis at about the time he wrote *Myths After Lincoln*.

Otto Eisenschiml

CHAPTER

5

They Hated—and Loved—
John Wilkes Booth

Soon after Lincoln's death, the Washington *Daily
Morning Chronicle*, reflecting the feeling of many enraged
Americans, expressed the hope that John Wilkes Booth would
be captured alive so he might be made to suffer for his crime.
His "agony should be 'long drawn out,'" the paper editorialized,
"through the process of trial, conviction, sentence, and after weeks
of contemplation of the gallows, execution, with the assurance
from the hangman that his body was to be delivered to the sur-
geons for dissection. . . . No humane man should object to ap-
ply such mental tortures to such a wretch." The *Chronicle*'s hatred
was so intense that when Booth was shot and killed the paper's
story denied him even the dignity of having met death bravely.
"He died like a coward, burned out of a trap like a rat; armed to
the teeth, but fearing to use his arms, either on his pursuers or
even on himself. He showed he could be a bravo before a theatrical audience, but failed to show that he could face death with
the common courage of a bandit. Like many another actor, he
could not act to a poor house." Perhaps it was just as well that
Booth was dead, the *Chronicle* concluded, "for such carrion only
infects the earth and makes a noisome stench throughout the
moral atmosphere."[1]

Other observers, however, assuming that Booth was only the
trigger man in a grand conspiracy, felt less repugnance for him
than for the individuals they believed had hired him, or for abstract forces like the spirit of rebellion or the spirit of slavery
that they thought had provoked him. Even at the conspiracy
trial, where Special Judge Advocate John A. Bingham referred

to Booth as the tool "by whose hand Jefferson Davis inflicted the mortal wound upon Abraham Lincoln," there was no abuse of the assassin's character. Indeed, defense counsel described him as a man of glamour and fascination in order to account for his influence over their impressionable clients. [2]

Very little about Booth appeared in the first book on the assassination, published in Cincinnati by J. R. Hawley & Co. late in the summer of 1865. A summary or digest of newspaper stories compiled for commercial purposes largely before May 26, 1865, when relatively little was known about either Booth or the conspiracy, the book necessarily concentrated upon acts of treason and disloyalty committed by enemies of the United States in both the North and the South, and it treated the assassination as but the last of many crimes. One of its anonymous authors (internal evidence suggests more than one) was the well-known Washington reporter Ben: Perley Poore, who contributed a flattering description of Booth. The assassin, wrote Poore, was a genius on the stage; he possessed "a voice musically full and rich, a face almost classic in outline, features highly intellectual, a piercing black eye, capable of expressing the fiercest and the tenderest passion and emotion, and a commanding figure and impressive stage address." In his personal relations, Booth was entertaining and agreeable, and he had many friends. Poore did refer to Booth as "the infamous" and suggested that at the time of secession he had "escaped" from the South in order to avoid conscription in the Rebel army. But the real villains of the book were not Booth and his band but the "fire-eating Southerners" in Richmond and Canada and their friends in the North. [3]

The early practice of condemning Booth's crime while writing surprisingly favorable accounts of his personality was continued in George Alfred Townsend's *Life, Crime, and Capture of John Wilkes Booth* (1865), a collection of articles Townsend had published in the New York *World*. One of the country's best-known war correspondents, Townsend began to collect data about Booth immediately after the assassination and was able to publish in the *World* a sketch of "The Murderer" on the very day the news of his capture and death was carried in the press. [4]

Like Poore, Townsend was chiefly dependent for information about Booth upon members of the theatrical world, the assassin's colleagues and friends, who praised him as an actor and were obviously fond of him as a man. Townsend passed along their assessments and more biographical detail—much of it inaccurate—than would be published for many years. In order to balance the reports of Booth's friends, Townsend also consulted some of the assassin's enemies. One of them, a black man who lived with his family near the Booth farm, reported that as a boy Booth had been so cruel and bloodthirsty he used to shoot cats for fun, killing off "almost the entire breed in his neighborhood," according to Townsend. The story has been frequently reported (with easily predictable elaborations) by writers seeking to demonstrate how early Booth's murderous disposition had manifested itself. Sister Asia Booth Clarke angrily denied that any such thing ever took place and attributed the man's hostility to a feud growing out of some typical Halloween pranks.[5]

A resourceful investigative reporter, Townsend must have had contacts in Joseph Holt's Bureau of Military Justice, for he published material about Booth's activities before the information was officially made public. On May 2, 1865, the day of Andrew Johnson's proclamation stating that the assassination was part of a grand conspiracy, Townsend published an article stating that it was part of a simple conspiracy. Unlike the administration, Townsend believed that Booth really had intended to kidnap Lincoln and take him to Richmond, or, if that proved impossible, to hide him in a house in Washington. The kidnapping scheme had failed because Booth had been unable to attract men of sufficient boldness and character to execute it. Out of this failure and the vanity of an actor who began to see himself in the real-life role of Brutus, Booth "grew into the idea of murder."[6]

Townsend included some censure in his portrait of Booth. He described the darkening of Booth's mood when he determined upon assassination, "a purpose consonant with his evil nature," and he held that Booth deserved "no respect for his valor, charity for his motive, or sympathy for his sin."[7] But the overall effect of Townsend's book was favorable to Booth—so favorable that Townsend was accused of "canonizing" him—and readers might easily conclude that Booth did deserve respect, charity, and sympathy. Almost anyone would concede that there was valor in attacking Lincoln in a theater crowded with his friends. Almost anyone would be willing to extend charity to a man who had been motivated by the principle of *"Sic Semper Tyrannis!"* The assassin Townsend portrayed was a talented and thoroughly likable young man who committed a monstrous crime with the best of intentions. What could be more pitiable?

Pity for Booth is the dominant emotion aroused in a long poem written in 1865 by J. Dunbar Hylton. Composed in the first person as if written by Booth during his escape attempt, it describes the actor's agonizing regrets at killing a man he now recognizes as supremely kind and noble. He curses himself for having been an easy mark for the Confederates in Canada, who persuaded him it would be no crime to kill Lincoln and the cabinet.

. . .

> Ah, my God! What fool was I
> To herd with men so vile,
> And swallow down each crafty lie

. . .

From Canada Booth is directed to Mary E. Surratt in Washington, who agrees enthusiastically to help him. Three times he goes to the theater to kill Lincoln, but each time Lincoln's eyes happen to turn upon him, and he is unable to pull the trigger. Finally, Booth fortifies himself with liquor and shoots Lincoln from behind. At the end, he welcomes his own death, for hell could be no worse than the torment of his own self-damnation.[8]

The idea that the goodness reflected in eyes is capable of preventing evil is no doubt an old one. It appears occasionally in the literature of Lincoln's assassination, for the first time in a newspaper editorial on April 24, 1865. "A life-long friend of Mr. Lincoln's said, after hearing of his assassination, that he did not believe that any man could look in his face and strike him; that the genial and kindhearted nature that looked out of his eyes and beamed in every lineament of his face would disarm the most ferocious and determined assassin. This is true. Mr. Lincoln was shot from behind."[9]

Julia Ward Howe, a friend of the Booth brothers and an admirer of their mother, condemned John Wilkes in a poem, "Parricide," written on the day of Lincoln's funeral. But eight days later, when she read of Booth's death, she wrote another poem praying for her friend's "Pardon."[10]

. . .

Death brings atonement; he did that whereof ye accuse him, —
   Murder accurst;
But, from the crisis of crime in which Satan did lose him,
   Suffered the worst.

. . .

So the soft purples that quiet the heavens with mourning,
   Willing to fall,
Lend him one fold, his illustrious victim adorning
   With wider pall.
Back to the cross, where the Saviour, uplifted in dying,
   Bade all souls live,
Turns the reft bosom of Nature, his mother, low sighing,
   "Greatest, forgive!"

The hatreds that Lincoln had inspired during the war were
by no means obliterated by his assassination, and there were a
great many men and women who thought Booth was entitled to
much more than pardon. Within a short time, when national
grief had subsided, it was even possible to say so. Those who
did—in passages which are surprising to modern readers—reveal not only their admiration for Booth but also demonstrate
how deeply divided the people of the wartime North had been.

In a book addressed to the youth of the country, the New York
publisher Rushmore G. Horton exclaimed in 1866 that Lincoln's
emancipation of the slaves meant the end of America's greatness. Emancipation would lead inevitably to racial equality and
amalgamation, and "every nation on the face of the earth where
such a mixture has taken place . . . has declined in its civilization, and gradually sunk down in ruin, as if wasted by a slow
poison." The races were not equal; to treat them as if they were
was as wicked as it would be "to take an ox and try to make it go
as fast as a horse." In taking the life of the man who had acted
thus against the law of God, Booth was no common murderer.
He had understood what was happening to the country, and he
had acted from "no thirst for blood, no mean personal revenge,
no expectation of gain or reward."[11]

"We think we are safe in saying," wrote Chauncey Burr in his
redoubtable *The Old Guard* in 1867, "that there are more intelligent white men and women in this country today who respect

the name of John Wilkes Booth, than there are who respect the name of Abraham Lincoln." Burr regretted that there had not been a hundred men with Booth's courage and patriotism to save the country from the "stinking slough of African despotism" into which Lincoln's policies had plunged it.[12] In 1866 a New Englander, who had not forgotten Lincoln's violations of constitutionally protected civil liberties, declared, "The time is coming when there will be a monument erected to Booth higher than the spire of Lincoln."[13]

Henry Clay Dean, an anti-slavery Methodist preacher from Iowa who had served as chaplain of the U.S. Senate in the 1850s, also believed Booth was justified in killing Lincoln for his transgressions against the Constitution. Assassination, he said in his *Crimes of the Civil War* (1868), was hideous. "But who is the assassin? the man who in frenzied madness strikes the fatal blow; or the tyrant who overthrows all government—destroys his own safety in his rage to torture his enemies; . . . who gratifies his spite by plunging the country into civil war and universal anarchy; who regards nothing of law except its power to punish and inflict its penalties to satiate his malice?" America had been built upon two fundamental principles: that governments derived their just powers from the consent of the governed, and that "Resistance to Tyrants is Obedience to God."[14] Lincoln had scorned the first principle; Booth had acted upon the second.

In his extraordinary description of the act of assassination, Dean cast Booth in the role of champion of southern civilization and made the part every bit as heroic as the actor could have wished. The sun had scarcely set on that Good Friday in 1865 before the president and his guests drove to one of the fashionable haunts of their licentious capital. Ignoring the churches and cathedrals they passed en route, they proceeded to the theater, which had been selected as a fitting place "to obliviate all the recollections of Calvary." In the audience were officers promoted from gambling dens and "sinks of vice"; contractors who had plundered their fortunes; women who had "emerged from low estates, and brought everything with them to their new positions, but their virtue." The mammoth chandeliers reflected the dazzling light of bracelets, rings, chains, watches, and silks and cashmeres studded with diamonds. In the pit were soldiers and teamsters who had walked for months upon the ashes of burned plantations and who had shot herds of domestic animals in order to starve the southern people. "Inflamed with lust and drunken on blood," they were surrounded by abandoned women clothed in the stolen garments of southern ladies. Assembled in one motley gang, all were paying homage "to the usurper of the New Nation" as he sat in his box before them.

In the midst of this unfeeling merriment, Dean continued, there appeared, "a lithe, strong, beautiful form. His broad, pale forehead stood out from a rich crest of coal black hair that fell in luxuriance around his neck." He had seen the national rottenness, corruption, and crime for which the pretender in the mock royal box was responsible and without suggestion from any man had decided upon what he must do. As he stepped into Lincoln's box, "his eyes, like bursting balls of fire, fell full upon the object of his rage; he fired his pistol, his victim fell lifeless, and spoke no word to be remembered. Booth leaped upon the stage, crying *sic semper tyrannis.*"[15]

Another writer, John A. Marshall, in *American Bastille* (1869), recalled Lincoln's tyranny in terms that fully justified Booth's Brutus.

Some day the history of the political imprisonments . . . [of the Lincoln administration] will be written, and what a sad chapter to be read by posterity. It makes my heart weep to think that in this land of so-called liberty there has been so much oppression. . . . Citizens were arrested by thousands, and incarcerated without warrant. Judges were torn from the bench, bruised and bleeding. Ministers of the Gospel . . . were stricken down. . . . Women were incarcerated, and subjected to insult and outrage. Doctors were ruthlessly taken from the bedside of the dying patient, . . . and lawyers [were] arrested and consigned to the same cells with their clients whose release they were endeavoring to effect. Post offices were searched; newspapers seized and suppressed, while the editors were handcuffed and secretly hurried to prison.

According to Marshall, not one of the victims of Lincoln's persecution whose cases he reviews in his book had committed any act disloyal to the United States; they were all arrested simply because they were Democrats and dared to oppose Lincoln's tyranny.[16]

Lincoln-haters in the occupied South had to be circumspect in their public reactions to the assassination, but in late April

1865, before the arrival of federal troops in Galveston, Texas, the *Daily News* dared to speak. "We would have no obloquy cast upon the name of the man who did the deed," the paper declared. "Inspired by patriotic impulse and believing he was ridding the world of a monster, his name will be inscribed on the roll of true-hearted patriots."[17] "All honor to J. Wilkes Booth," wrote Kate Stone, who had fled to Texas from her family's Louisiana plantation when the district was occupied by the Union army. He "has rid the world of a tyrant and made himself famous for generations. . . . What torrents of blood Lincoln has caused to flow, and how Seward has aided him in his bloody work. I cannot be sorry for their fate. They deserve it." A few days later she added in her journal, "Poor Booth, to think that he fell at last. Many a true heart at the South weeps for his death."[18]

In Arkansas in 1869, the year after the state's "reconstruction," when federal troops had been removed, a former Confederate army officer wrote a novel on the assassination. Booth was no common murderer, wrote R. H. Crozier in *The Bloody Junto*, and he deserved better than to go down in history as a villain without a defense for his crime. His defense, of course, was that he had killed a tyrant. Lincoln's whole administration, the novelist arranges for Booth to explain at the end of a long discourse on the president's dictatorship, "has been one grand tragedy of systematical aggressions and encroachments upon rights, the violation of which would have hurled a despot from his throne in the old world."[19]

Not many Southerners were so outspoken so soon, but many would like to have been. "Today I speak of the murdered President as 'great and good,'" wrote a Confederate Marylander in the 1890s; "thirty years ago I regarded him only as the enemy of my country."[20] At the end of the century, John S. Wise, son of a governor of Virginia and a former Confederate soldier, said that he was ashamed of what he had said and thought when he first heard of Lincoln's assassination. But he proceeded to put his reactions in their historical setting. "For four years we had been fighting," he wrote. "In that struggle, all we loved had been lost. Lincoln incarnated to us the idea of oppression and conquest. We had seen his face over the coffins of our brothers and relatives and friends, in the flames of Richmond, in the disaster at Appomattox. In blood and flame and torture the temples of our lives were tumbling about our heads. We were desperate and vindictive, and whosoever denies it forgets or is false. We greeted his death in a spirit of reckless hate, and hailed it as bringing agony and bitterness to those who were the cause of our own agony and bitterness. To us, Lincoln was an inhuman monster."[21]

During Reconstruction, even when they had come to believe that the assassination had been unfortunate for the South, many Southerners continued to think of Lincoln as a monster and to resist the policies of national supremacy and emancipation with which he was associated. It was necessarily so, for if Lincoln had not been an oppressor and if his policies had not been detestable, how could the South's four-year resistance be justified? When Chicago was nearly destroyed by fire in 1871, some Southerners hailed it as a divine retribution upon the city for having been the site of Lincoln's first nomination to the presidency. Well into the twentieth century it was common in the South for Lincoln to be denounced as a despot and a "nigger lover," and that meant that Booth was necessarily a hero.[22]

One of the popular speakers on the southern Chatauqua lecture circuit in the 1880s and 1890s was Richard B. Garrett, a Baptist minister whose father had owned the Virginia farm where Booth spent the last two nights of his life. A boy of eleven years at the time, young Garrett shared his room with the friendly stranger who had arrived on the afternoon of April 24, 1865, and the following morning he observed him asleep. "I remember vividly the impression made upon me at that time," he said in one of his lectures. "I had never seen such a face before. Jet black curls clustered about a brow as white as marble and a heavy dark mustache shaded a mouth as beautiful as a babe's. One hand was thrown above the head of the sleeper, and it was as white and soft as a child's." After breakfast, the visitor had lounged on the grass beneath some apple trees, talking and playing with the children of the household. He showed them his pocket compass and laughed at their puzzled faces when he made the needle swing by moving his pocket knife back and forth above it.[23]

That night Booth and David Herold, planning to make an early start the following morning, slept in a tobacco curing shed in which furniture, including beds, had been stored. Then the U.S.

soldiers arrived, roused the Garrett family, surrounded the barn, and set it on fire. Like the soldiers, young Garrett rushed forward to look inside through the cracks. "It was a fearful picture," he recalled. "Framed in great waves of fire stood the crippled man leaning upon his crutches and holding his carbine in his hand. His hat had fallen off and his hair was brushed back from his white forehead. He was as beautiful as the statue of a Greek god and as calm in that awful hour." Boston Corbett claimed to have shot Booth because the trapped man was about to shoot one of the officers. "It was not true," said Garrett. "He made no movement to fire upon anybody." Booth had been shot down in cold blood. Moments after Booth breathed his last on the farmhouse porch, Garrett's mother washed the blood from his face and neck, placed a handkerchief over his face, and cut off a curl of his hair. At this point in his talk, Garrett would send shivers down the backs of his audience by holding up a locket. "I have a part of it here . . . ," he would say. "The rest I sent to his mother."[24]

Sometimes Garrett would conclude his lecture by reading a poetic tribute to Booth believed to have been written by Alexander W. Terrell, a Texan, in 1865, and originally published in Brick Pomeroy's LaCrosse *Democrat:*

. . .

He had written his name
In bright letters of fame
In the pathway of liberty's portal;
And the serfs who now blame
Will crimson with shame
When they learn they have cursed an immortal.

He hath died for the weal
Of a world 'neath the heel
Of too many a merciless Nero;
But while yet there is steel,
Every tyrant shall feel
That God's vengeance but waits for its hero.[25]

In 1904 in Troy, Alabama, an unreconstructed Rebel, Joseph Pinkney Parker, set up on his front lawn a four-foot granite monument bearing the inscription

Erected by
PINK PARKER
In honor of
John Wilks
Booth
for killing old
ABE LINCOLN.

When word of the monument reached the North, public protests forced the Troy town council to order it removed, but for
years Parker continued to celebrate April 15 by parading through
town with a placard announcing the anniversary of Lincoln's
death.[26]

Pink Parker had his counterparts in the North—even in
Springfield, Illinois, even in Lincoln's old home. Near the turn
of the century, Robert Todd Lincoln was distressed to learn that
when one of Osborn H. Oldroyd's successors as custodian of the
Lincoln house moved out he left a portrait of Booth behind on
the mantelpiece.[27]

Booth may have had his admirers among the people of the
North and South, but by the end of the century the simple conspiracy theory of the assassination had replaced the grand conspiracy theory, and Booth alone was held responsible for Lincoln's
death. That fact, in turn, meant that he alone had to bear the
hatred of increasing millions of Americans who were discovering
that they loved Lincoln. No longer was it fashionable to soften
criticism of Booth's crime with observations about his political
principles or his winning personality or his artistry upon the
stage. For most Americans, as Lincoln's reputation rose to the
level of a national deity about whom nothing too good could be
thought or said, Booth's reputation sank to the level of a common ruffian about whom there *was* nothing good to be thought
or said.

The public's image of Booth grew out of an emotional reaction, but it was sustained by the characterizations of serious
writers. John T. Morse, the New England scholar and Lincoln
biographer, called Booth "a disreputable fellow" and "an unworthy member of a distinguished family who drank excessively and
had little professional ability." A combination of melodrama and

brandy had so saturated his brain with "a passion for notoriety, which grew into the very mania of egotism," that the "ignoble tippler had dared to cut the life-thread from which depended no small portion of the destinies of millions of people."[28] Booth had been inspired with a "mad, unreasoning, malignant hatred of everything representing Freedom and Union," declared the soldier-politician John A. Logan.[29] The historian James Schouler dismissed Booth as a young man of "histrionic parentage, foolishly fanatical for secession, and the self-appointed avenger of a South whose Brutus he theatrically thought himself."[30] John G. Nicolay and John Hay said that "partisan hatred and the fumes of brandy" had worked Booth's brain into such a morbid state that he killed Lincoln in an outburst "of malice and rage."[31] Oldroyd was of the opinion that Booth killed Lincoln "solely to immortalize himself."[32] In *The Judicial Murder of Mrs. Surratt,* David M. Dewitt called Booth's kidnapping scheme "wild," and said, "It was a plot of the kind to emanate from the disordered brain of a young, spoiled, dissipated and disappointed actor." Plunged to the depths of despair by the plot's failure and by the fall of Richmond, Booth "suddenly, as a mere after-thought, the offspring of a spirit of impotent revenge, seized upon the idea of murder."[33] In *The Assassination of Abraham Lincoln,* Dewitt referred to Booth's "vengeful spirit" and his "canine appetite for distinction," which could only be satisfied by the commission of some deed of daring that would command "the wonder of contemporaries and the plaudits of posterity."[34]

Worshipping Lincoln, the American public found it easy to accept Booth as a madman and ham actor who possessed no redeeming qualities. But even as this image was being fixed on the national consciousness, evidence was accumulating that would someday make possible a better understanding of the kind of man and assassin Booth had been.

In the early 1880s the writer George Alfred Townsend made the first systematic attempt to trace Booth's movements from the time he left Dr. Samuel A. Mudd's home on April 15 to his arrival at Garrett's farm on April 24. Among the individuals he interviewed was Thomas A. Jones, who had cared for Booth and Herold for six days in a pine thicket in southern Maryland. Jones described Booth as a brave and appealing man, lying on the ground in constant pain. The actor truly believed he had killed a tyrant, and he read with anguish in the newspapers Jones brought him that most people did not agree. Determined to make every effort to escape, he knew that his chances were not good, and he swore that he would not be taken alive. When it was finally safe for Jones to escort the fugitives to the Potomac, where he supplied them with a boat, Booth took a grateful farewell. "God bless you, my dear friend," he said to Jones, "for all you have done for me. Goodbye, old fellow!" Many of Townsend's readers must have felt a quite unexpected sympathy for so game a hunted and crippled man.[35] In 1893 Jones, a former Confederate agent who had ferried mail and passengers across the river during the war, attempted to tell his own story in a book for sale at the Columbian Exposition in Chicago. But he was virtually mobbed by Union veterans who denounced him as "the dirty rebel who helped Booth escape," and only a few copies were sold.[36]

Some aging actors and actresses, upset at the way they believed Booth's character and abilities were being misrepresented, came to his defense. Clara Morris, who had once appeared with Booth in *The Marble Heart*, was playing in Boston in 1890 when the last installment of Nicolay and Hay's biography of Lincoln was serialized in *Century Magazine*. Because the authors had commented disparagingly upon Booth's talent as an actor, she contacted the editor of a local newspaper to set the record straight. Booth "had more than mere talent as an actor," she told the editor. "In his soul the fire of genius burned brightly, and he promised to top them all in the profession to which he was born. He had by inheritance the fire, the dash, the impetuosity, the temperament, and the genius of his great father, and he more nearly resembled the elder Booth in those qualities which go to make up a great actor than any of the other sons of the eminent sire." Then Morris proceeded to talk about Booth as a man, first explaining that she was not apologizing for him or excusing his crime. "At this late date," she hoped, "the country can afford to deal justly with John Wilkes Booth. He was not a bravo, a commonplace desperado, as some would make him. . . . It was impossible to see him and not admire him; it was equally impossible to know him and not love him."[37]

The interview did not attract much attention, though it represented a turning point in the public evaluations of Booth in the North. One reader whose attention it did attract was Edwin Booth, who sent a grateful acknowledgment. "My heartfelt thanks, Clara. I am so glad it was for you to say the first word of compassion for John Wilkes."[38]

In her autobiography, published in 1901, Morris continued to praise Booth as a man and declared she could not believe he was the leader of a band of assassins. The kidnapping plot, she thought, might well have appealed to him—though she did not believe he had conceived it—for there was in his character "an exaggeration of spirit—almost a wildness," a craving for dramatic situations in life as on the stage. In addition, "there was his passionate love and sympathy for the South—why, he was 'easier to be played on than a pipe.'" But when the kidnapping failed, she continued, "I truly believe he was a tool—certainly he was no leader. Those who led him knew his courage, his belief in Fate, his loyalty to his friends; and, because they knew these things, he drew the lot, as it was meant he should from the first. Then, half mad, he accepted the part Fate cast him for—committed the monstrous crime, and paid the awful price."[39]

Another actress, Kitty Blanchard, remembered simple and endearing acts of kindness performed by Booth on stage and off and must have impressed readers of *American Magazine* with how hard it was for his friends to accept the fact that he was a murderer.[40] Perhaps Blanchard was one of the friends who, unable to believe early reports that Booth was Lincoln's assassin, gathered in the lobby of his hotel and remained there until dawn on April 15, waiting vainly for him to saunter in.[41]

E. A. Emerson, who had often played with Booth and whose performance as Lord Dundreary in *Our American Cousin* was so unexpectedly interrupted on April 14, called Booth a "kind-hearted, genial person. . . . Everybody loved him on the stage, tho he was a little excitable and eccentric."[42] "Wilkes Booth was as manly a man as God ever made," declared John Ellsler, another actor, "but it seemed as if some evil star crossed his path and seized him for its purpose, or that the seed of inherent, uncontrollable madness took possession of him, transforming the normal man, filled with love, into an insane creature." In his private associations, said Ellsler, Booth was "firm as a rock, honest, sincere, and unassuming."[43] W. J. Ferguson, a young stagehand at Ford's Theater, remembered Booth's vitality, his joyousness, and his love of fun. "I held him in admiration and high esteem. With me the extent of my regard and respect for Booth fell nothing short of hero-worship."[44]

In her fond memoir of her brother written in the years before 1874 but not published until 1938, Asia Booth Clarke had much to say about his warm heart and generous nature. She could have said much more, she noted, but she did not, for she feared to sound fulsome. Besides, he had "crowds of friends" and when the time was fitting they would speak up.[45] They did, but Asia, who died in 1888, did not hear them, and the American people did not listen. Unable to think well of the man who had killed Lincoln, most people continued to view Booth as an actor without talent who had killed for the meanest of reasons—revenge.

Nevertheless, by 1909, when the nation settled in for a period of eulogies marking the centennial of Lincoln's birth, the Civil War president's position in the hearts of his countrymen was so secure that it was possible for Clara Laughlin, in *The Death of Lincoln*, to portray Booth as the charming and talented man his family and friends had known. Perhaps Booth was also the beneficiary of a sentiment expressed by President Theodore Roosevelt and felt by most other Americans. In an editorial in *Collier's Magazine*, Roosevelt paid tribute to the soldier of the Civil War who had fought so gallantly "for the right as it was given him to see the right, whether he wore the blue or whether he wore the gray."[46] In the interests of reconciliation between North and South, that the veterans of both sections had had the courage to fight for their convictions was considered more important than what their convictions had been. So it may have been with Booth; by 1909 it could be conceded that, he, too, had acted for what he believed to be right. In his case, however, neither Laughlin nor any writer who followed in her tradition failed to point out that what he had believed to be right was wrong.[47]

Laughlin appeared to be as much attracted to Booth as the star-struck women of his own time. "He was tall [in fact, he was about 5'8"] and full of slender grace," she wrote; "his features were classic in their perfectness; his big black eyes were teasing, tender, laughing, bewitching; a crown of slightly curling jet-black hair was worn pushed boyishly back from a brow of rare intellectual and physical beauty. He was elegant in his dress, blithe and winsome in his manner. Indeed, he was only too winsome—too easy to love and too hard to scold; too quick to charm and too charming to be judged. He was generous and kind, affectionate and gay."[48] "John"—which is what Laughlin most commonly called him until the abduction plot turned into an assassination plot, when she switched first to "John Booth" and finally to "Booth"—"was universally considered the most gifted of his family." He was adored by his mother, and he loved her so much in return that he made her a promise difficult for him to keep: "a promise that he would never take up arms against the Union." In plotting to kidnap Lincoln, Booth was, of course, violating this promise. But his purpose was to bring an end to the terrible war, and he knew that if he was successful his mother would forgive him and that he and his associates in the plot would be cheered as heroes. Booth was known to have associated with the Confederate representatives in Montreal, but there was "not a scintilla of reliable evidence" that his conversations with them had anything to do with a conspiracy against Lincoln.[49]

Curiously, Laughlin does not speculate in *The Death of Lincoln* about when Booth decided upon assassination, or even about what he hoped to accomplish by it. To the readers of the *Ladies' Home Journal*, however, she explained that as Booth paused outside of Lincoln's box that fatal night, "he knew so little of the great heart beating close beside him . . . that he thought it responsible for the war." Then, "this gentlest and winsomest and most cruelly-misguided of boys," opened the door and proceeded "to kill the man he believed to be a tyrant and archfiend."[50]

In the last part of her book, Laughlin granted Booth redemption through suffering and good intentions. Lying on the farmhouse porch, the blood pouring from the wound in his neck inflicted by Corbett and "suffering the most excruciating agony a human being can know," Booth struggled to speak. "'Tell mother—I die—for my—country,' he gasped. 'I did—what I thought—was—best.'" Later, "as the dawn was breaking into brilliant day, he indicated by a look, a feeble motion, that he wanted his paralyzed arms raised so he could see his hands. This was done, and he said, very faintly, as he looked at them: 'Useless—useless!' Those were his last words. Whether he bemoaned the uselessness of his hands to fight for him, or the uselessness of their mad crime, God only knows. But he could not more accurately have epitomized his insane deed. Never— except Once—was vengeance so misdirected. Never was sacrifice of a brilliant young life so worse than 'useless.'"[51]

Equally sympathetic and personal in tone was Francis Wilson's *John Wilkes Booth. Fact and Fiction of Lincoln's Assassination* (1929), the first book-length biography of Booth. A child actor at the time of the assassination, Wilson spent his long life almost entirely in the theatrical world. Among the professional organizations of which he was an officer was the Players Club, founded in New York by Edwin Booth. Although Edwin had a picture of John Wilkes near his bed in his rooms at the Club, he seldom talked of his brother, and then only to his closest friends. But Wilson knew Booth family history and tradition and set for himself the task of explaining why John Wilkes should have committed a deed so remote from his "innate qualities, his childhood environment, and the artistic refinements of his family." Whatever the qualities of his character may have been, Wilson declared, "brutality and vulgarity had no part in his nature. . . . Despite much absurd statement to the contrary, revenge or punishment played no part in his plotting against Lincoln."[52]

While previous writers had described Booth's plan to kidnap Lincoln and take him to Richmond as romantic or preposterous, Wilson believed it plausible and realistic, except for the thought of accomplishing the capture in a theater. No insuperable difficulties were involved in taking the underguarded president prisoner on the open highway, and travel to Richmond through southern Maryland was relatively simple. With Lincoln as a hostage, Wilson believed it was not crackbrained for Booth to assume the Confederacy could have forced some concession from the United States, which would either end the war at once or provide the means by which the South could win it soon. Judging from the amount of opposition to the Lincoln administration in the North, Booth was justified in believing that both sections would rejoice if the conflict could be ended.

The kidnapping conspiracy, the "masterstroke" to which Wilson claimed Booth had devoted himself heart and soul for four years, ended in humiliating failure, and Booth hated himself for

it. It was probably at the time he heard Lincoln advocate enfranchising some southern black men that Booth determined,
"if the opportunity arose, to destroy the President." It was not
too late to save the South, but it was too late for half-measures.
Then, in a sweep of madness "unquestionably induced by despair, drink, and inherited mental imbalance," he did destroy
Lincoln.

Why? What was his motive? Not the promise of wealth. There
was not enough money in the world, Wilson was certain, to tempt
Booth into either the kidnapping or assassination conspiracies,
or into any act of violence. Nor had he been motivated by vanity
and a desire for fame, "though, being an actor, that has been
charged against him." When Booth killed Lincoln, "it was the
act of a madman, driven insane by the sudden collapse of his
patriotic ambition, the maddening fear of the total failure of
cherished plans to save his country—and by the sudden exaggeration of hereditary imbalance."[53]

If Laughlin's and Wilson's portraits of Booth as a good-humored,
high-spirited, kind, and generous man marked the beginning of
a trend that would eventually change the public image of Lincoln's assassin—and also lead to a more sophisticated understanding of the furies of the Civil War—the trend was abruptly
halted by Lloyd Lewis's *Myths After Lincoln*. Published in the
same year as Wilson's biography, and far more widely read, *Myths
After Lincoln* reaffirmed Booth's position as the evil genius of
American history. Drawing upon Sir James George Frazer's *The
Golden Bough* (1890), a study of ancient cults and folklore, Lewis
showed that Lincoln had become an American folk hero similar
in many ways to the Dying God figure found in the mythologies
of peoples since antiquity. The Dying God was the "one hero
brighter and more beautiful than the rest, [the] one dear, friendly
god who had sacrificed his life for the race." The American people,
Lewis correctly observed, were far less interested in learning
about the historical Lincoln than about the mythological Lincoln, the Dying God who had suffered through the war for their
sake and mankind's, and who had given up his life upon the
completion of his mission. When Lincoln made his "ascent into
immortality," Lewis went on, "he took J. Wilkes Booth with him."
And that, too, was according to the ancient pattern, for most

Dying Gods were the victims of treachery and conferred upon those who had betrayed them an immortality of infamy. Booth was America's demon-hero, its folklore Judas, and so long as Lincoln was revered, Booth was destined to be despised.[54]

Although Lewis was well aware that the mythological Lincoln and the historical Lincoln were not the same, he made no effort to distinguish between the mythological and the historical Booth. Indeed, his chapters on Booth and his conspiracies, grouped under the general title "The American Judas," exceed in vituperation any extended analysis of Booth ever published.

Drawing upon such sources as Townsend's early dispatches and his own imagination and disregarding well-established facts, Lewis makes his readers dislike John Wilkes from the beginning. The elder Booth had taught his sons never to kill animals, even the opossums and poisonous snakes found on the family farm, and he served no meat at his table. His sons Junius Brutus, Jr., and Edwin, "serious toiling fellows," obeyed their father and prepared themselves to enter his profession. But John Wilkes, the wild son, the "old man's darling, hopelessly spoiled, an extraordinary naughty little boy who was allowed to do whatever he pleased," took special delight in violating the family taboo. He enjoyed shooting dogs and cats. "A good spanking administered to the boy at almost any point in this line of shootings," Lewis suggests, "might have been the means of saving the life of Abraham Lincoln in 1865. But no reproof was forthcoming." The boy was also spoiled by his mother, who saw him as "the flower of her flock, the most beautiful, the most spirited, the most winning, . . . the most loving," and she reconciled herself to the "captivating way he had of disobeying her commands" with the thought that he was, after all, a genius (131, 140–41, 144).

John Wilkes grew up believing in his own genius, believing that every Booth was a great actor and that he would be the greatest of them all. Adopting the attitude that since greatness on the stage was his destiny there was no need to prepare himself for it as his father and brothers had done, he bungled his theater debut in Philadelphia. He could not memorize even such simple lines as "Here comes the Duke," and in subsequent performances he was laughed and hooted off the stage for clumsiness and incompetence. "Perhaps it was then," Lewis imagines, "that he began hating the Northern people" (145).

Although Booth gained some popularity as an actor in the provinces, especially in the entertainment-starved cities of the South, he was a joke on the big city stages of the North and turned to liquor and women for solace. Despite his disappointment at his failure to achieve greatness, he "could never bring himself to learn the secret of good acting." He hated to read prompt books and was widely known for forgetting his lines. "When these lapses came, he imagined that he could cover them up with violent bellows and sword-wavings. In such moments he would prance and jump about the stage in picturesque displays. When dramatics failed, he would fall back upon athletics. Poor man, he made the mistake of training in the gymnasium instead of the study!" (152–53).

Booth's pro-southern sympathies, and those of other actors, were tolerated in the North with amused disdain, says Lewis, and "Booth's own family thought his Southern talk funny" and laughed at his "rantings." But all the while, Booth was secretly planning that "grandiose political melodrama with himself as hero," which he revealed to Samuel B. Arnold and Michael O'Laughlin in September 1864—the kidnapping of Lincoln. But as a political activist, as in his plays, Booth "failed to study his part." He did not consult Confederate authorities to discover if they would accept Lincoln as a prisoner; he did not realize that physically he was no match for the ex-frontier wrestler, "who was still, at fifty-six, one of the most powerful of living men"; and he recruited a group of incompetent nonentities to help him. But he was in his glory, and he spent hours "with his morons" playing with pistols and knives and false moustaches, "like so many Tom Sawyers in haymows across the world" (155, 167).

After the collapse of the kidnapping conspiracy in March 1865, and the near-collapse of the Confederacy in early April, Booth "decided that his one remaining way to command the public eye was to murder Lincoln and to explain the deed as an act of a Brutus liberating his people from a Tarquin's oppressions." This lust for renown, Lewis asserts, "by all the evidence that time has amassed, was the motive for the assassination" (169).

After shooting Lincoln and fighting off Major Henry R. Rathbone with his knife, Booth, "frantic to be down in front of the audience with his claim to fame," poised on the edge of the president's box. It was only a short leap, less than he had made many times in Macbeth, "but never in his whole life had Booth made himself wholly ready for the stage and [he] could not now, at twenty-six years of age, be expected to change. Just as he had bungled his first stage appearance, so he now bungled his last, catching his spur in a draped flag and hitting the floor, ignominiously, on all fours. It was a very funny fall, yet the audience did not laugh." But Booth was up in an instant, struck a dramatic pose with his bloody knife in the air, and took time to address the crowd with "'The South is avenged,'" and "'Sic semper tyrannis.'" Then he dragged his broken leg across the stage and disappeared out the back (174).

For twelve days Booth and Herold wandered south, dodging federal search parties, boasting of their deed whenever the opportunity arose, Lewis tells us, and eagerly reading the newspapers to see what the critics had to say about the performance at Ford's Theater. The critics did not like it, and nothing, not even the unrelenting pain of his broken leg, hurt Booth so much. They "put him down variously as a fool, a cut-throat, a 'Cain,' a hireling thug, or at best a weak tool of Confederate desperado-rulers. They left him no shred of dignity or of political position." In retaliation, Booth poured into his diary "all the hatred that any bad actor can feel for the critics who have skinned him alive. Furiously he wrote down his scalding disappointments in tragic bombast, protesting his sincere love of country, straining to establish his sincerity, as anxious as Hamlet to have himself cried aright to posterity." Knowing escape to be impossible because of his injury, he had no choice but to leave a record which "might palm off his personal ambition as patriotism" (182–83).

In short, Lewis described Booth perfectly as the demon-hero of American history and did not scruple against malicious exaggeration and fabrication. In folklore, after all, anything goes. Unfortunately, Lewis called his folklore biography.

It is interesting that Lewis's friend and fellow Chicago journalist Carl Sandburg, who incorporated so much folklore in his six-volume biography of Lincoln, should have rejected Booth folklore and made a serious effort to portray the assassin as an historical figure. "Wilkes Booth could not be polished off as summarily as I believed," Sandburg wrote his publisher on August 28, 1938, explaining a delay in the completion of his last volume. "I am about half thru the final chapter, having done a more extended miniature biography of our American Judas than any other [Lincoln] biographer has attempted."[55]

If his *Myths After Lincoln* had been published in 1939 instead of 1929, Lewis might also have recognized that Booth could not be summarily "polished off." For in 1938, Asia Booth Clarke's *The Unlocked Book* and newspaper installments of Stanley Kimmel's researches—later incorporated into *The Mad Booths of Maryland*—were published, and Sandburg made use of them. Added to Wilson's biography, these works made it impossible for any serious writer to continue to identify the historical Booth with the folklore Booth. Yet even in 1929 Lewis should have known enough to distinguish between the two.

The John Wilkes Booth who emerges from Sandburg's pages is likable and talented, though impulsive; he was a fanatic for the southern cause, but he was no demon. He hated Lincoln personally, believing his scorn to be "that of a fine-haired patrician for a plebeian mongrel," and he truly feared that Lincoln was a dictator intent upon making himself king. Sandburg pointed out that such views were shared by many educated individuals and had been stated constantly throughout the war. If Booth had been entirely ignorant of what was thought about Lincoln in the South and had drawn his knowledge of the president exclusively from the columns of the New York *World,* the Detroit Free *Press,* and the Chicago *Times,* Sandburg declared, "he would have felt himself correct and justified to go forth with a brass pocket pistol." Booth was, in short, a reflection of the widespread hatred for Lincoln in the North.[56]

But Sandburg did not altogether hide his contempt for the actor. The kidnapping conspiracy originated, Sandburg states, out of Booth's "deepening sense of guilt over keeping himself in safety and comfort while the war raged and the Southern cause sank lower." Of the "To Whom It May Concern Letter," in which Booth had sought to explain why he was trying to make a prisoner of Lincoln, Sandburg writes: "More than any other document perhaps this letter gave the key to J. Wilkes Booth, his scrambled brain, his vanity and self-importance, *his level of ideas and reasoning about that of an eighth-grade schoolboy, his ham-actor habit of speech and phrase,* his desire to show the South that he was a Confederate hero even though they no longer loved him or cared about him." Sandburg omitted the italicized words (together with many other dispensable passages) from the 1954 abridgement of his six volumes, *Abraham Lincoln. The Prairie Years and the War Years.*[57]

Sandburg was a great deal more generous to Booth than another Lincoln scholar, Emanuel Hertz. In April 1940, the seventy-fifth anniversary of the assassination, Hertz wrote that Booth, "the neurotic, the mediocre scion of a distinguished acting family, [and] unworthy brother of the great Edwin Booth, was an embittered Southerner who had never forsworn his Union allegiance, had never served in the Confederate Army, and had never, in fact, put himself to any inconvenience for the Southern cause." When he shot Lincoln, it was "the final insane act of a man whose twenty-six years of life had been weak and futile, who was a second-rater in his own profession, and who wanted to win the glaring floodlight of notoriety."[58]

If Hertz's assessment was a restatement of the traditional view of Booth, Philip Van Doren Stern, a New York writer and editor, came up with an entirely new interpretation in his popular *The Man Who Killed Lincoln* (1939). Although in reality a work of fiction, the book was generally accepted as biography, and Stern himself described it as "my first historical work."[59] In an afterword Stern declared he had invented nothing "other than conversation, internal and external," and five minor incidents that he duly identified.[60] But in fact he invented far more, for, like a novelist, he described the changing facial expressions, moods, mannerisms, and even the nightmares of his characters. The most outlandish of the inventions that Stern represented as the truth was Booth's alleged hatred for his father.

As described in *The Man Who Killed Lincoln*, Booth's boyhood years were scarred by the eccentricities and the sudden appearances and disappearances of his father. The little cottage in which the family lived "would suddenly be filled with a cantankerous old man who stormed about, criticized everything, and then, just as suddenly, was gone again on one of his acting tours." The father's death in 1852 had been a great relief to young John Wilkes, "removing the ever-present threat of his return to a household that, so far as Booth was concerned, managed to get along very well without him." Booth also hated his father, according to Stern, because he had learned, when a child, that the celebrated actor was still legally married to a woman he had left in England. That meant that John Wilkes and all of his brothers and sisters were illegitimate. Booth "hated his father for this crime against his mother," and he was miserable with fear that "someone would call him bastard to his face." (The existence of Adelaide Booth—and of her son, Richard—became known to the Maryland children in 1846, when she came to America and took up residence in Baltimore. After numerous stormy encounters between the two families, a divorce was obtained in April 1851. On May 10 of that year, John Wilkes's thirteenth birthday, Junius Brutus and Mary Ann Holmes were married. All of the Booths were understandably secretive about this bit of family history.)[61] Stern plods on, intimating that Booth hated his father because the elder Booth had not been entirely sane, and John Wilkes was haunted by the fear that he might have inherited a tendency toward madness.[62] Any student in Psychology 1 could pick up the hypothesis: Booth shot Lincoln—Father Abraham—because he identified him with his own father, whom he hated.

Stern saw the assassination in just such sophomoric terms. In his dreams, Stern writes, Booth confused Lincoln with his father. The president would appear to him not in Washington but in the cottage on the farm where he spent his boyhood. He would see him "lurking in the dark twisted rooms, ready to spring out at him from the shadows around the chimney corner. He had seen his figure stalking across the fields like a giant, searching for him under trees and bushes, and reaching his enormous hand through the windows to pluck him out of his own bed. He remembered him asking his mother where she had hidden her son . . . the creature had seized her violently . . . her screams still rang in his ears . . . and he heard the Lincoln demon's voice booming. . . . Strange, he thought suddenly, Lincoln has a high-pitched voice, not deep at all—and then, quickly, he forced himself to stop thinking of his dreams."[63]

The last months of Booth's life were dominated by his hatred for Lincoln. He was determined to kill him no matter what the sacrifice, and he admitted to himself that his kidnapping plan had been merely a blind; if Lincoln had become his prisoner, he would have murdered him forthwith. "The very thought of the man's face, of his hideous and repulsive body, made him want to stamp him out like a spider."[64]

Stern was the first writer to suggest that Booth killed Lincoln because he hated his own father, but the idea proved irresistible to psychiatrists. The very next year, 1940, George W. Wilson published a short article on Booth as a "Father Murderer." Though he regretted not having read Stern's book until after having completed his article, his reasoning and conclusions were remarkably similar.

Wilson's Booth experienced extreme envy and hatred for his father and brothers. These emotions, Wilson explained in a paragraph almost devoid of punctuation, were

expressed very early in life in his identification with Brutus from Shakespeare's "Julius Caesar." Booth's delusion that Lincoln wanted to become king was probably based on his early relationship to his own father, the same as was that of Brutus to Caesar. Booth was extremely afraid of his father who was a stern aggressive domineering man and as a consequence repressed his hostility for the father and the older successful brothers as well. . . . With the return of the South to the Union like the return of the father to the mother following one of his long theatrical engagements there was reactivated in Booth's unconscious all of the hatred that he had felt as a child for his father and his fantasy became that of rescuing the oppressed mother (the South). . . . When Booth entered the box occupied by the president and his wife . . . , he unconsciously murdered his own father (brother).[65]

Punctuation was not Wilson's only deficiency. In his brief article, he misspelled the names of Surratt and Eisenschiml, declared that Booth shot Lincoln with a carbine, that Herold tried to murder William H. Seward, that Booth and Herold were fleeing to Richmond at the time of their capture, that Booth was from Virginia, that his mother had a master's degree in art, and that his father had played the role of Asa Trenchard in *Our American Cousin* in Ford's Theater. (Junius Brutus Booth died in 1852. *Our American Cousin* was first produced in 1858, and Ford's Theater opened in 1863.)

In 1958 the theme of Booth as a father murderer was picked

up by another psychiatrist, Philip Weissman. Past generations, Weissman observed, had insisted upon dismissing Booth as a madman. That was because they did not understand "that John Wilkes' delusion in which he perceived and hated Lincoln as a reigning king was derived from the denial of rage against his brother Edwin." During his frantic effort to escape, Booth had written in his diary a note that revealed "a direct expression of the unconscious aim of his murderous act. 'I do not repent the blow I struck . . . I think I have done well. Though I am abandoned, with the *curse of Cain* upon me, when if the world knew my heart, that one blow would have made me great, though I did desire no greatness.' In this desperate, defiant utterance, John labels his own act as the act of Cain, in which the good brother Abel was slain. This was not, as so many had thought, the act of a Brutus who killed a ruler, but the act of a brother who kills a brother unconsciously."[66]

Since Junius Brutus, Jr., accompanied his father on theatrical tours, Weissman's analysis continues, Edwin, five-and-one-half years older than John Wilkes, was the oldest male at home "and must have appeared to John as a father as well as a brother. Therefore, Edwin occupied the double dais of a rival heir and substitute father." When Edwin was fourteen, he became his father's touring companion and began his apprenticeship on the stage. For the next four years, from the time that John Wilkes was growing from ages nine to thirteen, he was like a fatherless boy playing wild games. "John felt that he had been badly treated and neglected and that he was not accepted as a man [at the age of thirteen!] and an actor by his father." How could he ever hope to learn elocution and declamation, he complained to Asia, stuck on the farm raising food for the family? "He began to plan defiantly for himself, for his acting and subsequent fame. From now on, in every way and at every moment, his acting developed a stealthy, surreptitious, aggressive quality." Rebelling against his apparent fate, John Wilkes determined to compete on the stage with his father and brother.[67]

But he was no match for Edwin, whose performance as Shylock in the *Merchant of Venice* greatly impressed Lincoln, and who was entertained at dinner by Secretary of State Seward. "To dine with the Secretary of State and lure the President to an unplanned visit to his performance would be any actor's dream.

What feelings would this stir in a rival actor brother?" Historians had been puzzled, Weissman notes, about why Seward had been selected as co-victim of Booth's assassination conspiracy. Had it been "exclusively a political plot, Vice President Johnson or Secretary of War Stanton would have been much more suitable targets. . . . The choice of Seward as victim exposes the emotional origins of the crime. He [Seward] was hated because, like Lincoln, he admired Edwin."[68]

On one occasion, after Edwin had completed an extended run in the role of Hamlet, Junius Brutus Booth, Jr., congratulated him, saying even their father could not have done so well. Weissman picks up the story: "Finally, the silent, younger rival, John Wilkes, with a tinge of psychotic unreality and extraordinary keenness, says, 'No, no, no! There's but one Hamlet to my mind; that's my brother Edwin. You see, between ourselves, he is Hamlet—melancholy and all.'" Such a characterization would seem to be an extremely generous appreciation coming from a brother supposed to be consumed with jealousy. But Weissman refers to its "psychotic unreality" and then, quite irrelevantly, reminds us "that Lincoln too had a 'melancholy' quality."[69]

Edward J. Kempf—still another psychiatrist without any conspicuous knowledge of Lincoln, Booth, or the Civil War—explained that Booth, "a dissipated actor out of work," hated his father and killed Lincoln in his place, while having "Mrs. Surratt and her gang kill Vice-President Johnson and Secretary Seward at the same time." As Kempf saw it, Junius Brutus Booth, the father, recognized and was proud of Edwin's great ability, making him a partner in his productions, "but he scorned John's ambitions to act and treated his efforts with contempt, and punished him cruelly for disobedience. Naturally John's self-defensive reactions accumulated irrepressible hate of his father for his injustice, favoritism and tyranny, and jealousy of the superiority of his illustrious brother. . . . As usual, under such conditions of extreme family deformation of the character development of a child, an intense instinctive compulsion grew in his mind to destroy the cause by killing his father in order to liberate himself from the effect of his tyranny." Because his father was dead, Booth's "irrepressible compulsion turned upon a surrogate father, the President of his country whom he condemned as an unjust tyrant."[70]

Perhaps the psychiatrists should not be too severely criticized for such nonsense; they derived their insights, after all, from Philip Van Doren Stern, who had a reputation as a scholar and who had claimed to have invented nothing in *The Man Who Killed Lincoln* except some dialogue and five specified incidents. Nowhere does Stern cite evidence for his theory that Booth hated his father. None of the books listed in his bibliography lends it any support whatsoever, and several help to establish the exact opposite.

In fact, Junius Brutus Booth and his son John Wilkes seem to have been especially close. Adam Badeau, General Ulysses S. Grant's aide-de-camp and a close friend of Edwin, knew that the actor had received much training from his father. "I asked him whether he was the favorite, but he said no: his father always preferred John Wilkes."[71] The drama critic and historian William Winter reported the same. "John Wilkes was (so Edwin told me) his father's favorite child."[72] "From the moment of his birth," writes Kimmel, historian of the Booth family, John Wilkes "was the darling of his father's heart. Indeed, both his parents so idolized and spoiled him that by comparison they seemed indifferent to the older children." As the most vivacious of the children, he was the center of the family's attention, and when his father returned from one of his tours "it was to shower 'his well-beloved, his bright boy Absalom,' with tender-hearted adulation."[73]

John Wilkes returned his father's love. A schoolmate, who slept in the cot next to him for two years, wrote, "John had one of the most lively and cheerful of dispositions; was kind, generous and affectionate in his nature, with an admiration for his father and his abilities that amounted almost to idolatry."[74] In the middle 1850s John and Asia, aware that most of the stories and anecdotes about their famous father were untrue, determined to write his biography and began collecting letters, playbills, and criticisms. Mary Ann, afraid to have too much of her husband's private life recorded, destroyed most of his personal letters, but she could not stop the project. In 1866 Asia completed it on her own: *Booth Memorials: Incidents and Anecdotes in the Life of Junius Brutus Booth.*[75] When John Wilkes's body was returned to the family for reburial in the Booth plot in Green Mount

Cemetery, Baltimore, in 1869, it was—according to Asia—placed in an unmarked grave next to the father Booth had so loved and admired.[76]

Another psychological explanation of the assassination is worthy of consideration if only because it comes from Stanley Kimmel's fact-filled and authoritative *The Mad Booths of Maryland* (1940, 1969). Kimmel begins by repeating the well-known circumstances of Booth's early acting career. John Wilkes, eager to follow his father and older brothers on the stage, was well endowed for stardom. He was handsome, he radiated a restless energy, and he possessed agility and originality in movement upon the stage. But his acting was crude; it had force but not finish. Unlike his brothers, he had not prepared himself for the profession but had simply launched himself upon it. He plunged into each part with determination rather than with subtle understanding. Worst of all, he had never learned to use his voice properly. Kimmel quotes a Boston critic who wrote in May 1862 that Booth was "apparently, entirely ignorant of the main principles of elocution. We do not mean by this word merely enunciation, but the nature and proper treatment of the voice, as well. He ignores the fundamental principle of all vocal study and exercise—that the chest, and not the throat or mouth, should supply the sound necessary for singing or speaking." If Booth had read the criticism, Kimmel comments, it might have warned him "that he was striding toward an abyss," for Kimmel says it was his lack of voice control which ultimately forced him off the stage.[77]

By March 1864, when his appearance in New Orleans in one of his father's most admired roles, *Richard III*, was cancelled because of a "bad cold," Kimmel believes Booth knew the truth. He knew that he was not simply suffering from a bronchial infection brought on by a cold, but that he was paying the price of his failure to learn how to project his voice properly. "He knew," says Kimmel, "his future as a star was doomed. He might continue his engagements at intervals, perhaps play a few benefit bills, but soon the curtain would fall before him for the last time and in the dim light of some empty theatre he would make his final exit. The name of Booth would still dominate the boards, but it would be filled in by Edwin—not by John Wilkes" (181).

Tormented by the inevitability and imminence of the end of his career, Booth could not bear the thought that he was "to be forced off the stage by so intangible an enemy as his voice! He could not believe it! What was he to do now? He had always been an actor, he knew no other craft. Where was he to win fame, fortune, immortality if not in the theatre?" (185).

Hiding from his friends the fact that his acting career was almost over, Booth made several trips to the oil fields of Pennsylvania and invested heavily. But his dreams of power and profit in this highly speculative field of business never materialized, and he sought desperately for some other shortcut to fame.

In Washington he was angered by the sound of people cheering marching soldiers, for it reminded him of "the plaudits he had received in the theatre" but would no more. "This and Edwin's success irked Wilkes," Kimmel explains, "and set him planning some heroic deed which would lift him to immediate fame and compensate for the loss of his voice." Grant's order stopping the exchange of prisoners-of-war "crystallized the project" that was forming in his mind: he would kidnap the president of the United States and use him to force the release of Confederate prisoners (185–87).

It was true, Kimmel concedes, that Booth had revelled in the acclaim he had received in the South before the war and that "he became more violent in his verbal defense of her cause than most rebels." But those who knew him intimately "never regarded his remarks as sincere, nor indicative of any deep feeling" (160, 262). He turned to political action, not out of conviction, but out of psychological necessity.

Booth was easily able to enlist his boyhood friends Arnold and O'Laughlin in his "preposterous scheme." His own enthusiasm for it soared when he suffered another attack of bronchitis and was unable to speak above a whisper. He travelled to Canada and was seen conspicuously in the company of the Canadian representatives, and he spoke mysteriously of big plans afoot (191).

One by one, he assembled his little band of conspirators. But bad luck, bad roads, insufficient funds, and discouraging delays caused his mental condition to become increasingly unstable. He began to drink heavily and "became the victim of morbid impulses, delusions, and manias." After the fiasco on the road to the Soldiers' Home, the conspirators disbanded, and Booth gave up the kidnapping plan. Then came the fall of Richmond, the surrender of General Robert E. Lee, and Lincoln's April 11th speech calling for limited black suffrage. Booth realized "that to become a hero he must act quickly or sink forever into insignificance" (262).

Booth shot Lincoln, according to Kimmel, because he was losing his voice and could think of no other way to become famous. "A voice which had been applauded night after night by appreciative audiences, a voice which had been unable to withstand the ordeal of constant performances, a voice which had mocked his desire for fame, drove him to that act of madness. There can be no doubt that this was the underlying cause of his determination to kill Lincoln" (262–63). This theory, unworthy of Kimmel's impressive research and knowledge of the Booth family, trivializes Booth and ignores the fact that a great many people sincerely believed that Lincoln deserved killing. Surely it is foolish to say "there can be no doubt" the loss of his voice was the underlying cause of Booth's action.

In classifying Kimmel's idea with other farfetched theories, George S. Bryan points out that Booth did not have to kill Lincoln in order to win the fame that the loss of his voice would deny him on the stage; he was already famous on the stage. And his career was by no means over. Recovering from his bad cold in New Orleans, Booth completed a successful engagement of five weeks in Boston in May 1864. In November he played in *Julius Caesar* with his brothers in New York, and he appeared in two productions in Washington in 1865. By managers and theater-goers alike, he was regarded as a star.[78]

Of course, it was true that during the 1864–65 season Booth played much less frequently than usual, but that was not because he could not play. It was because, as Kimmel well knew, he was consumed by another interest. There is reason to believe, furthermore, that some of the talk about Booth's bronchitis may have been inspired by the actor himself as a way of explaining his infrequent appearances on stage. Early in 1865 John H. Surratt asked his friend Louis J. Weichmann to write an article for the press saying that Booth had retired from the theater because of erysipelas of the leg, and was engaged in the oil business.[79]

But, of course, he had not retired and did not intend to. In November 1864 he had taken his theatrical wardrobe to Montreal for shipment to Richmond, where he expected to join it and use it. At a meeting in his room at the National Hotel on March 31, 1865, Booth told Arnold that he had given up the kidnapping plan forever. "Among the last words uttered by Booth on this occasion," Arnold remembered, "were, that he intended returning to his profession upon the stage."[80]

It is no coincidence that Bryan, who wrote the most balanced and reasonable account of the assassination as a simple conspiracy, should have written in the same book—*The Great American Myth*—the most balanced and reasonable analysis of Booth's conduct. Avoiding the simplistic and sensational explanations of earlier writers, Bryan allows Booth nearly one hundred pages to grow from the high-spirited young boy who so admired his famous father and older brothers into the angry, quick-tempered zealot who shot Lincoln. Following his theatrical career in greater detail and conceding him a greater measure of success and recognition than did Kimmel, Bryan shows how closely Booth identified himself with the pro-Confederate sympathies of his native Baltimore and Maryland. On the other hand, he fails to pay sufficient attention to Booth's deep aversion to Lincoln and his policies.

Bryan believes that the frustration that Booth felt following the failure of his kidnapping conspiracy was compounded by his belated recognition that the plan had probably been doomed to failure from the start. It was extremely unlikely that the president could have been seized and carried off without somebody being alerted and giving an alarm, and Booth knew it would have taken a much larger group than the one he commanded to fight its way out of Union-held territory.[81] He had wasted his time and his money in a futile enterprise; and he was furious with himself and with friends like Arnold who were deserting him. Ordinarily genial and even-tempered, he became quick to anger; ordinarily temperate, he began to drink excessively. Given to undisciplined emotional excesses and physical violence on stage, these traits of character, held in check through four years of war, now burst forth and took control of him offstage. When he heard the tyrant whom he hated advocate the ballot for certain southern black men, it was too much. "That means nigger citizenship," he muttered. "Now, by God, I'll put him through."[82]

But by the time Bryan wrote, interest had already shifted from Booth and his simple conspiracy to a new villain and a new grand conspiracy.

6

Otto Eisenschiml's Grand Conspiracy

$\mathbf{B}$Y THE LATE 1930s the general outline, if not the details, of John Wilkes Booth's kidnapping conspiracy and its objectives had been well established. There was a consensus, too, that the conspiracy to assassinate had grown out of the failure of the abduction plot and that it had been a simple conspiracy originating with Booth.

Booth himself, however, remained a riddle. The general public thought of him as the folklore demon, the American Judas described by Lloyd Lewis. Turn-of-the-century writers like John G. Nicolay and John Hay, David M. Dewitt, and Osborn H. Oldroyd explained his killing of Lincoln by emphasizing negative features of his character: he was full of malice and hatred, he struck to avenge the South, he was vain and sought notoriety. Somewhat later, Clara Laughlin and Francis Wilson, almost as much captivated by Booth's personality as his friends had been, reasoned that he had been misled and misinformed and that, made desperate by the failure of his plans and by the Confederacy's impending defeat, he had suffered an attack of mental imbalance and committed an out-of-character crime. Philip Van Doren Stern and Stanley Kimmel offered psychological explanations of his action.

The assassin Booth had thus been analyzed by many writers from a variety of perspectives. But the assassination of Lincoln had never been adequately explained as the political act that Booth had believed it to be. "*Sic semper tyrannis!*" he had cried, echoing an old and defensible tradition. The trouble was that most Americans were simply incapable of thinking of Lincoln as a tyrant, or of taking seriously anyone who thought he was—especially his murderer.

It was perhaps no coincidence that one of the first writers to make an association between Lincoln's political actions and his assassination was a Southerner and a Democrat who had experienced the Civil War as a boy in Georgia: Woodrow Wilson. In his *A History of the American People* (1901), Wilson wrote that Booth had been "half-crazed by blind enthusiasm and poignant regret for the lost southern cause." But he conferred a measure of respectability upon the assassin by noting that "Mr. Lincoln had acted oftentimes with the authority almost of a dictator. . . . Individual rights had seemed for a time suspended." Men close to Lincoln and the people at large had trusted him; they had understood that he acted from "sober motives," and they expected a restoration of their civil liberties. "But men who were not near him could not so see him."[1]

Wilson did not dwell on the point. But leading revisionist historians of his generation who were critical of Lincoln's usurpations of power—for example, William A. Dunning and James Ford Rhodes (both born and raised in the North), and John A. Burgess (a Union veteran born in Tennessee)—did not relate the assassination to the usurpations at all. Few historians did. Ellis Paxson Oberholtzer labelled the assassination political but did not discuss it as such, and in his 1931 biography of Lincoln Edgar Lee Masters said only that "Booth's bullet was the last one fired for States' Rights."[2]

With such exceptions, Lincoln's assassination had never been interpreted in the political terms essential to any understanding of Booth's motivations. Since the interpretations that had been proposed of why Booth killed Lincoln were inadequate and unsatisfactory, knowledge of one of the most important events in American history also remained inadequate and unsatisfactory. "The student is as puzzled as the man on the street," wrote Otto Eisenschiml in 1937. "A great political crime was committed without an adequate motive."[3] In his *Why Was Lincoln Murdered?* Eisenschiml sought to fill the conceptual vacuum that existed in the history of Lincoln's assassination by formulating an entirely new political hypothesis.

Although born, raised, and educated in Austria, Eisenschiml was an American citizen by birth. His father had emigrated to

California at the time of the gold rush and during the Civil War saw action at Shiloh as an officer in an Illinois regiment. He next became an Indian scout and, while living in Nevada, an American citizen. Moving to Chicago, he worked as a butcher until 1872, when he returned to Austria and married. His son Otto was born in Vienna on June 16, 1880. The senior Eisenschiml, always proud of his U.S. citizenship, talked to his son about Lincoln and Ulysses S. Grant and his experiences in America and advised him to emigrate as soon as his education was complete. Young Eisenschiml took the advice. Upon receiving a diploma in Chemical Engineering from the Polytechnic School of Vienna in 1901, he sailed for the United States.[4]

Starting out as a chemist in a steel factory in Pittsburgh and in a linseed oil plant in Chicago, Eisenschiml soon began to act as a consultant for businessmen with chemical problems—how to keep the transparent address windows in envelopes from clouding over, for example, and how to make an oil cloth flexible, waterproof, and heat resistant for use in hospitals and elsewhere. Opportunities for chemists with an eye for business were plentiful, and shortly after World War I he left his laboratory and, as president of the Scientific Oil Compounding Company, became the distributor of raw materials used in the manufacture of paints, varnishes, and fungicides. Within a few years he had made a fortune.[5]

Eisenschiml was glad to give up his career in chemistry, for he craved a recognition not received by members of the profession. Chemists were responsible for breathtaking improvements in medicine and agriculture and in thousands of products consumed every day, yet they were unknown to the public, looked down upon by those who profited from their skills, and paid the wages of stenographers. He became a businessman, Eisenschiml said, out of necessity; "my choice might have been different, had chemists been regarded with more respect, and had the financial returns been anywhere near adequate."[6]

As a boy in Austria, Eisenschiml's interest in American history had been aroused by his father's stories. As a man in the United States, it was stimulated by his own travels. In 1913, after inspecting as a consultant some abandoned mines in the Black Hills, he continued west to Montana, where he visited the site of the famous Custer massacre of 1876. The weather-blanched bones of men and animals were still exposed, and Eisenschiml picked up cooking utensils, a loaded revolver, and other relics. The experience moved him deeply, more deeply, he said, "than anything had ever done before." He resolved to visit every battlefield in the United States and later rejoiced that he had been lucky enough to see many of them "before paved roads and peanut stands turned their hallowed soil into picnic grounds." With the time and means to indulge his interest, he studied the battles intensively before making his field trips, and in the absence of the uniformed guides of a later day he trudged over the battlegrounds listening to the tales of old-time residents. In 1946 he published a vivid little book about one such investigation which had special meaning for him, *The Story of Shiloh*.[7]

It was not military history, however, but Lincoln's assassination that most fully occupied Eisenschiml. He approached the subject with an energetic and imaginative mind, and, so he maintained, with the methods and objectivity of a scientist. "Research should be undertaken with a microscope, not with a brief case," he insisted. In history, "facts, facts and more facts are needed and should be unearthed." In commenting upon his work as an historian he frequently spoke of his chemical training and "chemical thinking" and observed that "once a chemist, always a chemist." "I suffer from an inborn vice of asking questions," he wrote, "a vice which is the birthright of every chemist, and should be that of every historian, but rarely is." The writing of history, he found, "was fascinating work, and, after all, not unlike the solving of chemical problems."[8]

The circumstance that aroused Eisenschiml's curiosity about the assassination was why General Grant had first accepted and then declined Lincoln's invitation to attend Ford's Theater as his guest on April 14, 1865. It was a momentous change of mind, for Eisenschiml believed that if the general had been by the president's side "the attempt on Lincoln's life would not have been made." Grant's staff was never far away from him and would undoubtedly have prevented Booth or anyone else from entering the box. At the very least, the negligent guard assigned to Lincoln "would have hesitated to leave his post when standing sentry for the lieutenant general." He might take that liberty with Lincoln, but he had been a soldier and would not have done so with Grant. Even if it had been possible for Booth to talk his way past the guard or guards, he probably would not have tried, for he would have known that "with a thousand eyes constantly focused on the Presidential box—the men to see what Grant looked like, the women what Mrs. Grant was wearing," his action would be observed and he could not possibly escape. Since Booth was no martyr, but a "vanity-mad actor, who wanted to be feted by the South as its hero," he would not have attempted the assassination. Therefore, whoever induced Grant to change his mind about going to the theater, "played—knowingly or unknowingly—straight into the hands of the conspirators."[9]

"How could Grant have broken his promise," Eisenschiml wondered, "without being rude, if not actually insubordinate? . . . My curiosity increased when I discovered that Grant's own explanation, given in his autobiography, was trivial, evasive, highly improbable. I tried to shut my mind against the challenge of this riddle; but in my heart I knew I would not be able to rest until I had satisfied myself as to why Grant had left Washington an hour and a half before the curtain rose in Ford's Theater that fatal night."[10] The inspiration came to him one day while driving along a Chicago boulevard. As he described it in a book of informal essays, it startled him so "that involuntarily I put my foot on the brake pedal. The car came to an abrupt stop, and the one behind bumped into me. Out of it stepped a six-footer with the meanest face in six states. He lumbered up to my open window. 'Say, fellow,' he bellowed, 'what you been thinking about?'

"'I'll tell you, my friend,' I replied. 'I've been thinking that for the first time I have an inkling why General Grant did not accompany Lincoln to the theater on the night of April 14, 1865.'

"The giant staggered as if I had hit him on the chin, ran back to his car, jumped in and raced away at sixty miles an hour. I have never seen him again."[11] (Eisenschiml might not have seen the man again, but he had apparently seen him before. In his autobiography he described the same encounter taking place when he was a consulting chemist mulling over some other problem.[12])

What startled Eisenschiml was the conviction that Grant would not have altered his plans to accompany Lincoln unless he had been so ordered. The only man from whom Grant took orders, besides Lincoln himself, was Secretary of War Edwin M. Stanton. Had Stanton ordered Grant to change his plans? To his astonishment, Eisenschiml discovered that he had. Two clerks in the War Department had heard Stanton give an "implied order" to Grant not to go to the theater, and since both were on friendly terms with the secretary their testimony could be considered free from malice. The suspicion thus aroused led Eisenschiml in 1933 to the archives of the judge advocate general's office in the War Department, Washington. There he discovered a dust-covered filing cabinet containing the material collected by Joseph Holt and his Bureau of Military Justice and now known as "Investigation and Trial Papers Relating to the Assassination of President Lincoln." "I have always been proud of my steady nerves," he wrote years later, "but in this instance I admit that I trembled like a dope addict. I was holding in my hands priceless source documents which would change the accepted accounts of Lincoln's assassination and force the rewriting of an important chapter in history."[13]

In exploring the possibility that Stanton might have been involved in the assassination conspiracy, Eisenschiml determined to follow the method of the Russian chemist Dimitri Mendeleyev, who nearly a century before had observed that if all the known elements were arranged in the order of their atomic weights they displayed a regularity of periodicity, except that there were gaps between them. Mendeleyev proposed to fellow scientists that if these gaps could be filled by the discovery of new elements and that if the properties of the new elements followed the existing periodical arrangement, then the periodicity was not a mere coincidence but a scientific truth. The scientific world rose to the challenge, Eisenschiml wrote, and "today Mendeleyev's table hangs in every chemical laboratory worthy of its name."[14]

For many years Eisenschiml labored with the help of a research staff to discover, arrange, and weigh the various elements that seemed to link Stanton to the assassination. One after another fell into place, but "I have not succeeded to this day in filling all the gaps," he admitted in 1963, the year of his death. "If I had received the same help as Mendeleyev did, the chances are that history today would be much nearer to the truth about

Lincoln's assassination; but I was not, for most historians do homage to principles which differ sharply from those of scientists."[15]

It is fitting that in the title of the book which made him famous—*Why Was Lincoln Murdered?*—Eisenschiml should have asked a question, for he prided himself on asking questions that he said historians had not bothered to ask. Indeed, questions were such a prominent feature of the book that the volume's flavor and major supposition can be suggested by a simple listing of some of those it raised. Since the existence of conspiracies against Lincoln's life was known to the War Department, why were not the strictest measures taken to protect the president? Why did Secretary Stanton deny Lincoln the protection he requested at the theater? Why was the bodyguard who was assigned—a man "guilty of the grossest negligence"—never punished? Why was the telegraph service out of Washington interrupted for two hours at approximately the same time as the attack on Lincoln? Was it only a coincidence that Stanton should have issued orders blocking every route of escape out of the capital except the one that Booth took? When Booth was captured, why was he killed in violation of orders? Why was the soldier who claimed to have fired the shot never punished? After Booth's co-conspirators had been captured and imprisoned, why were they forced to wear canvas hoods over their heads, cutting them off from communication with the outside world? Why were the four conspirators who were not hanged sent to a prison on a remote island eighty miles off the coast of Florida instead of to Albany, New York, where it had been originally intended to send them? Why was Lincoln murdered?

The following condensation of the Eisenschiml thesis gives his answers to many of these questions and his speculations about others for which the evidence is inconclusive. Lengthy as it is, it does not do the thesis justice, for it necessarily slights the details and documentation with which Eisenschiml embellished his plots and subplots. Depriving it of this elaboration lessens its impact and persuasiveness but does not alter its substance.

If, in giving an "implied order" to Grant not to attend the theater with Lincoln, Stanton had knowingly played into the hands of the conspirators, then he would have taken other actions as well to facilitate their work. When the secretary denied

Lincoln the escort he requested in Grant's place, was it "just boorishness," or did he have some other reason?

The member of the Washington Metropolitan Police Force who was detailed to stand guard outside Lincoln's box on April 14 was John F. Parker, whose record included such violations of police regulations as drunkenness and sleeping while on duty. Lincoln, "a shrewd judge of human nature," doubted Parker's reliability and, upon learning that Grant was not going to accompany him to the theater after all, stopped off at the War Department and "asked Stanton to let him have his chief aide, Major Thomas T. Eckert, as escort for himself and his guests." He was impressed with Eckert's strength, Lincoln said, having seen him break five iron pokers over his arm, one after another. "This request Stanton refused pointblank; he had some important work for Eckert that night, he said, and could not spare him." When Lincoln asked Eckert directly, the major "also very decidedly refused to go, . . . pleading work that could not be put off." Disappointed, Lincoln said he would invite Major Henry R. Rathbone instead and left.[16] Neither Stanton nor Eckert ever appeared at the War Department that evening, and both were at home when informed of the assassination. When Stanton told the president that he expected to do a lot of work that night, "he seems to have evaded the truth" (38).

And what of police officer Parker, whose "unbelievable carelessness" in leaving his post outside the door to Lincoln's box was immediately responsible for the assassination, and for whose conduct "no mitigating circumstances could be pleaded?" Although Stanton had been mercilessly severe during the war with poor country boys who had fallen asleep on sentry duty after long marches, he was inexplicably generous with Parker, who was not punished, reprimanded, or even immediately relieved of his White House duties. "There is no evidence that Parker was in any way involved in the murder conspiracy," but that he should have escaped Stanton's wrath is "one of the unexplained mysteries of those eventful days" (17–18).

After being shot by Booth, the unconscious Lincoln was carried to a roominghouse across the street, where he died the following morning. Stanton spent the long night in the back parlor of the house interrogating witnesses and issuing orders to military units around the capital for the capture of the fleeing assassin. To all appearances, the measures taken were thorough. But in all the telegrams sent out by the War Department that night, no mention was made of the road that led directly south from the capital to Port Tobacco, Maryland, on the Potomac. "The only road that Stanton failed to bar was the one by which Booth escaped from Washington; and there never should have been the slightest doubt that he would use it" (91–96).

Within a few minutes after the assassination, "a bizarre incident" occurred: the "interruption of all telegraphic communication between Washington and the outside world, lasting about two hours." The interruption, the result of a short circuit in the main batteries of the commercial telegraph, seemed to be an inside job, for only an insider could have had access to the batteries. "The mere suspicion that there might be a traitor in the ranks of the telegraphic corps should have been enough to warrant a painstaking inquiry. But evidently no alarm was felt by Eckert or by Stanton, and no investigation was ever made." For the two critical hours immediately following Booth's flight, "few telegrams pertaining to Lincoln's death left Washington. But when Stanton got ready to send out the first of his dispatches, the telegraph was functioning again" (78–83).

If the assassin of the president was to be caught, it was of vital importance "that his name and description be instantly flashed as far as the powers of the Washington government extended." According to Corporal James Tanner, who took down in shorthand the testimony of the eyewitnesses questioned by Stanton, enough had been said in fifteen minutes to make it certain that Booth was the guilty man. Since Tanner began his work at midnight or shortly after, "by half past twelve at the latest, Stanton could have sounded the general alarm for Booth's capture. Instead of doing this, he waited three hours before disclosing the name of the assassin, and for two hours he did not send out any news at all." In the meantime, the nation's morning newspapers went to press, most of them with stories telling only that the president had been shot. Not until the afternoon papers came out did the bulk of the American people learn who had done the shooting. In other ways, too, Stanton "hampered the newspapers . . . instead of enlisting their aid in the capture of the assassins" (64–77, 435).

Through an incredible error, "if error it can be called," the photograph introduced by the government in May at the trial of the assassination conspirators as that of John Wilkes Booth was in reality a picture of his brother Edwin. In April, when questioned by army officers, Samuel A. Mudd, the physician who treated the leg Booth had injured on his jump from Lincoln's box, admitted an acquaintance with the wanted man, but stated that he could not recognize him from the picture shown. If the picture shown to Mudd had also been that of Edwin Booth, then other pursuing officers were probably also furnished with a copy of it. "If this supposition be correct, it follows that *all the pursuers of Booth were equipped* with the wrong pictures. . . . How many other people [besides Mudd] who had seen John Wilkes Booth may have been misled when Edwin Booth's picture was held before their eyes? And how many detectives might have met J. Wilkes Booth in person and let him pass as not being the man they were after?" (265, Eisenschiml's italics).

A great many military and civilian units participated in the search for Booth and David Herold, his companion in flight, but because of the large rewards offered there was little cooperation between them. "Avarice, jealousy and ambition soon overcame patriotism, and each group kept to itself whatever facts it was able to gather." Thus General Christopher C. Augur, commander of the Department of Washington, learned on April 21 or 22 from his men in the field that Booth had broken his leg and been treated by Dr. Mudd, but the general did not share this crucial information with the War Department. Stanton did not learn of it until April 24, when one of Augur's men in southern Maryland, Major James R. O'Beirne, confided it to a telegrapher, Samuel Beckwith, who wired the news to Eckert (120–22).

At the time, O'Beirne later declared, he was hot on the trail of Booth and Herold, who had crossed the river into Virginia, "and had he held to it for a few more hours would probably have captured them. . . . One can imagine his surprise and despair when orders came over the wire from Washington to discontinue his expedition and remain on the Maryland side of the Potomac." A farm girl near Bryantown had reported seeing two men, one of them using a crutch, emerge from some woods and ask for food, and O'Beirne was directed to investigate. Though he conducted a vigorous and thorough search of the neighborhood, he discovered nothing but crutch marks, and "while he literally walked around in circles, looking for these two phantoms who never materialized," a force representing Stanton and Colonel Lafayette C. Baker, whom Stanton had placed in charge of the search for Booth, took up the trail where O'Beirne had left it "and came home with the Big Prize" (122–23).

The successful expedition was headed by ex-Lieutenant Luther B. Baker, a cousin of Colonel Baker, and Everton J. Conger, a former lieutenant-colonel close to Stanton. It consisted of a detachment of twenty-five cavalrymen from a New York regiment, under the command of Lieutenant Edward P. Doherty. "You are going after Booth," Colonel Baker said to his cousin as they parted on the afternoon of April 24. "Lieutenant, we have got a sure thing" (124).

They did. Before dawn on April 26 they surrounded the tobacco shed on the farm near Bowling Green, Virginia, where Booth and Herold were sleeping. Herold surrendered, but Booth announced his intention to fight his way out. The barn was set on fire. As Booth moved toward the door, a shot was fired and he fell to the ground, paralyzed by a bullet in the neck. He died on the porch of the farmhouse just as the sun rose. Baker and Conger, commanding twenty-five experienced soldiers and an officer, should have been able to capture the crippled Booth alive, as their orders had directed. They could have waited until daylight and then stormed the shed, or laid siege to it and let hunger force Booth out. "Was it fear that the rewards would have to be shared with reinforcements which might arrive" that made them act so precipitously? "Or did Conger have secret orders to kill the fugitive? Did Lieutenant Baker suspect something of this sort?" (159–60).

Since Booth's broken leg made his ultimate capture inevitable, it was essential to the same authorities who had wanted him to escape—and who had conducted the search for him in such a way that, uninjured, he would have—that he be silenced before he had an opportunity to incriminate them. As the ranking officer, Conger's proper place was in front of the shed, at the door through which Booth would emerge, but Baker had occupied this position and Conger was around at the side. What good reason could there have been for Conger to take that position except that he wanted to be able to kill Booth without attracting attention? "And Booth had to be killed before he could talk."[17]

After dragging Booth from the flaming barn, Baker asked Conger why he had shot the assassin. Conger replied that he had not shot him, that Booth must have shot himself. "No, he did not," declared Baker, who had been watching him all the time. Then the idea flashed through his mind, he later testified before a Congressional committee, that if Conger had fired the shot, "it had better not be known." What could such an enigmatic statement mean except that Baker suspected Conger had shot Booth on secret orders from Stanton? Upon returning to Washington, Baker made a full statement before Judge Advocate General Holt about the manner of Booth's capture and death, but the statement mysteriously disappeared. Baker feared foul play; perhaps his suspicions of Conger were responsible (158–60).[18]

One thing was certain: the shot that killed Booth had not been fired by the emotionally unbalanced trooper, Boston Corbett, who claimed to have fired it at God's direction. Corbett and the other soldiers surrounding the barn had been assigned positions about thirty feet away from it. If Corbett had been the killer, he would have had to crawl close to the building in order to fire his revolver or carbine through one of the cracks. With the shed ablaze, he would have been seen by other soldiers, but not one of them ever supported his story. Nevertheless, Corbett's eccentric confession had been a godsend to Conger, who must have been wondering how he could fasten the blame on someone for violating orders. Back in Washington, Stanton dismissed the complaint against Corbett and called him a patriot who "has saved us continued excitement, delay and expense." What kind of excitement did Stanton think Corbett had spared him? Still, it had to be admitted that the "shooting of Booth could have been an accident"(153–56, 185).[19]

If Stanton were a member of the assassination conspiracy, it would have been as important to him to silence the eight conspirators known or believed to have been in Booth's confidence as it was to silence Booth himself. Why else would he have ordered the seven male prisoners tried for their part in the conspiracy to wear hoods over their heads as "better security against conversation"? Why was it the government wished to keep them from talking? After they were removed from temporary imprisonment aboard monitors in the Potomac to the old penitentiary on the grounds of the Washington Arsenal, security was increased. The prisoners were shackled at the wrist by a rigid iron bar that prevented the movement of one arm without a similar motion by the other. These shackles made it impossible for the prisoners, already blinded and silenced by the hoods, to write out legible messages. For all practical purposes, they were "blind, deaf, dumb, and paralyzed," cut off from communication with everyone. Torture is usually employed "to extort confessions from the accused; this mad invention of Stanton's made confessions impossible. Was there method in this madness?" (175–79).[20]

As a woman, Mary E. Surratt was not required to wear stiff wrist shackles or a hood, but other means were found to silence her. "In all likelihood, a promise of clemency was held out." Few observers at the conspiracy trial believed she would be sentenced to death, and neither did she herself. When at last she learned she was to be hanged, "it was too late to talk, even had she intended to do so. She collapsed and remained in a semi-delirious condition until the end" (179–80).[21]

If it were true that the male prisoners had been hooded and shackled to insure their silence, "and no direct proof for this assumption exists," it would be necessary for all to be condemned to death, for they could not be kept permanently in hoods and stiff shackles. Certainly the government prosecutors made vigorous efforts to have death penalties pronounced for all eight defendants. But the "military commission balked at this wholesale hanging" and sentenced four of the men to prison at Albany, New York. "Delivered from the clutches of military discipline, and confined in a state jail, the victims of Stanton's wrath would soon have been at liberty to talk." Therefore, at the secretary's instigation, they were shipped away to the island military prison on the Dry Tortugas, where there would be no danger that they might talk to reporters (181).[22]

But even at the Dry Tortugas they could talk to their guards and to other prisoners, and the day of reckoning would only be postponed. Under the guise of preventing an escape, the four state prisoners were accordingly confined to a small dungeon and denied communication with others on the island. When smallpox broke out, patients were placed so close to them that they expected to become victims of the disease themselves. "What evidently was required was *Silence*" (181–83). [23]

At this point Eisenschiml abruptly stops his discussion of the ways in which the War Department sought to silence its prisoners. Perhaps he recognized that he had already gone too far, much too far, that there were no grounds whatsoever for suggesting that Stanton tried to keep any of the conspirators from talking. If Eisenschiml really did try to function like a chemist in a laboratory, he knew that this and all his other major points could not stand a fair test against the evidence, that the entire "Eisenschiml thesis" rested upon the twisting and stretching of facts, that the questions he asked were both leading and misleading.

The story about Stanton denying Lincoln the company of Eckert at Ford's theater comes from the memoir of David H. Bates, one of the two War Department clerks whose memory of how Stanton had given an "implied order" to Grant to change his plans had so impressed Eisenschiml. Eisenschiml admitted that Bates's "charge," published forty-two years after the event, could have been the product of an old man's imagination. But since Bates had admired Stanton and been a lifelong friend of Eckert, he considered it unlikely.

The truth is that Bates made no "charge" against Stanton. He stated that upon hearing that the Lincolns were planning to attend the theater in company with General and Mrs. Grant, Stanton "made a vigorous protest" against it on grounds of security. Because Lincoln, as usual, made light of the secretary's fears, Stanton privately asked Grant not to make the public appearance and to try to persuade Lincoln to give it up as well. Grant, who said he was only looking for an excuse, agreed readily enough. Lincoln had not been eager to attend the play either, but, since it had been announced in the papers that both he and Grant would be there, he felt an obligation to go so as not to give the audience a double disappointment. When he asked for the company of Eckert, Stanton refused, according to Bates, because he was "still unwilling to encourage the theater project," and Eckert, "knowing Stanton's views," declined for the same reason. The point of Bates's story was that Stanton had earnestly sought to discourage Lincoln from attending the theater, not that he had lured him defenseless into a trap.

Bates wondered if "the alert and vigorous Eckert" might not have been able to save the president's life if he had been in the box instead of Major Rathbone. He might have. But it must be remembered that Eckert was to have been a guest inside the box rather than a guard outside of it, a distinction Eisenschiml blurs by referring to Eckert as an escort for Lincoln and his "guests." The chances are that no one could have stopped Booth from pulling the trigger once he stood behind the president's chair.[24]

The second clerk who heard Stanton talk to Grant about breaking his theater engagement was the telegrapher Beckwith, whose story, published in 1913, was identical to Bates's and possibly inspired by it.[25]

The man who allowed Booth to reach Lincoln's chair was Parker. Why was he not punished? According to Eisenschiml's own interpretation, it could have been because Parker had not really failed in his duty. An eyewitness cited by Eisenschiml testified that Booth stopped outside the door to Lincoln's box, took some visiting cards from his pocket, selected one, and showed it to the president's "messenger," who was seated one step down next to the door. Eisenschiml assumes that the messenger was Parker and wonders what Parker did with the card.[26] If the messenger really was Parker, it would appear that his offense was not that he had abandoned his post, but that he had given Booth permission to approach the president. Had he remained standing by the door, there would have been no reason for him to act differently, for Lincoln's interest in actors and the theater was well known.

But Eisenschiml was almost certainly mistaken about the identity of the man to whom Booth showed his card. Shortly before Booth's arrival, Simon P. Hanscom, editor of the Washington *National Republican*, had called at the president's box to deliver a document. In his newspaper he reported that the only one present at the door was Charles Forbes, well known in Washington as Lincoln's messenger and footman.[27]

Early in May 1865 charges were brought against Parker for neglect of duty, with Forbes as one of the witnesses, and a trial was held before a Metropolitan Police board. There is no known record of the trial, but Parker must have had a reasonable defense, for the charge against him was dropped in June, and he remained on active duty on the police force. Perhaps he had not been ordered to stand guard outside the president's door at all, but only to escort the president to and from the theater. Perhaps he could show, as James O. Hall has suggested, "that the President [had] dismissed him and told him to take a seat and enjoy the play. This would have been in character for Lincoln."[28] Perhaps it was recognized that Booth could have talked his way past Parker as both he and Hanscom had talked their ways past Forbes and that any possible neglect of duty was thus of no practical consequence.

In his allegation that Stanton closed all of the roads leading out of Washington except the one to Port Tobacco that Booth took, Eisenschiml admits there were no telegraphic facilities and no significant body of troops in that part of southern Maryland.[29] How, then, could Stanton be held responsible for not having closed this route, as he had closed the others, by a few well-directed telegrams? Before midnight on April 14 Stanton did warn the naval station at St. Inigoes, Maryland, near the mouth of the Potomac—the telegraph station closest to Port Tobacco—that the parties to the assassination "may escape or attempt to escape across the Potomac."[30] A writer as partial to Stanton as Eisenschiml was hostile could claim that Stanton had thus "blocked" the river. Although Eisenschiml cites this telegram, he states incorrectly that it urged the commander only to bottle-up the outlet of the Potomac.[31]

Since he concedes that the lack of telegraphic facilities made it impossible for Stanton to throw "a cordon across the culprit's path" in southern Maryland, Eisenschiml proceeds to ask, "Why, then, were the troops from Washington not thrown into the breach and put into motion at once?" In the same extraordinary paragraph, he explains why: with his substantial head start, an uninjured Booth could easily have outridden any pursuing soldiers. By early morning on April 15 he would have been near King George Court House, Virginia, "and out of immediate reach of all organized pursuit. It would not have mattered, therefore, that the government had blocked the road behind him."[32]

One other possibility remained. "If the pursuers had subjected their problem to an intelligent analysis," Eisenschiml says they would have recognized that Booth would be in Virginia early the next morning. "The proper thing, therefore, would have been to mobilize the Richmond troops at once." Soldiers from Richmond could have arrived at Fredericksburg "by dawn and, within a few hours would have been in a position to guard all crossings of the Rappahannock river. This would have bottled Booth up, no matter how fast he traveled."[33]

Here Eisenschiml is guilty of ignoring the true nature of the problem Stanton faced in the hours following Booth's attack. With so much happening in Washington and with so many rumors circulating about what might happen next, it was utterly impossible for Stanton and his aides to sit down and subject their problem to the kind of calm and intelligent analysis Eisenschiml says they should have given it. Even had they been able to do so, they would by no means have concluded that Booth would continue to ride directly southward toward a section of Virginia controlled by the U.S. Army. If troops had been immediately deployed from Richmond, they might have arrived at the Rappahannock in time to stop Booth, providing he had taken the same route as an uninjured rider that he did take when hobbled by his broken leg. Whatever his escape plans may have been, his timing and his itinerary were, of course, altered by his unforeseen accident.

For several pages Eisenschiml occupies his readers with a discussion of the "bizarre incident" of the interruption of the telegraph. He begins by stating that "all telegraphic communication" was cut off for two hours and ends by stating that "few telegrams" left Washington during the same two hours. But, as he himself shows, it was only the commercial line between Washington and Baltimore that was inoperative; the War Department's lines were never affected. Why did Eckert make no investigation? He explained to a Congressional committee, "It did not at the time seem to be sufficiently important, as the interruption only continued about two hours. I was so full of business of almost every character that I could not give it my personal attention. . . . I could not ascertain with certainty what the facts were without making a personal investigation, and I had not time to do that." In short, the temporary interruption of one branch of the commercial telegraph line was not worth investigating.[34]

Whether Stanton should have released the news that Booth was the man who shot the president more promptly than he did is simply a matter of opinion. Against Eisenschiml's suggestion that the secretary deliberately withheld the news from the public for three hours in order to increase Booth's chances of escaping, one must recognize that it would have been inexcusable to send an angry citizenry after the wrong man. Under the circumstances, a delay of three hours was perhaps not excessive. Besides, as Corporal Tanner stated in the source cited by Eisenschiml, the witnesses interrogated by Stanton were so horrified that they would say no more than that they believed the assassin to be Booth; none would make a positive identification. Similarly, Stanton's censorship of news about the assassination sent out of Washington was justified or not, depending upon whether or not one feels it was important to contain the excitability of the people. Although it was one of the most sensational stories in American history and came at a time when public emotions were already overwrought, there were remarkably few lurid reports in the press, a fact for which Stanton deserves the credit or blame.[35]

Among the papers that Eisenschiml consulted in the office of the judge advocate general is an envelope marked "Ex no 1 Booth's photograph."[36] Inside it, undeniably, is a picture of Edwin Booth. But it does not follow that the picture was presented at the conspiracy trial as one of John Wilkes, for the papers had been shuffled by many military and civilian hands through the years, and it is impossible to say what photograph was in the envelope in 1865. Moreover, if the pictures of the two brothers had been deliberately switched in order to confuse witnesses, the War Department could easily have covered its deception by switching them back after the trial. In that case, no one except those responsible would ever have known about the treachery.

If, deliberately or not, the wrong picture was shown at the trial, it follows that it could also have been given to the various search parties and been shown to Dr. Mudd and others. But it does not follow that all of Booth's pursuers were equipped with it, and evidence with which Eisenschiml was familiar makes it certain that they were not. On April 25 Lieutenant Baker showed the picture he carried to the fisherman who ferried him across the Rappahannock and was told that it looked like the lame man who had crossed the day before except that that man had not worn a moustache. Since Edwin Booth never did have a moustache, the picture could not have been of him. Baker had never seen Booth until the night he captured him, but he told Congress he recognized him at once from his picture. Lieutenant Doherty was convinced by the reaction of Virginians to whom he showed the photo he carried that the assassin was close at hand.[37] Many copies and reproductions exist of the posters distributed by the War Department to advertise the rewards for the capture of Booth, Herold, and John H. Surratt. These posters, scattered throughout the countryside, were the first "Man Wanted" broadsides ever published with photographs.[38] None has ever been found with the picture of Edwin Booth.

In speculating about how Colonel Baker picked up Booth's trail, Eisenschiml suggests as an "intriguing hypothesis" that the colonel had known for several days where Booth and Herold were hiding and was thus enabled "to time Conger's pursuit to a nicety." But in the absence of evidence he declares it safer to assume that Baker acted upon the information that telegrapher Beckwith learned from Major O'Beirne and wired to the War Department on April 24. O'Beirne, who insisted that he would have caught the fugitives if he had not been ordered to pursue the false lead near Bryantown, believed he had been shouldered aside so that favorites of the War Department could collect the reward.[39]

Documents cited by Eisenschiml indicate that there is no basis in fact for O'Beirne's story. In addition to giving the War Department its first information about the injury to Booth's leg, Beckwith's telegram of April 24 reported that O'Beirne was investigating two possible leads to Booth and Herold. The first was that the two men had crossed the Potomac in a small boat at Swann Point on April 16, and the other was that they were still concealed in the swamp near Bryantown. If O'Beirne had crossed the Potomac on April 24, he would have been following the wrong men. But since the fugitives had in fact crossed the river not far away on April 22, he might have caught them by accident. For this reason, and because he believed he had furnished the War Department with the information that led to the capture, O'Beirne argued that he was entitled to part of the reward.[40]

No copy of the telegram O'Beirne said he received from the War Department was ever found in the records, but "O'Beirne proclaimed its existence," Eisenschiml tells us, "—which no one denied—even in official letters to Stanton himself." Eisenschiml takes O'Beirne at his word, declaring that "orders to have him abandon the pursuit of Booth" were sent to him "immediately" upon receipt of Beckwith's telegram. "It is significant," Eisenschiml concludes, "that of all the telegrams pertaining to this matter, this one in particular is not on file."[41]

Evidence cited by Eisenschiml and presumably familiar to him indicates that no such wire was ever sent to O'Beirne. In his April 24 telegram Beckwith stated that he and O'Beirne "propose first to thoroughly scour swamp and country [in the Bryantown area] today, and if unsuccessful and additional evidence will justify it, we then propose to cross with force into Virginia and follow up that trail as long as there is any hope." Early on the morning of April 26 he telegraphed optimistically that he and O'Beirne had found enough evidence of the presence of Booth and Herold near Bryantown "to justify the belief they are still in [the] same vicinity."[42] In short, it was not the War Department that kept O'Beirne from crossing into Virginia but the fact that by far the more promising of his two leads was in Maryland. Unless one is to believe that Colonel Baker's "sure thing" was the eight-day-old trail that O'Beirne himself chose not to follow, O'Beirne had nothing whatsoever to do with the location and capture of Booth. This conclusion was reached by a committee of the House of Representatives, whose report Eisenschiml quotes at length.[43] O'Beirne's story was designed to win him a share of the reward money. Eisenschiml seems to have reported it at length to support his allegation that the War Department wanted the capture of Booth to be made by a party that included its own trusted agent. Other parties—O'Beirne's would do for an example—had to be called off so that Conger could be in at the kill.

In order to establish the likelihood that Conger fired the shot that killed Booth, Eisenschiml dismisses the case against Corbett by declaring that the sergeant was standing thirty feet away from the shed when the shot was fired. It is true that Corbett and the other soldiers had been originally ordered to assume positions that far away, but it is easy to imagine that as the drama neared its fiery climax the temptation to move in for a closer look would have been overpowering, especially since the brightness of the fire inside the shed made those outside of it invisible to Booth. Lieutenant Doherty's 1890 statement that he had stationed Corbett "at a large crack in the side of the barn" is untrustworthy,[44] but if, as Eisenschiml points out, it is significant that no soldier ever said he saw Corbett shoot Booth, it is also significant that none ever said he could not have shot him.[45]

When carried or dragged from the burning shed and placed on the grass beneath a tree, Booth was unconscious. But a splash of water revived him, and he spoke in gasps and whispers to his captors both there and upon the farmhouse porch where he was soon taken. There is no disagreement among the three officers present—Doherty, Baker, and Conger—about the substance of his remarks. He wanted his mother to know that he had acted for his country and that he had done what he thought was best; he asked to be put out of his misery; he asked that his hands be raised and pronounced them useless; he asked how his presence at the farm had been betrayed.

But in other respects each of the three men described the scene in such a way as to stress his own central role in it. Thus Doherty claimed to have overruled Baker about the acceptance of Herold's surrender, to have grabbed that frantic prisoner by the wrists himself and pulled him from the barn, and to have had exclusive custody of him during the hour or two that Booth lay passively dying. He also claimed to have been the first to reach Booth after the shot was fired and in his 1890 reminiscence even claimed to have caught him before he touched the ground.[46] In a joint affidavit Baker and Conger deprecated Doherty as "the mere commander" of the badly disciplined troops, to whom, as a matter of fact, Conger often gave orders directly. They stated that Baker alone had communicated with Booth about surrender and that it was Baker who pulled Herold from the barn and who was the first to reach Booth inside it. Doherty, they said, "was absent from the door when Booth was shot." In independent testimony Baker stated that Conger had left him in charge of Booth at three different times: when Conger attempted to put out the fire in the barn, when he went to find the soldier who had shot against orders, and when, shortly before Booth's death, he gathered up the articles taken from Booth's pockets and departed with them for Washington.[47] Conger, who received $15,000 as the leader's share of the reward money, was asked by a Congressman if he had ever left Booth after the attempt to put out the fire. "No, sir; I did not," Conger replied. "I may not have staid directly by his side all the time until he died; but I did not leave the porch, so far as I remember."[48]

Whatever the evidence suggests about the rivalries and the greed of the three officers, it contains no hint that Conger was Booth's secret murderer or that he hovered close to his victim ready to clamp his hand over his mouth if he should start to say the wrong thing. Whoever fired the fatal shot—whether it was Corbett or somebody else—it is certain that Conger did not do it in order to keep Booth from talking.

What, then, did Baker mean when he said of the missing testimony he had given to Holt about the capture and death of Booth that he suspected foul play? There was never the slightest doubt what he meant. "My impression is," he told the Congressional committee, "that it was destroyed in order to suppress the facts which it proved as to my having charge of the party, so that my claim to the chief share of the reward would not be so good." A committee member then asked, "It is with reference to the distribution of the reward that you think there was foul play?" "Yes," Baker answered.[49]

Lieutenant Baker may be excused some resentment, for he had been given command of the expedition by Colonel Baker. After receiving the assignment, he encountered Conger, formerly an officer in his own regiment, and either asked him to come along or was asked by Conger if he might. It soon became apparent that Conger was unhappy serving under one of his former junior officers, and, because he was more experienced and knew the Virginia countryside, Baker relinquished the command to him. The gesture cost him dearly; his share of the reward money was only $3,000.[50]

Nor is there the slighest substance to Eisenschiml's argument that the hoods, the executions, and the treatment of the prisoners at the Dry Tortugas were all calculated to keep Booth's friends from talking. If Stanton had really feared that they, or any one of them, might expose his role in the assassination conspiracy, he would have had to silence them all in the same way Eisenschiml intimates he had Booth silenced—by killing them at the time they were captured. Otherwise, it would be too late. As it was, all eight prisoners were not only taken alive but also were interrogated by military or civilian police at the times of their arrests and repeatedly afterward, and all were represented by counsel at their trial. It is absurd to state they had no opportunity to talk. If the hoods had been designed to prevent the male prisoners from telling what they knew, they would not have been ordered permanently removed on June 10 when the weather became hot.[51] Mrs. Surratt's "semi-delirious condition" did not prevent her from protesting her innocence on her way to the gallows and is hardly likely to have prevented her from revealing the guilt of someone in the War Department who was responsible for her impending death. The three men hanged were not delirious at all, and each (like Mrs. Surratt) had been visited by relatives or clergymen the night before the hanging. George Atzerodt wrote a confession in his cell, supplementing the one read by his attorney at the trial.

The four prisoners sent to the Dry Tortugas had abundant opportunity to talk to guards and members of the crew of the ship that transported them, and, upon their arrival, to guards and other prisoners. When they were confined after two or three weeks, it was in response to a real possibility of a rescue attempt from New Orleans. Mudd, a southern gentleman who found it intolerable to be guarded by black soldiers, did in fact attempt to escape. When a yellow fever epidemic broke out, Mudd took over the work of deceased Army physicians and had unlimited opportunity to talk to his patients and others. Michael O'Laughlin succumbed to the fever, but the three survivors were pardoned in 1869 and returned to their homes. Edman Spangler lived for a year and a half, Mudd till 1883, Samuel B. Arnold till 1906. If they had had anything to say, they could have talked at any time during these years.

Of all the conspirators, the one closest to Booth was John H. Surratt, who escaped to Europe. If he knew that Stanton or anyone else in the government was involved in the conspiracy he could have revealed it at any time, and might have been expected to do so to avenge his mother's execution. Yet, according to Eisenschiml, it was not until after two years, when Surratt was captured and brought back to the United States, that "the old fear that the prisoner might talk seemed to take hold of the authorities."[52] Whether or not Surratt's trial was the mockery Eisenschiml called it, it was a civil trial, and Surratt was never hooded and had unlimited opportunities to talk. After the jury failed to reach a verdict, charges against him were dropped. He lived until 1916.

When scrutinized point by point, Eisenschiml's grand conspiracy thus falls apart, and one wonders how Eisenschiml, professing scientific objectivity all the while, could present it as a work of honest scholarship. Perhaps he justified his misrepresentations to himself by so often citing and even discussing the evidence that exposed them, and by observing that he was, after all, only raising questions that had been ignored by historians. Indeed, he concludes a summary chapter with the modest admission that "there is not one point in this summary that can be proven; it is all hypothesis. . . . In view of all facts known at this time, an indictment against Stanton cannot be sustained for lack of material evidence."[53] At the end, after having cruelly misrepresented Stanton for several hundred pages, Eisenschiml thus assumes the pose of the dispassionate scientist and dismisses his victim in two sentences.

Possibly his judgment was warped by the excitement of discovering long-neglected documents, and by the expectation of winning as an historian the recognition he had failed to receive as a chemist.[54] Most likely, he was simply carried away by the anti-Radical bias that still characterized writing about the Civil War era, and by the novelty of his inspiration that one of the leading Radical villains might have been guilty of the ultimate villainy.

Eisenschiml's Stanton, the logical outgrowth and ultimate extension of a whole generation of revisionist wrath and resentment, was villainous indeed. He was not only the possible mastermind of a Radical grand conspiracy to assassinate Lincoln, but he was also a leader of an earlier Radical conspiracy to prolong the Civil War and make himself the supreme power in the United States. In chapters entitled "Not Wanted—Victory in the East" and "Not Wanted—Victory in the West," Eisenschiml explains that at the beginning of the war the Radical abolitionists were only a small minority. If the war had ended after only a year or two, the majority of the people of the North would have welcomed the southern states back into the Union without recrimination or punishment. "Therefore, the war had to last long enough to embitter the Northern sections to a point where the populace, saturated with propaganda and embittered by the loss of relations and friends, would become as vindictive as the Radical leaders. Secretary of War Stanton was quite outspoken about this."[55]

As the secretary of war, Stanton was obviously in a position to make a major contribution to the success of this conspiracy. He could prevent Union armies from defeating the Rebels by simply withholding the troops and supplies necessary for victory. In this way and for this reason, Eisenschiml charges, he assured the defeat of General George McClellan in the peninsular campaign outside Richmond in 1862. Stanton could also delay the Union's victory by having inept generals appointed to important military commands. It was through his influence, for example, that Henry W. Halleck—who "willingly took orders from Stanton"—was appointed general-in-chief. "The selection of Halleck as head of the Federal armies," Eisenschiml wryly observes, "made it all but certain that the war would be just one military fiasco after another."[56]

The Radical conspiracy to prolong the war would do more than lead to a harsh peace for the South. It would also, Eisenschiml says Stanton recognized, serve the secretary's own interests. For as the war dragged on and on, a huge army—which he would control—would necessarily be created. When the war was finally allowed to end, Stanton would be in a position to exercise vast power. His reading of history had shown him that after every war the people rewarded the man they considered responsible for victory by elevating him to the highest position within their power. "That he would be the one to emerge in the end as the popular leader was undoubtedly his cherished dream."[57] Nor need he fear that the United States would lose the war, leaving him in disfavor with the people. "Barring a miracle," Eisenschiml confidently states, "the enormous preponderance of the North's numbers, its unlimited resources and the ever tightening blockade must eventually bring the Confederacy to its knees, no matter how badly the Union generals handled the campaigns."[58]

In assessing his chances of becoming the nation's ruler after the war, Eisenschiml tells us, Stanton saw no potential rival for that position in the cabinet. Nor did he think of Lincoln as any threat to his ambitions, for he considered the president an "uncouth country lawyer" and treated him "with more or less open contempt." Stanton believed a military hero was his most likely competitor, but he knew how to take care of generals. After 1862 McClellan, whom Stanton had helped to destroy, was no longer popular. Grant, whom Stanton belittled and bullied, was considered a dull and colorless man, not the sort to fire the public's imagination. He "might win battles—no one knew how he did it—but as a politician he would be like clay in the hands of the War Minister." General William Tecumseh Sherman, who led the victorious march to the sea, was something else again. "But Stanton soon had an opportunity to sink his stiletto into him to the hilt," by disavowing the surrender terms he had extended to Joseph E. Johnston's Rebel army in such a way as to make Sherman seem to be a traitor. "Thus, with one blow, the idol of the western armies was vanquished by Stanton's artifices and was prevented from becoming a dangerous rival." At war's end Stanton "was second only to Lincoln in popular acclaim."[59]

Then comes Eisenschiml's sudden climax. "Unexpectedly the blow fell. . . . The future which had looked so bright was suddenly shrouded with gloom." For the president began taking steps to restore the South to its old position within the Union, threatening to wipe out the entire Radical program for Reconstruction and with it Stanton's hope for leadership.

"It was then that Lincoln was shot."[60]

It is perhaps unnecessary to inform readers that Eisenschiml establishes the Radical conspiracy to prolong the war—and Stanton's key participation in it—by the same techniques he used to establish his hypothesis of Stanton's involvement in the assassination. Again he has shaped the facts to fit his theory, rather than his theory to fit the facts. His assertion that Stanton aspired and plotted to become the nation's postwar leader is pure fiction.

The manuscript of *Why Was Lincoln Murdered?* was accepted by the first publisher to whom Eisenschiml submitted it,[61] became a Book-of-the-Month Club selection, and was widely recognized as original and controversial. It has long been out of print and is probably not often read today. But the Eisenschiml thesis is known to many thousands of individuals who have never heard the name of its progenitor, for it has been popularized and expanded upon in books (two of which were condensed in the *Reader's Digest*), articles, and TV dramas, and it has a powerful appeal to people who see the sinister hand of conspiracy and cover-up in the assassinations of the 1960s. If, to Eisenschiml's intense irritation,[62] it was from the beginning rejected by most professional historians (without, it must be admitted, close critical analysis), it is not because historians "do homage to principles which differ sharply from those of scientists," but because in *Why Was Lincoln Murdered?* Eisenschiml himself departed from the principles to which both historians and scientists do do homage. Mendeleyev's table would never have been completed if scientists had yielded to the temptation of filling in the gaps by distorting the evidence.

Following the Leader:
The War Department and Booth's
Abduction Plot

Otto Eisenschiml believed that his discovery of the "Investigation and Trial Papers" relating to the assassination, which he found in the judge advocate general's office in Washington, "would change the accepted accounts of Lincoln's assassination and force the rewriting of an important chapter in history."[1] However, he made very little use of the papers himself. Of the approximately 1,000 footnotes in *Why Was Lincoln Murdered?* only forty are citations to the papers, and none of them is of significance. The fact is not surprising, for one would hardly expect to find evidence linking the secretary of war to the assassination conspiracy in the War Department's own archives.

Yet, as a matter of fact, Eisenschiml did incorporate into his thesis one fact that he learned from the papers: that in the envelope marked "Ex no 1 Booth's photograph" was a photograph of Edwin Booth, not John Wilkes Booth. The extraordinary and unwarranted conclusion to which Eisenschiml jumped from this fact was discussed in the previous chapter. What is significant about it here is that Eisenschiml did not cite the papers as the source from which he learned of it. The only part of the Eisenschiml thesis that grew out of Eisenschiml's research in the War Department papers went unacknowledged.

The sources from which Eisenschiml largely wrote *Why Was Lincoln Murdered?* were not newly discovered documents and manuscripts—not the War Department's, not those of the Washington Metropolitan Police, not his own collections—but published works long available to the public: government doc-

uments, newspapers, diaries, and memoirs. It is a tribute to
Eisenschiml's resourcefulness in amassing these sources—many
of them unknown to previous writers—and to his authoritative-
sounding interpretations that some of the conclusions he based
upon them have influenced nearly every writer on the assassination since 1937. One of his assertions—that the War Department knew of Booth's abduction plot—has become generally
accepted as a truth.

Since the publication of Eisenschiml's book, there has indeed
been a rewriting of the history of Lincoln's murder. But it has
not come about as a result of the War Department's papers. It
has come about, instead, as a result of the boldness of the Eisenschiml thesis itself, which, like the Big Lie, generated its own
credibility. For many people, the thesis was simply too audacious to be disbelieved. Popular writers eagerly embraced all or
parts of the new grand conspiracy theory and diligently searched
for new facts or incidents to be used to arouse suspicions against
Edwin M. Stanton and the Radicals.

The direct influence of Eisenschiml was seen in the very next
book published on the assassination, Philip Van Doren Stern's
The Man Who Killed Lincoln (1939). According to this study of
Booth, the War Department knew of the actor's determination
to kill Lincoln and sought to encourage it by promising to assist
him in his escape. Originally Booth's contact with the unnamed
department officials was John H. Surratt, who was sworn to secrecy and could not tell his friend their names. By 1955, when
a revised edition was published, Stern had become convinced
that Surratt had not been in Washington at the time of the assassination, and so he invented a "John Smith" to act as go-
between.

Were the conspirators whom Stern imagined in the War Department Confederate spies or Radical Republicans who disapproved of Lincoln's Reconstruction program? In one place in his
lengthy afterword Stern states that Booth would not have conspired against Lincoln to put Radicals in power. Booth might
have been a fool, Stern observed, but his love for the South was
so great "that he was surely not knowingly a traitor to his own
cause." The conspirators in the War Department must therefore
have been pro-Confederate. But a few pages later Stern declared they could have been either Confederates or Radicals,[2]

and in his text he resolved the confusion in favor of the Radicals. During his flight Booth was uncertain about how his unknown allies were helping him, but he saw signs of their assistance in many incidents: in the interruption of the telegraph, in the delay in releasing his name to the newspapers, in the failure of the government to organize a prompt pursuit along the most obvious of the roads leading south out of the capital. These were all matters for which Eisenschiml had held Stanton responsible.

Like Eisenschiml, Stern was suspicious of the government's failure to introduce Booth's diary as evidence at the conspiracy trial, calling it a "clue" pointing to Stanton's involvement in the assassination.[3] He was also disturbed by the missing pages and by Booth's statement that he was tempted to return to Washington and to try to clear his name. "How could this self-confessed assassin 'clear his name,'" Stern wondered, "unless he knew something that would implicate people who were so important that the sensational nature of his disclosures would dwarf even the enormity of his own crime?"[4] Neither Stern nor Congressman Ben Butler, who called attention to the same diary entry in his 1867 effort to incriminate Andrew Johnson, seems to have reflected that Booth could not have cleared his name by implicating others, no matter how eminent they might have been. He had simply meant that he was tempted to return to Washington "and in a measure clear my name[,] which I feel I can do," by explaining the altruism of his motives.[5]

"I am really enchanted with your book," Eisenschiml told Stern, "and whatever lies within my power to enhance its sales I shall do with genuine pleasure."[6] Little wonder.

Emanuel Hertz, the Lincoln collector and writer, was also enthusiastic. Stern, he wrote, had told the story of the assassination "with more fairness and truth than it has ever been told before. . . . [He was] content to deal with the facts as they were and not with what might have been"—a strange comment to make about a book in which there was so much fiction. Equally strange is that, despite his admiration for Stern's book, Hertz summarily rejected the conspiratorial theory which Stern had borrowed from Eisenschiml and without which there was not much left of The Man Who Killed Lincoln. The "grotesque supposition," Hertz wrote, "that Secretary of War Stanton wanted to get rid of Lincoln, took no precautions to protect him and was dilatory in pursuing the conspirators is not worth an argument."[7]

The fact is that both Hertz and Stern enjoyed contemplating a good conspiracy.

In 1938, the year before publication of *The Man Who Killed Lincoln,* Hertz had edited *The Hidden Lincoln,* a selection of letters and other documents about Lincoln from the voluminous files of William H. Herndon, Lincoln's law partner for twenty years and the author (with Jesse W. Weik) of an important biography, *Herndon's Lincoln* (1889). Much of what Herndon had to say of Lincoln's parentage and early life was based upon unreliable reminiscences and idle gossip, and his description of Lincoln's marriage reflected the personal dislike he and Mary Lincoln felt for each other.

Robert Todd Lincoln, the Lincolns' only surviving son, was well acquainted with Herndon's ideas and believed them to be false and objectionable. Accordingly, when John G. Nicolay and John Hay were writing their biography, it was arranged that Lincoln would be entitled to review—blue pencil in hand— what they wrote about his father's first forty years. The two former presidential secretaries were willing to grant him this privilege because he, in turn, was permitting them—and no one else— to use his vast collection of his father's papers in the preparation of their work. When the Nicolay and Hay biography was published, Herndon scoffed at the presentation of Lincoln's early years and accused the authors of suppressing the truth. The title that Hertz chose for his selections from Herndon's papers—*The Hidden Lincoln*—shows that he agreed. Unlike Nicolay and Hay, Hertz declared, Herndon had not tried to hide Lincoln; he "put the passion for truth before any 'kid-glove' considerations."[8]

As a way of boosting the importance of the Herndon papers he was publishing, Hertz charged that before Robert Lincoln deposited the Abraham Lincoln Papers in the Library of Congress—with the proviso they not be opened to the public for twenty-one years after his death—he "subjected the papers to a purge." Hertz's reason for thinking so was that in 1923 two friends of Lincoln called upon him at his summer estate, Hildene, in Manchester, Vermont, and found him burning papers in the fireplace. Lincoln told one of the men, Horace G. Young, a businessman and golfing partner—according to a friend of Young who related the story fourteen years later—that the papers contained evidence of the treason of a member of his father's cabinet and were best destroyed. He told the other, Nicholas Murray Butler, president of Columbia University, that he was burning private family papers.[9]

As related by Hertz, the incident would probably have attracted little attention. It was Stern who turned it into a sensation by implying a connection with Lincoln's assassination. In the afterword to *The Man Who Killed Lincoln,* Stern repeated Hertz's story, noted that the Abraham Lincoln Papers would be opened in 1947 (Robert Todd Lincoln having died in 1926), and stated flatly that then "we shall find out who it was that sat at the Cabinet table betraying the President and the people he served. Perhaps we shall even be able to trace some connection to the men who shared with John Wilkes Booth the responsibility for the murder of Abraham Lincoln." In the 1955 edition of *The Man Who Killed Lincoln,* Stern observed regretfully that when the Lincoln Papers were opened, "Nothing of interest concerning the assassination was found among them. Whether Robert Todd Lincoln had destroyed important evidence or whether such evidence had never existed . . . will probably never be known."[10]

It was a cruel and irresponsible comment, well calculated to stimulate appetites whetted by the Eisenschiml thesis. David C. Mearns, chief of the Manuscripts Division of the Library of Congress at the time the Lincoln Papers were opened, stated that to believe that Robert Lincoln would have shielded Stanton or anyone else involved in his father's death by destroying incriminating evidence "violates what is known of Robert Lincoln's character."[11] Even the thought of it "would have horrified Robert Lincoln to the depth of his soul," protested S. L. Carson.[12]

While Hildene was being restored as an historical museum in the 1970s, Carson discovered there a large, ornately framed portrait of Stanton. In addition, Robert Lincoln had kept above the fireplace in his library a copy of Francis B. Carpenter's famous painting of Lincoln reading the Emancipation Proclamation to his cabinet. At Hildene, Lincoln must have looked upon

Stanton's image almost daily; he could not possibly have done so had he believed the secretary had had anything whatsoever to do with his father's murder.[13]

Nor could Nicolay and Hay, who had studied the Lincoln Papers and whose love for the president was nearly as great and personal as Robert's, have participated in a cover-up of evidence implicating Stanton in the assassination. In their biography they praised Stanton for his "outspoken counsel and robust energy" and for his loyalty to Lincoln. Though members of the cabinet differed from Lincoln in many respects, "they returned his courtesy and kindness as a rule with warm friendship, and none of them more sincerely than Mr. Stanton."[14] A few months after the assassination, Hay wrote to Stanton, "Not everyone knows, as I do, how close you stood to our lost leader, how he loved you and trusted you, and how vain were all the efforts to shake that trust and confidence, not lightly given and never withdrawn. All this will be known sometime of course, to his honor and yours."[15] There had been nothing in the Lincoln Papers to alter this judgment.

In a vain effort to scotch Stern's shameless innuendo, Nicholas Murray Butler himself announced in 1939 that there was not "the slightest ground" for suspecting that Robert Lincoln had burned anything but private family papers.[16] Nine years later, Mearns subjected the story to a critical analysis that should have stamped it out once and for all.[17] But it was no use. Stern's base and baseless suggestion was greedily seized upon by writers on the assassination—including Eisenschiml—and was repeated in popular journals like the *Reader's Digest*.[18]

The spectacle of Robert Todd Lincoln burning papers was promptly incorporated into the new grand conspiracy theory and, in a perverse way, seemed even to confirm the truth of it. Believers in conspiracy are not discouraged by the lack of evidence, because they can easily convince themselves that the evidence has been destroyed by conspirators seeking to protect themselves or others. The twist that Stern gave to Hertz's story—the president's son actually destroying "evidence"—thus contributed to the growing irrationality of the popular view of Lincoln's assassination.

What makes the canard doubly regrettable is that there was no basis in fact for even Hertz's interpretation of the burning episode. Whatever Robert Lincoln set afire that day in 1923, it had nothing to do with a "purge" of the Lincoln Papers. Lincoln had deposited that collection in the Library of Congress four years before, in 1919.[19]

George S. Bryan's *The Great American Myth* was being written at the time *Why Was Lincoln Murdered?* was published, and Bryan did not recast it to deal in any comprehensive way with the Eisenschiml thesis. But he left no doubt that he considered it as but the newest of the many myths that surrounded the assassination. The suggestion that Stanton might have been involved in the conspiracy and that he sought to assist Booth's escape, said Bryan, was "as inapt as it is malicious." The widespread hatred for Lincoln and the intensely emotional climate of the Civil War era were such that there was "no need to imagine vain things or to assemble a *melange* of scandalous inferences against any particular individual or small group, whether of the North or of the South. The whole affair cuts deeper than that."[20]

In 1955 the journalist Jim Bishop published his enormously successful *The Day Lincoln Was Shot,* the most widely read of all books written on the assassination. Bishop confessed that he considered his manuscript "a pile of ———," but it became a Book-of-the-Month Club selection, was condensed in both the *Reader's Digest* and *Blue Book,* was translated into fourteen languages, went through many printings in paperback, and made its author lots and lots of money.[21] It was still in print in 1982, its errors still uncorrected. As in the popular "Day" books that followed—*The Day Christ Died* (1957), *A Day in the Life of President Kennedy* (1964)—Bishop divided Lincoln's last day into one hour segments, which built suspense and made for easy reading. Although Bishop presented the assassination as a simple conspiracy—he states categorically that "there were never more than seven persons" involved in the kidnapping plot[22]—Bryan does not appear in his brief bibliography. Eisenschiml does (though he was unaccountably dropped from the paperback edition), and throughout his narrative Bishop brings up points that Eisenschiml had introduced into the literature of the assassination.

There was the matter of Stanton's "delay" in releasing the assassin's name. Although Corporal James Tanner, recording the testimony at the Petersen house in shorthand, had said that he had heard enough in fifteen minutes to hang Booth, Stanton waited. "Many fine literary minds have read into this an assent to the assassination on the part of War Secretary Stanton," Bishop notes. "There is no evidence in any record to support this," a point Eisenschiml would have been quick to concede. Bishop believes that Stanton was slow to release Booth's name for another reason. The simultaneous attacks on Lincoln and William H. Seward and the interruption of the commercial telegraph had convinced Stanton that he was faced with an imminent and widespread Confederate uprising. As he saw it, therefore, Booth was small game; it was more important to take action to "stop the *pending* assassinations . . . than to apprehend the perpetrators of the Lincoln shooting."[23]

Bishop did think it odd that Stanton should have sent out the telegraphic alarm "almost everywhere except on the fat foot of Maryland which lies between the Potomac and the Patuxent. And that's where Booth was." The only road out of the capital left "uncovered, unwatched, unpatrolled" was the road to southern Maryland that Booth took. But he offers no explanation.[24]

According to Bishop, Stanton was at first "frozen with fright"; but the secretary rallied, and during the eight hours he used the Petersen house as his command post, "he did as well as anyone could have—perhaps better."[25] His most serious mistake was his assumption that he was dealing with a Confederate grand conspiracy. Bishop believes that by 3:00 A.M. on April 15 Stanton had recognized the error, for in a telegram he sent to General John A. Dix at that hour he stated that every effort had been taken "to prevent the escape of the murderer." The secretary's use of the singular noun, Bishop declares, revealed that Stanton now realized that he was pursuing only one man. "If this new thesis was correct," Bishop continues, "then Stanton, with all the majesty and power of the United States Government behind him, was a damned fool. He had been outwitted, was being outwitted, and might continue to be outwitted by a lone actor. Because of this, and for no other reason, the Secretary of War would, in the days ahead, insist that this was all part of a huge conspiracy, inspired and approved by the defunct Confederate States Government. He could not admit, even to himself, that he was not battling Davis and Benjamin and Seddon and Stephens. It was big, or Stanton was ridiculous."[26] Altogether, it was a heavy theory to hang on a singular noun in a telegram, but it is a measure of Eisenschiml's influence: rejecting Stanton as a conspirator, Bishop felt it necessary to present him as a fool.

Others have felt the same compulsion. The noted Lincoln scholar, Paul M. Angle, wrote that Eisenschiml's description of the ineptitude of the War Department at the time of the assassination went far "to explain why four years passed before the North was able to subdue a South greatly inferior in both men and resources."[27] In a book clearly inspired by Eisenschiml, Theodore Roscoe maintained that "if the fantasia which permitted Booth's escape was unintentional, one must attribute to War Secretary Stanton a head of almost solid bone, a plethora of unadulterated stupidity."[28] But Roscoe did not believe that Stanton was stupid. Quite the contrary; adhering slavishly to the Eisenschiml thesis, he places Stanton at the very center of his intricate *Web of Conspiracy* (1959).

The simple conspiracy theory of the assassination, Roscoe begins, was "a towering edifice of so-called history . . . erected on sand. It made popular reading, but it lacked the exacting foundations of true historicity." Still, the historians were not to blame, for they were dependent upon the information available to them, "and for many years the United States War Department kept the records on Lincoln's assassination locked in files marked 'secret,'" withholding them even from Senators and members of the House of Representatives. However, determined students "could discover enormous incongruities and gaping holes" in the traditional interpretation, and by the 1920s they were beginning to ask questions. As a result, the War Department's papers, or what was left of them "after sedulous 'screening,'" were transferred to the National Archives in the 1930s and opened to researchers, the first of whom was Eisenschiml. Why the secrecy? The secrecy, says Roscoe, "covered a betrayal. The betrayal of Abraham Lincoln is as obvious as the situation at Ford's Theater."[29]

That the Lincoln assassination papers were classified Secret, an assertion often encountered in books and articles published since 1959, apparently originated with Roscoe. The truth is that the papers were never classified at all, though one can imagine

War Department officials, wary of invasions of their files, giving
the impression that they were. Eisenschiml himself told how he
persuaded a colonel to allow him to see the papers by convincing the officer that his interest was more than casual.[30] Others
had done the same before him. One researcher wrote in 1924,
"Two guards stood over me in the dusty attic of the War Department in Washington last July as I fumbled through masses of
yellowed documents, over sixty years old, which had to do with
the plot to assassinate Abraham Lincoln and with the part which
John Wilkes Booth played in the assassination."[31] If David M.
Dewitt had not been permitted to study the papers in the 1890s,
he could not have described—so damningly for the reputations
of Stanton and Holt—the positioning of the petition for clemency for Mrs. Surratt among the papers that Joseph Holt submitted to President Johnson. The "Investigation and Trial Papers"
were accessioned by the National Archives, not in the 1930s,
but in 1941, along with other records from the judge advocate
general's office dating back to 1812.

In attempting to prove his assertion that "the criminals responsible for Lincoln's death got away with murder,"[32] Roscoe
relates in elaborate detail most of the mysterious incidents and
circumstances with which Eisenschiml developed his grand
conspiracy: Stanton's refusal to allow Thomas T. Eckert to accompany Lincoln to the theater, the delay in the release of Booth's
name, the failure to launch a prompt pursuit, the efforts to keep
the defendants from talking, the suppression and mutilation of
Booth's diary, and so on. He added nothing of significance to the
Eisenschiml thesis, although he devoted nearly one hundred
pages to a description of some of the material found in the assassination papers. Naively, he attempted to weave their inevitable
inconsistencies and contradictions into his web.

In one particular, however, Roscoe did venture an original
contribution. In *Why Was Lincoln Murdered?* Eisenschiml noted
that John F. Parker, the guard who left his post outside the door
of Lincoln's box, had been selected for duty at the White House
"by none other than President Lincoln's own wife," although in
fact all Mary Lincoln had done was to scrawl her signature on
an appointment order written by someone else. Nevertheless,
Eisenschiml considered the circumstance "mystifying." Uncriti-

cal, as always, of Eisenschiml's generalizations, Roscoe wondered if this evidence of Mary Lincoln's relationship with Parker might not indicate a deeper involvement with him in the assassination conspiracy. Lincoln had left his wife moderately well provided for, and yet in her later years she was constantly beset by financial problems. "Could her continual impoverishment suggest blackmail?" asked Roscoe.[33]

It was a wild and vulgar suggestion—framed, in the Eisenschiml manner, as a question.

One of Eisenschiml's ideas that has been generally accepted by writers on Lincoln's assassination—and, one may believe, by many Civil War scholars who have not written on it—is that the War Department knew of Booth's conspiracy to kidnap Lincoln. The idea is properly called Eisenschiml's, even though he was not the first to suggest it. Indeed, some evidence dating from as early as 1865 appears to indicate that the department did have knowledge of the abduction plot.

Within a few hours after the assassination, agents of the War Department entered and searched Booth's room in the National Hotel and found the letter to Booth from Samuel B. Arnold dated March 27, 1865, and signed simply "Sam." "You know full well," the letter read, "that the G——t suspicions something is going on . . . ; therefore the undertaking is becoming more complicated. Why not, for the present desist[?]"[34]

In the lecture that he delivered in 1870 about his involvement in the abduction plot, John H. Surratt claimed to have warned his fellow conspirators that the government knew of their plans. It was at that midnight supper at Gautier's Restaurant to which Booth had invited his little band in mid-March 1865. A stockade was being built at the Navy Yard Bridge—across which they had planned to carry Lincoln—and Surratt thought it was significant that the gates opened toward the south, as though the danger was expected from within the city rather than from outside it. "At this meeting," said Surratt in 1870, "I explained the construction of the gates, etc., and stated that I was confident the government had wind of our movement and that the best thing we could do would be to throw up the whole project. Everyone seemed to coincide in my opinion, except Booth." At the 1865 trial of the conspirators, Surratt went on, it was learned that he had been right about the government's knowledge of the plot. One of his mother's boarders, his erstwhile friend and college classmate, Louis J. Weichmann, had told a clerk in the War Department what he knew about it.[35]

Clara Laughlin rediscovered Surratt's lecture and published most of it in 1909 as an appendix to her *The Death of Lincoln*. She, too, believed the government had known about the abduction conspiracy. As early as April 17, only two days after Lincoln's death, Arnold was arrested at Fort Monroe, Virginia, and Michael O'Laughlin at Baltimore. How could they possibly have been picked up so quickly, Laughlin wondered, unless the government knew about the kidnapping plan and "quite naturally jumped to the conclusion that the men involved in it were those implicated in the President's murder."[36] But she did not pursue the point.

The first writer who did pursue it was Eisenschiml, who praised the "keen insight" of Laughlin, his Chicago friend and neighbor, in explaining the prompt arrests of Arnold and O'Laughlin. In addition, he reasoned that when Booth and his friends intercepted the president's carriage on the Seventh Street road "it is almost certain" that the coachman and whoever was inside instead of Lincoln "sensed their peril when they observed the suspicious actions of the plotters. The chances are that the horses were whirled around and driven at top speed back to Washington, where the adventure must have been reported to the secret service. . . . That Booth's band thought its intention had been correctly interpreted," Eisenschiml observed, "is plainly shown by the haste with which its members scattered in all directions—to Baltimore, to Richmond, to New York."[37]

But, Eisenschiml continued, there was a further indication, unknown to Laughlin, "that the War Department—charged with the responsibility of protecting the President—knew about this bold attempt to kidnap him."[38] He was referring to a memoir written by the War Department clerk mentioned by Surratt, to whom the boarder Weichmann had spoken about activities at the Surratt boardinghouse. Although the memoir had been published in 1911, Eisenschiml was the first writer to use it.

The clerk, Daniel H. L. Gleason, was a discharged Army officer with an outstanding war record, who had begun early in 1865 to work as a civilian in Washington in the office of the Commissary General of Prisoners, where he occupied a desk next to Weichmann. In his memoir Gleason recalled that Weichmann had on several occasions spoken to him of the Surratt boardinghouse as being a stopping place for Rebels and Rebel sympathizers, men and women who came and went at all hours, day and night. Booth called frequently and held secret meetings with Surratt and his mother and with men who Weichman felt sure were using false names and had some connection with the Confederate government. One day late in February 1865, Weichmann, visibly disturbed, told Gleason he had discovered a cache of pistols and knives at the house and had asked Surratt about it. Surratt then told him that he and Booth and the others were planning to kidnap the president and his cabinet on Inauguration Day, March 4. Though "stunned and amazed" by Weichmann's report, Gleason found it difficult to believe the conspirators would attempt anything so foolhardy, and yet he recognized that the Rebels in Washington were bitter and incorrigible. Further talks with Weichmann convinced him that the situation was indeed serious and that "the only thing to do was to see Mr. Stanton."

Instead of seeing Stanton himself, however, Gleason talked over the problem with his roommate, an assistant provost marshal on the staff of the military commander of Washington, General Christopher C. Augur. The roommate then arranged through channels to inform Stanton of the plot, with the result that the secretary ordered two companies of cavalry to accompany Lincoln's carriage. At about the same time, Weichmann told Gleason that he himself had spoken of the conspiracy to a U.S. Enrolling Officer, one McDavitt, "who in turn had notified the authorities." These officials were also on the alert, "though not fully believing his story." But when March 4 passed without incident, Gleason and Weichmann concluded that they had been fooled or that the plan had been abandoned.

Upon learning of the assassination on the night of April 14, the 1911 reminiscence concluded, Gleason went immediately to General Augur's headquarters and "advised the arrest of

Weichmann and everyone found at the Surratt house." Later Gleason visited Weichmann in the Old Capitol Prison and advised him to tell officials all he knew about the plot and the plotters. "He promised to, and did; it was through his evidence alone that the conviction of the conspirators was secured."[39]

If Gleason's 1911 statements are true, then Eisenschiml was fully justified in asserting that before March 4 and nearly two weeks before the date of the kidnapping fiasco, the War Department "had been fully advised" that Lincoln was in danger from Booth and that "it is practically certain that they also knew the identity of the entire group."[40] It seemed a reasonable conclusion, confirming the suspicions expressed by Arnold in the "Sam" letter and by Surratt in his 1870 lecture, and supporting Laughlin's supposition about the prompt arrests of Arnold and O'Laughlin. Writers on the assassination since 1937 have disagreed among themselves about whether or not the War Department responded properly to Gleason's warning, or whether it responded at all, but with rare unanimity they have accepted Eisenschiml's judgment: the War Department had known about Booth's abduction conspiracy.

Central to the plot of Stern's *The Man Who Killed Lincoln* was the knowledge of Booth's plans by powerful officials in the War Department who encouraged Booth to carry them out by promising to assist in his escape. In *The Mad Booths of Maryland*, Stanley Kimmel expressed wonderment. "Why such information did not lead to a quick round-up of the plotters before the assassination instead of after it is amazing." Even Bryan in *The Great American Myth* declared there was no reason to doubt the truth of Gleason's reminiscence.[41]

In *The Day Lincoln Was Shot* Bishop embellished Gleason's story with imaginary details, and concluded by asking, "Is it too much to suggest that the United States Government, on one level or another, was aware of John Wilkes Booth and his band . . . ? Is it too much to suggest that the government officers would give . . . [Gleason's] report more than casual attention because it could not be classified with the crackpot anonymous letters which usually told about such plots, but came, rather, from a trusted clerk who worked for the War Department?" Stanton had arrested thousands of people on far flimsier evidence, Bishop noted, and "it would have required only a nod to put Booth and his band, and the Surratts too and their boarders, behind bars."[42]

"Why did the War Department fail to act?" asked Roscoe in *The Web of Conspiracy*. "Why were not Army detectives immediately dispatched to trail Booth night and day? Why did not the Federal Secret Service promptly descend on Mrs. Surratt's boardinghouse?"[43] In a rare lapse of scholarly precision Stanton's biographers, Benjamin P. Thomas and Harold Hyman, described Gleason relating Weichmann's story to Stanton in person. In response to the warning, the secretary "increased the guards protecting Lincoln, over the President's protests. With the war coming to a victorious end, there was no reason to do more."[44] In *Mask for Treason* (1965) Vaughan Shelton agreed that Stanton and other officials had heard of "the rumor circulated" by Weichmann but explained that Washington was "one great rumor-mill, and no one in the War Department took the revelations seriously until after the assassination."[45]

In *Twenty Days*, Dorothy Meserve Kunhardt and Philip B. Kunhardt stated positively that the War Department had been told about Booth's abduction plot, but that "Stanton had paid it no heed," except to keep track of Arnold and O'Laughlin.[46] Robert H. Fowler made the same two points in *Album of the Lincoln Murder:* the War Department had been informed of the kidnapping conspiracy, and "the first persons to be arrested in the assassination conspiracy were those who had been involved in the plot to capture the President."[47] In *Anatomy of an Assassination* (1966) John Cottrell declared that as a result of Weichmann's warning War Department detectives had put the Surratt house "under surveillance for weeks. And yet no direct action was taken. The suspects were not even brought in for questioning."[48] Edward Hyams wrote in 1970 that Stanton knew of Booth's plans and made no effort to block them. "If this was not, on Stanton's part, a case of assassination by refraining from, instead of taking, action," he exclaimed, "then it is remarkable it should look so very like it."[49] In *Assassination in America* (1977) James McKinley stated that "Stanton's War Department had known for several weeks that Booth, the Surratts, Arnold, O'Laughlin, Atzerodt, Herold, and, at the end, Paine, intended to harm

Lincoln. Weichmann had told them."[50] Finally, John K. Lattimer concluded in *Kennedy and Lincoln* (1980) that as a result of Weichmann's warnings the authorities knew enough to go directly to the Surratt boardinghouse after the assassination.[51]

In the years since *Why Was Lincoln Murdered?* repetition has thus confirmed Eisenschiml's assertion that the War Department knew about Booth's conspiracy to kidnap Lincoln. Like Bishop's conclusion about the use of the singular noun in Stanton's telegram, it was a large assumption to rest upon a dubious source—in this case a reminiscence published forty-six years after the event. It is also a personal tribute to Eisenschiml that his conclusion should have been accepted without question by so many writers, some of whom ought to have known better.

As is true of all sources used in writing history, Gleason's memoir cannot be accepted without critical analysis, and critical analysis reveals that it cannot be accepted. It is contradicted by reliable contemporary evidence, some of it originating with Gleason himself and preserved in the War Department's assassination papers that Eisenschiml so prided himself on discovering. If Eisenschiml did not see it there, he should have.

What Gleason wrote in 1911 is very different from what he said in a deposition made for the War Department on April 18, 1865. At that time, so soon after the assassination, Gleason testified that toward the end of February or early in March Weichmann had told him he was acquainted with blockade runners, young fellows, not secessionists, who were out for money and excitement. Now they were engaged in a different kind of enterprise that aroused his suspicions. "He never gave me to understand what the nature of the plot was," said Gleason on April 18. Although Weichmann's friends had not asked him to join them, Weichmann believed it might be possible to become a member of the group, and he asked for Gleason's advice. Gleason told him that he ought to join for the purpose of finding out what they were up to and of exposing them. He suggested that Weichmann speak to the provost marshal and get his approval, but Weichmann said that the role of spy would be too risky. A short while later Weichmann told Gleason that whatever operation had been planned seemed to have been abandoned, for the group had dispersed. "After the assassination of Mr. Lincoln," Gleason concluded, "I told the authorities of this."[52] If, weeks before the assassination, Gleason had reported Weichmann's conversations to his roommate who passed the information on to Stanton, as Gleason wrote in 1911 had been done, then surely he would have said so while being interrogated in April 1865. Instead, he said under oath, "After the assassination of Mr. Lincoln I told the authorities."

There is more. In November 1865, a few months after the trial in which Weichmann's testimony had been so influential in the conviction of the conspirators, Gleason wrote and congratulated Weichmann "for the manly way in which you discharged your disagreeable duties in regard to the Surratt family. You have done nobly and are deserving of all credit. When I last saw you," Gleason continued, "my feelings were anything but true, friendly ones, as you must know, but the course you pursued, the testimony you gave, which I assure you was critically read by me, has a long time since completely changed my opinion, and I beg your pardon for all unjust suspicions which I have ever entertained toward you."[53]

One judges from this letter that immediately after the assassination Gleason was angry with Weichmann, suspecting that he had known more about Booth's conspiracy than he had reported at the office. But if what Gleason wrote in 1911 had been true—that Weichmann had told him about the conspiracy to kidnap and that Gleason had then seen to it that Stanton was informed—there would have been no cause for anger. Each man would have fulfilled his duty, and Gleason would have had no reason to hold "unjust suspicions" against Weichmann. Gleason's 1911 reminiscence is thus discredited by Gleason's own 1865 deposition and letter.

Was it a case of an old man's memory betraying him? Possibly. But it is far more likely that in 1911 Gleason was reacting to the account of his conversations with Weichmann as described in the first book to pay any attention to the talks, Osborn H. Oldroyd's *Assassination of Abraham Lincoln*.

At the 1865 conspiracy trial Weichmann had testified that he and Gleason had speculated only casually about what might be going on at the Surratt house, and that, whatever it was, Gleason had not taken it very seriously. In fact, Gleason had "laughed and hooted" at the idea that the kidnapping of the president might be being planned. This testimony, which was probably close to the truth, was satisfactory to Gleason, for in his letter of apology to Weichmann he said he had read it critically and that it had set his mind at rest.

The version of the Weichmann-Gleason talks in Oldroyd's well-known book, however, was anything but satisfactory to Gleason. According to Oldroyd, there was nothing in the least casual about Weichmann's speculations or Gleason's response. On the contrary, Gleason was thoroughly alarmed by what Weichmann told him. "By God, that is strange," Oldroyd quoted Gleason as having said about the incident in mid-March when Surratt, Booth, and Lewis Paine returned so upset from their mysterious horseback ride, "there is something wrong going on there, Weichmann." The two men considered what the conspirators might be up to—including blockade running, releasing prisoners, and engaging in cotton and oil speculations—but reached no conclusion. "It was suggested," Oldroyd does not say by whom, "that probably it would be a good thing to go and tell the Secretary of War, but finally Gleason said that 'inasmuch as what these men were after had failed, it would be a good thing to keep an eye on them, and if anything again came up, to promptly report it to the authorities.'" But nothing further happened to alarm Weichmann.[54]

Oldroyd's version of the conversations thus stated categorically that Gleason made the decision not to inform Secretary Stanton, even though he was fully convinced "something wrong" was going on. In view of the fact that if he had alerted the War Department the Surratt house and all who visited it would likely have been put under close surveillance, someone, sometime, would almost certainly hold Gleason responsible for Lincoln's murder.

In his 1929 biography of Booth, Francis Wilson did. Taking his material from Oldroyd, Wilson wrote that Gleason's decision not to report Weichmann's story "was about as reckless an assumption of responsibility, not to say as brilliant a bit of stupidity, as could be imagined. A report to Stanton might well have saved Lincoln's life."[55]

Gleason probably did not know that Weichmann was the author of Oldroyd's account of the conversations and of all or most of the rest of the chapter about himself in Oldroyd's book,[56] but he might easily have suspected some kind of collusion. The chapter contained many details of Weichmann's biography not previously published, reprinted private letters to him, and vigorously defended him against his critics. If Gleason decided to protect his reputation by publishing his own account of the talks with Weichmann, making himself seem wise for reporting them to the War Department before the assassination rather than irresponsible for deciding not to, it is perhaps understandable and forgivable.

What is not forgivable is his apparent lack of concern for the reputation of Secretary Stanton, which has had to bear the burden so largely imposed upon it by Gleason's false memoir—that Stanton allowed Booth and his friends to remain at liberty in the capital even though he knew of their conspiracy against Lincoln.

Weichmann completed the writing of his own history of the assassination in 1901, but he died the following year and his manuscript was not published until 1975. His treatment of the conversations with Gleason is similar to his testimony at the conspiracy trial and is thus preferable to both the account he wrote for Oldroyd's book and to Gleason's memoir. "My only regret in this whole affair," he wrote, "is that when I spoke of the exciting events of the 16th of March [really the 17th] to Captain Gleason, he and I did not then go to Secretary Stanton and inform him." They had not done so, Weichmann said, because he could not believe that his friends the Surratts could really be plotting a violent crime against the president.[57]

In Weichmann's history there is no mention of a U.S. Enrolling Officer McDavitt. Gleason meant James A. McDevitt, a detective on the Washington Metropolitan Police Force, to whom Weichmann spoke about affairs at the Surratt house after breakfast on April 15.[58] Weichmann did tell McDevitt what he knew about the conspiracy, as Gleason said in his memoir, but not until it was too late.

In an effort to substantiate the truth of Gleason's memoir, Eisenschiml cited a statement made by Weichmann himself during the trial of John H. Surratt in 1867. "For once . . . ," Eisenschiml declared, Weichmann "lost his bland equanimity and went a little beyond his carefully rehearsed testimony." From a passage of cross-examination that he chose not to analyze, Eisenschiml quoted the following single question and answer:

Q. Do you recollect of stating . . . that if Captain Gleason had not betrayed you, you never would have said a word about this matter?
A. No, sir. . . . Mr. Gleason never went to the War Department until about ten days after I had first given the information.[59]

As presented by Eisenschiml, Weichmann appears to have said that Gleason went to the War Department about ten days after he had first confided in him, or weeks before the assassination. If so, Gleason's memoir might be trustworthy after all. But, in fact, Weichmann was not talking about what Eisenschiml implied he was.

At the time he made the statement, Weichmann was being interrogated by one of Surratt's attorneys, Joseph H. Bradley, Sr., about the testimony he had given two years before at the conspiracy trial and about remarks he was afterward alleged to have made concerning the testimony. In an affidavit dated July 7, 1865—the day of Mrs. Surratt's execution—John P. Brophy, a friend of Weichmann, swore that Weichmann had admitted to having given false testimony at the trial in order to avoid being tried as a conspirator himself. Further, Weichmann had stated that if Gleason had not informed upon him he would have said nothing at all about Mrs. Surratt or the other suspected parties.[60] At Surratt's trial, Lewis J. Carland, a costumer at Ford's Theater, testified that Weichmann had made similar statements to him.[61] It was about these allegations that Bradley was questioning the government's key witness in 1867:

Q. Do you know Mr. Lewis Carland?
A. Slightly.
Q. Do you recollect of having a conversation with him on the subject of your testimony, and your knowledge in regard to this alleged conspiracy?
A. I had several talks with him. . . .
Q. Do you remember a conversation with him when Mr. John Brophy was present?
A. Yes, sir; right in front of his house. . . .
Q. Do you recollect of stating in that conversation, or in any other with Mr. Carland or Mr. Brophy, that if Captain Gleason had not betrayed you, you never would have said a word about this matter?

A. No, sir.

Q. Have you seen an affidavit made by Mr. Brophy . . . ?

A. Yes, sir; I saw it two years ago. Mr. Gleason never went to the War Department until about ten days after I had first given the information.

Q. About three, perhaps four, weeks before the assassination—at all events after this horseback ride of which you have spoken—I want to know what you said to Mr. Carland or to Mr. Brophy?

A. I will just tell you what I did say. . . . I cannot say that I said that Mr. Gleason betrayed me, because Mr. Gleason never did betray me.[62]

The significance of this exchange is very different from that attributed to it by Eisenschiml. When Weichmann spoke of Gleason's going to the War Department "about ten days after I had first given the information," he was not referring to the information he had given to Gleason in their February and March 1865 conversations. He was referring, instead, to the information he had given to McDevitt the morning after the assassination. He was mistaken in thinking that Gleason did not go to the War Department until after "about ten days." Actually, Gleason gave his deposition after only three days, on April 18. But by that date, Weichmann was in Canada with McDevitt searching for Surratt, and he probably never did know exactly when Gleason made his statement. Weichmann's point was that he had not been "betrayed" by Gleason because he had, in fact, spoken to the authorities before Gleason did.

But Weichmann was being characteristically devious; Gleason did not give his deposition for several days after Weichmann had told his story to the Washington police, but the government witness well knew that his officemate had reported the fact of their conversations to the War Department within hours of the assassination. It may, then, have been true that Weichmann, knowing he had been incriminated by Gleason, spoke to the police on April 15 only because he had to do so to protect himself.

An interesting feature of the dialogue quoted from the Surratt trial is that attorney Bradley was misled by Weichmann's testimony in precisely the way Eisenschiml had expected his readers to be misled by it. In preparation for the interrogation, Bradley had studied Weichmann's testimony at the 1865 conspiracy trial, including the passages relating to the conversations with Gleason. When he heard his witness state, "Mr. Gleason never went to the War Department until about ten days after I had first given the information," Bradley jumped to the conclusion that Weichmann was referring to the information he had given to Gleason in March. He therefore interposed his comment, "About three, perhaps four, weeks before the assassination . . . ," and then immediately returned to his original line of questioning. His comment was offhand and irrelevant. There had been no previous mention of the Weichmann-Gleason talks, so Weichmann could not possibly have been alluding to them, and there was no subsequent mention of them, either. Weichmann's statement in response to Bradley's questioning was an attempt to clear himself of the accusations made by Brophy and Carland, nothing more.

What about the other evidence that the War Department knew of the abduction plot? Surratt believed the conspiracy had been exposed by Weichmann's telling that War Department clerk about it. But, alas, Gleason did not inform the authorities until after the assassination, so Surratt was mistaken in thinking the government learned of the plot from him. It might have learned of it from someone else, but the erection of a stockade at the Navy Yard Bridge is hardly proof that it had. If the government knew of the plot and wished to break it up, it could simply have arrested the men involved. If it was unsure of their identities and their plans, the building of a stockade at only one of the exits from Washington would have been useless; all of the exits would have to be blocked. If the government knew of the conspiracy and, for a sinister reason like that suggested by Eisenschiml, wished it to proceed, there would have been no need to build any stockade. It is difficult to understand what possible significance there could have been in the fact that the gates were constructed to open one way instead of the other, for presumably they would be closed well before whomever they were supposed to stop was about to pass through them. Perhaps Surratt, who said he wanted to "throw up the whole project," was simply looking for an excuse to do it.

The arrests of Arnold and O'Laughlin so soon after the assassination did not come about as a result of the War Department's knowledge of their participation in the kidnapping conspiracy, but as the result of quick thinking and quick acting on the part of James L. McPhail, provost marshal general of Baltimore. McPhail had known the O'Laughlin family for thirty years and knew that O'Laughlin and Arnold were friends of Booth. He telegraphed that fact to the War Department on the morning of April 15 and then proceeded to track down the two men himself.[63] A Congressional committee, whose reports were apparently unknown to Laughlin and Eisenschiml, officially credited the fast work of McPhail and his staff for the two arrests.[64] McPhail was, of course, also responsible for the prompt identification of Arnold as the author of the "Sam" letter found in Booth's room.

It is impossible to say why Arnold was so sure in this letter that the government "suspicioned" something was going on. Perhaps he was referring to Surratt's warning given at the meeting at Gautier's just two weeks before. He had become impatient with Booth because of the actor's ridiculous talk of seizing Lincoln in the theater, and at Gautier's he threatened to withdraw from the group if an attempt was not made within a week to capture the president on the open road. The attempt was made, it failed, and Arnold, like Surratt, may only have been looking for a way out.

Arnold's letter figures in another way in the hypothesis that the War Department knew of the conspiracy. "It appears from a letter found in Booth's trunk," Secretary Stanton stated in a telegram sent at 4:44 A.M. April 15, "that the murder was planned before the 4th of March, but fell through."[65] In fact, Arnold's letter said nothing about March 4, and Eisenschiml declares that Stanton "blundered" in mentioning the date (and also in arresting Arnold and O'Laughlin so quickly), for it pointed to some "secret knowledge possessed by the Secretary of War."[66] But it does not necessarily do anything of the kind. As Eisenschiml himself shows, there were rumors of several conspiracies against Lincoln circulating in Washington at the time of the Inauguration, and special security arrangements were then taken. Stanton could easily have mistaken the conspiracy revealed in the "Sam" letter for any of them.

There is still another possible explanation for Stanton's reference to March 4. In his reminiscence Gleason wrote that he had learned of the assassination shortly after it occurred and that he had rushed to General Augur's headquarters to recommend the arrest of Weichmann and everyone at the Surratt house. This

much of the memoir was true, for in his April 18 deposition
Gleason stated that he had informed the authorities about
Weichmann's story "after the assassination"—clearly indicating
that his deposition was not the first time he had talked. If his
reminiscence may be trusted on this point, it may also be true
that he told the officers on Augur's staff that some kind of a plot
had been planned for March 4. Neither Weichmann nor any of
the conspirators testified that it had been, but it was a natural
target date and might easily have arisen in conversations at the
Surratts'. If so, it could have been reported by Weichmann to
Gleason, and by Gleason to the authorities at headquarters. Augur could have passed the information to Stanton during any of
their several conferences assassination night.

According to Eisenschiml, the members of Booth's group believed that they had exposed their plot, if it was not already
known to the government, that March afternoon they intercepted Lincoln's carriage, forcing it to "whirl around" and speed
back to the safety of Washington. Why else would they have
"scattered in all directions—to Baltimore, to Richmond, to New
York"?[67]

The truth is that they did not intercept the carriage (all stories
that they did are fiction), which would not have had to "whirl
around" because it would have been on its way back to the city
anyway, and Booth and his friends did not scatter out of fear and
panic. Booth remained in Washington and on the following night
played the role of Pescara in *The Apostate* at Ford's Theater, his
next-to-the-last performance on that stage. After the play he
treated David Herold and Atzerodt to drinks. On March 21 he
went to New York, returning to Washington on March 25. Surratt did not leave for Richmond until March 26.[68]

It would be possible to illustrate with a tiresome number of
examples how post-Eisenschiml writers on Lincoln's murder have
blindly followed the leader. McKinley wanted to know why
Booth's most logical escape route was "left unguarded and open,
while the Northern roads were quickly blocked. Did Stanton
want Booth to escape?"[69] Kimmel thought John H. Surratt was
probably responsible for the interruption of the telegraph on
assassination night, because no other member of Booth's group
would have been smart enough to provide such assistance to the

fleeing assassin.[70] Shelton suggested that short-circuiting the telegraph wires might have been the important work which Stanton told Lincoln would not permit Eckert, head of the military telegraph, to accompany him to the theater on April 14.[71] Lattimer referred to Eisenschiml's "innuendo" that Stanton might have said Eckert had important duties to perform that evening because the secretary knew an attempt would probably be made on Lincoln's life, "and he did not want the President to be guarded in any special way. There is no proof for this allegation, of course, but implied bits of circumstantial evidence do seem to place Stanton in a peculiar light."[72]

These questions and suspicions and many, many more may be reasonably ascribed to Eisenschiml, who may also be held responsible for the literary climate that has induced so many writers to join in the fun of character assassination. The destruction of Stanton's reputation may have begun with the revisionist Dewitt (whose prestige remains unaccountably high despite his flagrantly partisan misrepresentations), but it was Eisenschiml's example that encouraged writers to shape evidence into grotesque preconceived patterns and to look for depraved explanations for routine events.

Since many of the books dealing with the assassination are popular, large numbers of readers are affected by the distortions deriving from Eisenschiml. The number is further increased by the fact that Eisenschiml-inspired works, with their titillating hints or assertions of conspiracy and betrayal, are the ones to which high school and college students, magazine freelancers, newspaper reporters, and the authors of TV scripts turn for material for their essays, articles, and dramatizations. Such productions, in turn, influence those who are exposed to them, thus further spreading the major and minor hypotheses of the Eisenschiml thesis, giving them additional authority with each additional repetition.

Eisenschiml's falsifications and perversions, camouflaged by the man's constant protestations of scientific objectivity, have thus erected a formidable barrier against an understanding of Lincoln's assassination. There is perhaps no event in their history about which the American people have been so shockingly misinformed.

CHAPTER
8

Reductio ad Absurdum

ALTHOUGH OTTO EISENSCHIML WAS ALWAYS QUICK to admit that no evidence supported his trumped-up case against Edwin M. Stanton, thereby winning for himself a reputation for both modesty and honesty, he professed to be bothered by the fact that no earlier writer—not even the reporters of anti-Radical newspapers—had shared his suspicions. Civil War reporters were not simpletons, he knew, and they "must have suspected that something was wrong, if there was something to suspect. If they had, it was reasonable to expect that they had put their suspicions into words, even though their publishers may have suppressed what they had written. But where were these words?"[1]

In 1948 a man found some of them. They were printed in a weekly newspaper the man said he had discovered in a hollow space behind a mirror that had fallen down in an old building in Baltimore. The newspaper, yellow and brittle with age and with some of its pages still uncut, was *The People's Weekly* for May 2, 1868, and it contained precisely the kind of article Eisenschiml had thought must exist. "THE REAL INSTIGATORS OF THE ASSASSINATION OF LINCOLN," proclaimed a story on the front page, "were Edwin M. Stanton, Joseph Holt, and Lafayette C. Baker," whose "brutal instincts" had been warmed into life by the "wicked vindictiveness" of the Radical leader in the House of Representatives, Thaddeus Stevens. Lincoln had been assassinated so "that they might have freer scope in hanging rebels and appropriating to themselves their property; to which they feared Lincoln's good nature and desire for conciliation would be an obstacle." No details or evidence of the alleged plot were presented, but they were promised for the paper's next issue. Possibly because he feared that the somewhat stagey manner in which the paper was discovered and the neatness with which the article appeared to fit his thesis might cause some readers to suspect a hoax, Eisenschiml published a photograph of part of the paper's front page. It showed the masthead and date, and the opening paragraphs of the article; Eisenschiml also commented upon other stories carried in the issue.[2]

Despite one of the thorough and imaginative investigations for which he was justly famous, Eisenschiml was unable to locate a copy of *The People's Weekly* for May 9, 1868, and only two other issues of the paper (neither containing anything about the assassination) were located. Eisenschiml's May 2nd issue, presented to him by its discoverer, proved to be the only known copy for that date. "Perhaps some day the missing [May 9] copy of *The People's Weekly* will be found," Eisenschiml commented; "if so, it will be a miracle, for one can hardly expect that some day someone [else] . . . will discover one of them hidden in a hole behind a mirror. Yet, what a find it would be!"[3]

In all probability, the lecture circuit audiences who heard Eisenschiml tell this story and the readers who read about it were more disappointed than Eisenschiml himself at his inability to find a copy of the issue of the paper that would supposedly present evidence to substantiate the Eisenschiml thesis. For Eisenschiml knew too much about Lincoln and the politics of Reconstruction to take the May 2nd article as seriously as he pretended.

The editor of the *Weekly* was Benjamin Edwards Green, son of Duff Green, prominent journalist, supporter of John C. Calhoun, and promoter of various industrial enterprises in the South. Born in Kentucky in 1822, Ben Green (as he was known) shared his father's extreme states' rights political principles and participated in some of his business ventures. During the Civil War he managed an iron works in Tennessee for the Confederate government. In 1868 he settled in Washington, D. C., and, beginning with the May 2nd issue, became editor of *The People's Weekly*.[4]

In the article charging that Stanton, Holt, and Baker had arranged Lincoln's murder at the urging of Stevens, Green stated that the idea had been suggested to him by one of the stenographic reporters at the 1865 conspiracy trial. At first Green said he had dismissed the idea as "a wild vagary," but "subse-

quent developments and an examination of the [trial] testimony"
convinced him that the man's suspicions were well-founded. Since
none of the trial testimony pointed in any way to Stanton, Holt,
or Baker, Eisenschiml assumed that it must have been the "subsequent developments" that won Green over. "But what particular developments did Green have in mind?" Eisenschiml
wondered. Unfortunately, it was one of those questions to which
there was no direct answer.

However, an analysis of the text of Green's article—quoted in
its entirety by Eisenschiml in 1950 in an historical journal but
not in a briefer discussion of the subject in one of his books—
suggests the kind of "developments" that Green had had in mind.
The article recalled that at the time of his visit to Richmond
early in April 1865, Lincoln had held frank discussions with various Southerners, including John A. Campbell, a former Justice
of the U.S. Supreme Court who had resigned and become assistant secretary in the Confederate War Department. According to the article, Lincoln had reproached Campbell and others
for their secession, for it had left him in the power of the abolitionists, who had forced him to issue the Emancipation Proclamation. He could not revoke the Proclamation, Lincoln had said,
but he would allow the Supreme Court to determine whether
or not it was constitutional. At this point, Campbell interrupted. He was satisfied to leave the decision with the court, he
told Lincoln, for, whatever the political views of Chief Justice
Salmon P. Chase, "he will be compelled to decide that you had
no Constitutional authority to issue that proclamation."

"I am perfectly willing that the Supreme Court shall decide
that it was unconstitutional, null and void," Lincoln rejoined.
"*Now* the question is whether you will come back into the Union
and sustain me in putting down the fanatics and abolitionists. I
don't want to take your slaves from you. If you want to keep
them, come back at once into the Union, vote against the Constitutional amendment abolishing slavery, and sustain me in my
efforts to rescue the government from the fanatics and abolitionists."

When, the article continued, on April 6, 1865, Lincoln ordered General Godfrey Weitzel, U.S. military commander in
Richmond, "to call the Virginia Legislature together," it was so
he could secure the state's vote against the Thirteenth Amend-

ment. Stanton forced the president to rescind the order and then "determined to get rid of him, as an obstacle to his game of rebel hanging and plundering." The agency to which the secretary turned to accomplish his objective was "that infamous adjunct of the War Department, the Bureau of Military Injustice."

Concluding with the promise to report full particulars of the conspiracy in the next issue, Green noted that if the secrets of Stanton's administration of the War Department and of Holt's management of his Bureau were ever known, they would "make one's hair stand on end."[5]

As Eisenschiml well knew—but did not state—the article was utter nonsense. Lincoln never said to Southerners in Richmond—or anywhere else—that he wanted their help in "putting down the fanatics and abolitionists," or that he did not want to take their slaves away from them. He never said to former Justice Campbell—or anyone else—that he wanted southern help to defeat the constitutional amendment ending slavery. Quite the opposite. Lincoln worked hard for the amendment, as Campbell himself reported. "His indispensable conditions [for peace]," Campbell informed Confederate General Richard Taylor in Mobile, on April 12, 1865, "are the restoration of the authority of the United States and the disbanding of the troops, and no receding on his part from his position on the slavery question as defined in his message in December and other official documents."[6]

In the December 1864 message to which Campbell referred, Lincoln had forcefully urged the House of Representatives to pass the Thirteenth Amendment, already approved by the Senate. When the House did so at the end of January, Lincoln expressed his gratification to serenaders at the White House. He had done all he himself could do to end slavery, he told them, when he issued his Emancipation Proclamation, though he was sure there would have been questions about the Proclamation's legality. "But this amendment," he exclaimed, "is a King's cure for all the evils. It winds the whole thing up." And then he congratulated "all present, himself, the country and the whole world upon this great moral victory."[7]

Nor did Lincoln ever give an order "to call the Virginia Legislature together." What he did do on April 6 was to authorize "the gentlemen who have acted as the Legislature of Virginia" to meet for the purpose of withdrawing Virginia's soldiers from the Army. Six days later he revoked the authorization, for Virginia's soldiers had by then surrendered at Appomattox.[8]

In short, Green's article, the work of an embittered southern Democrat at a time of extreme partisan controversy, was simply political propaganda. It was designed to influence public opinion against the "fanatics and abolitionists" who were in 1868 setting Reconstruction policy; Lincoln had opposed these same men, and that was why he was killed. The crudeness of the article permits one positive conclusion: it is almost certainly genuine, for the perpetrator of a hoax would not likely have been so careless in his misrepresentations of Lincoln's views on slavery and the Thirteenth Amendment. Green, on the other hand—like many another propagandist—would have felt no compunction against misrepresenting the truth, or making it up, if he believed doing so would serve his cause.

The misrepresentation of evidence, upon which the entire Eisenschiml thesis rested, is the falsification of evidence. The logical next step is the manufacture of false evidence.

In 1961 one Ray A. Neff, destined for notoriety, gave Eisenschiml fans something to become excited about when he published in the popular magazine *Civil War Times* the text of two cipher messages he said he had found written in a bound volume of an English military journal for the last half of the year 1864. Neff had purchased the volume in a Philadelphia bookstore for fifty cents. Allegedly written in 1868 by Lafayette C. Baker, the former War Department detective and secret agent, the messages disclosed that Lincoln had indeed been the victim of a grand conspiracy organized by Secretary of War Stanton. They also revealed that Baker believed he himself was to be killed to prevent him from exposing the conspirators. Lengthy as they are, the messages deserve to be reprinted in full, with punctuation and parenthetical options exactly as Neff presented them, for they caused a sensation.[9]

I am constantly being followed. They are professionals. I cannot fool them. 2–5–68 In new Rome there walked three men, a Judas, a Brutus and a spy. Each planned that he should be the kink(g) when Abraham should die. One trusted not the other but they went on for that day, waiting for that final moment when with pistol in his hand, one of the sons of Brutus could sneak behind that cursed man and put a bullet in his brain and lay his clumsey corpse away. As the fallen man lay dying, Judas came and paid respects to one he hated, and when at last he saw him die, he said, "Now the ages have him and the nation now have I." But Alas (as) fate would have it Judas slowly fell from g(r)ace, and with him went Brutus down to their proper place. But lest one is left to wonder what has happened to the spy, I can safely tell you this, it was I. Lafayette C. Baker 2–5–68

It was on the tenth of April, Sis(x)ty-five when I first knew that the plan was in action. Ecert (Thomas Thompson Eckert, an aide to Stanton?) had made all the contacts, the deed to be done of the fo(u)rteenth. I did not know the identity of the assassin but I knew most all else when I approached E. S. (Edwin Stanton?) about it. He at once acted surprised and disbelieving. Later he said, "You are a party to it too. Let us wait and see what comes of it and then we will know better how to act in the matter." I soon discovered what he meant that I was a party to it when the following day I was shown a document that I knew to be a forgery but a clever one, which made it appear that I had been in charge of a plot to kidnap the president, the vice-president being the instigator. Then I became a party to that deed even though I did not care to

(This could also read: "I had been in charge of a plot to kidnap the president, (and) the vice-president. Being the instigator then, I became a party to that deed even though etc.)

On the thirteenth he discovered that the president had ordered (that) the Legislature of Virginia be allowed to assemble to withdraw that states troops from action against the U.S. He fermented immediately into an insane tyrade. Then for the first time I realized his mental disunity and his insane and fanatical hatred for the president. There are few in the War Department that respect the president or his strategy but there (are) not many who would countermand an order that the pres(ident) had given. However during that insane moment he sent a telegram to Gen. Weitzel countermanding the presidents order of the twelfth. Then he laughed in a most spine chilling manner and said, "If he would to know who recinded his order we will let Lucifer tell him. Be off Tom (Eckert?) and see to the arrangements. There can be no mistakes. This is the first th(at) I knew that he was the one responsible for the assassination plot. Always before I thought that either he did not trust me, for he really trusted no one, or he was protecting someone until it was to his benefit to expose them. But now I know the truth and it frightens me no end. I fear that somehow

I may become the sacrificial goat. There were at least eleven members of Congress involved in the plot, no less than twelve Army officers, three Naval officers and at least 24 civilians, of which one was a governor of a loyal state. Five were bankers of great repute, three were nationally known newspaper men and eleven were industrialists of great repute and wealth. There were probably more that I know nothing of. The names of these known conspirators is presented without comment or notation, in Vol. one of this series. Eighty-five thousand dollars was contributed by the named persons to pay for the deed. Only eight persons knew the details of the plot and the identity of the others.

I fear for my life.   LCB.

After decoding these astonishing messages, Neff searched the volume for additional secrets. Noticing a number of discolored spots, he treated them with ultraviolet radiations. One of the spots emitted a purple glow; upon the application of a solution of tannic acid—like Eisenschiml, Neff had been trained as a chemist—the signature "L. C. Baker" gradually emerged. A handwriting expert compared it to one of Baker's known signatures and pronounced it genuine. The volume had belonged to Baker!

Even more impressive substantiation was a document Neff said he had found in a mountain of dusty records in the Philadelphia City Hall. The document was identified as the transcript of a hearing held in Philadelphia in 1872 on a codicil to Baker's will, which had been suppressed at the time of the detective's death in July 1868. At the hearing, one William Carter, who had served under Baker, stated that he had called upon him shortly before his death. "When I came into the room," Carter testified, "he had a stack of books by his bed and had one open and was making marks in it. I asked him what he was doing and he said, 'I'm writing my memoirs.' . . . Then I said, 'But General, them books is already wrote,' and he said, 'Right, they are going to have to get up early to get ahead of old Lafe Baker.' . . . I picked up one of the books and looked at it and I saw that he was writing cipher in it. . . . All the time that I was there he kept writing in the book. . . . It was an English military journal."

At the hearing Baker's physician testified that Baker had been followed during the last months of his life, that several attempts had been made to kill him, and that his death, certified as due to meningitis, could have been caused by arsenic poisoning. A servant who had been almost hit by a bullet shot at Baker through a window in his home testified that Baker had said they would get him yet. When the servant asked who they were, he replied, "My old friends . . . ," and explained that he had papers that could send them to prison.[10]

All in all, the transcript appeared to provide remarkable corroboration of the validity of Baker's ciphers and of the fears expressed in them. "The only question remaining . . . ," stated Robert H. Fowler, editor of *Civil War Times*, "is: Did Lafayette C. Baker tell the truth or was he merely trying to settle an old score with Stanton?" Baker was capable of such a deception, for "truthfulness was not his outstanding virtue. He was a scoundrel." Neff himself was becomingly modest about the significance of his discovery. He could not accept Baker at his word, he said, without additional evidence.[11]

The story of Neff's sensational find was picked up by the wire services and publicized in nearly every newspaper in the country.[12] Evidence had been found confirming the Eisenschiml thesis!

Eisenschiml was not so sure. He wondered what such a large number of conspirators could have contributed to the assassination plot and how Stanton could possibly have expected to keep so many men quiet. And why had Baker left his message in such an obscure magazine? The value of the ciphers, Eisenschiml recognized, depended entirely upon Baker, whose "unsavory character puts a question mark behind the results of Neff's fine piece of historical research." Still, he believed the ciphers had "somewhat strengthened" his thesis and quoted with satisfaction from an editorial in the Washington *Post:* "About a quarter century ago Otto Eisenschiml, an eminent Civil War buff, provoked a good deal of denunciation and derision from book reviewers and historians by advancing the hypothesis that the late Edwin M. Stanton . . . might have had something to do with the murder of President Lincoln. . . . Now comes Ray A. Neff . . . to give some documentary verisimilitude to Mr. Eisenschiml's hypothesis."[13]

As Eisenschiml had expected, professional historians were not much impressed with the ciphers, and not only because of their mistrust of Baker. Their attitude was influenced more by a profound change that was taking place at the time in how they viewed

Lincoln and the Radical Republicans and the subject of Reconstruction. The revisionist interpretation, so influential since the
end of the nineteenth century, had stressed an irreconcilable
antagonism between the compassionate president, who wanted
to make a generous peace with the South, and the vindictive
members of his own party, who wished to punish and humiliate
the Rebels. As late as 1945 the eminent James G. Randall, a
leading revisionist, went so far as to assert that Lincoln faced
greater opposition from the leaders of his own party than he did
from Democrats and Confederates![14]

David M. Dewitt interjected the revisionist slant into the history of Lincoln's assassination by stressing Stanton's vindictive
treatment of the conspirators, especially his ruthless persecution of Mary E. Surratt; subsequent writers added their own
contributions to the diminution of the great wartime secretary's
character and reputation. So far as Stanton was concerned, revisionism reached its supreme consummation in the Eisenschiml thesis. How could he possibly be made to seem more
despicable than as the man responsible for Lincoln's murder?

But revisionism was passing away at the very time Neff's discovery might have been expected to give it renewed vitality and
plausibility. During the civil rights revolution of the 1960s—
sometimes referred to as the Second Reconstruction—the nation was torn by many of the same conflicts that had beset it in
the post–Civil War era. The intrusion of the federal government
into areas traditionally left to the states in order to bring about
the civil equality of all citizens was precisely what the Radical
Republicans had attempted a century before. These long-
maligned leaders now began to seem more heroic (if premature)
than villainous; their objective had not been to punish or humiliate the South but to safeguard the results of the war and to
give meaning to the freedom won by the ex-slaves. On these
vital matters there had been no major differences between Lincoln and the Radicals, certainly no irreconcilable ones. That
Lincoln was murdered in order to remove him as an obstacle to
Radical Reconstruction was "rubbish!" exclaimed William E.
Baringer in commenting upon the Baker ciphers. "Lincoln's reconstruction policy could have been stopped a whole lot more
easily by voting it down in Congress." T. Harry Williams, whose
1949 book on *Lincoln and the Radicals* was a classic statement

of revisionism, had so far changed his mind by 1961 that he wrote of Stanton's alleged involvement in Lincoln's death, "I see no motive whatever."[15]

Old ideas die hard, however, and the public—educated for two generations in the anti-Radical tenets of revisionism and diverted for one generation by the conspiratorial postulates of the Eisenschiml thesis—was unaffected by this major shift of professional opinion. "From this point on," as Lincoln scholar Mark Neely put it, "the two worlds—academic and popular— did not collide; they simply never met again."[16] To professional historians, Neff's ciphers simply did not add up, apart from such trivial matters as the misdating of Lincoln's order concerning the Virginia legislature, an error easily attributed to fallible memory.

At about the same time as the publication of the Neff-Baker ciphers, and possibly as a result of them, Vaughan Shelton, a freelance writer, began a "microscopic" study of the Lincoln assassination with a view to revealing the truth about it. In 1965 the results of his investigations were published under the title *Mask for Treason. The Lincoln Murder Trial.*[17] Although Shelton dedicated the book to Eisenschiml and was indebted to him in many ways, he nevertheless claimed to be presenting "a substantially *new* version" of the assassination.[18]

It proved to be new, but not substantial.

Shelton's explanation of the assassination is labyrinthine and irrational, but it is worth consideration because it demonstrates the absurdities to which the post-Eisenschiml obsession with conspiracy can drive hyperactive imaginations and gullible minds. (It also demonstrates something about the gullibility of publishers and readers.)

Before considering the "Author's Conception of the Conspiracy"—included as an "addendum" after four hundred pages of a deranged analysis of sources—it is necessary to state that Shelton finds the key to the assassination mystery in the person of Lewis Paine, one of the defendants at the conspiracy trial about whose guilt, traditionally, there has been no doubt. Shelton believes that Paine was innocent, that he did not attack Secretary of State William H. Seward, and that he did not even know John Wilkes Booth. "Paine" was not the alias of Lewis Thornton Powell, as both he himself and the War Department insisted, but an altogether different individual, a Powell-look-alike. Indeed, he was Powell's cousin, and he was framed by the War Department so that Powell, a department agent, could escape punishment. Shelton is not entirely clear as to why Paine claimed he was Powell, or why he allowed himself to be hanged in Powell's place, but he thinks Paine had some kind of death wish. He states that Powell himself was not sure why his cousin was willing to make the supreme sacrifice; but one day he did show up in court, possibly, says Shelton, to ease a guilty conscience by giving Paine an opportunity to expose him publicly. In any case, an innocent man pretending to be Lewis Thornton Powell was put to death, and the real Lewis Thornton Powell, legally dead and thus able to assume a new identity and lead a new life, was free. [19]

So much for Shelton's "key." Now for his summary.

Baker had lied when he stated in the cipher messages given to the world by Neff that Stanton was responsible for the assassination plot; Baker himself was responsible for it. As Shelton saw the conspiracy, John H. Surratt had been a double agent whose contact in the North was Baker. For months he had kept the detective informed about Booth's plan to kidnap Lincoln in a theater. It was useful information for Baker, for if the abduction ever did take place, he could add to his laurels by quickly fingering Booth and his group. But nothing happened and nothing was likely to happen, so—with Baker's approval—Surratt introduced Powell to the little band of inept conspirators. Booth was very favorably impressed with Powell, but Powell could see that Booth was only "a posturing, prating egotist, obsessed with the idea of a grand gesture before an audience—but wholly incapable of bringing it off."

After the midnight dinner meeting at Gautier's restaurant in mid-March 1865, Booth's friends dispersed (Shelton does not believe the conspirators intended to intercept Lincoln's carriage on the highway), and Powell reported to Baker for instructions. The assassination plot resulted.

Why did Baker want Lincoln murdered? He wanted the president removed because he recognized that his own power was dependent upon the perpetuation of the national crisis, and Lincoln was planning a peace of reconciliation. He also knew that Stanton, Seward, and other leaders would like Lincoln out of the way for the same reason. "They might not collaborate in assassination, but they would give it their tacit approval." Booth was already primed to do something dramatic in the theater. Under "Powell's skillful direction" it became murder instead of abduction. It was planned that Booth, who would be recognized as the killer, would be eliminated after the assassination "—and that would be the end of it. No search for the culprit, no further investigation; case closed!"

In the execution of this new scheme, Powell enlisted the help of two members of the old kidnapping conspiracy, Mary E. Surratt and David Herold. "The widow had the actor's confidence and agreed to help mold his state of mind to the theme that Lincoln was the cause of all the nation's woes, and his death would be a blessing applauded by millions." Herold's function was to accompany Booth on his flight out of Washington and kill him by putting white arsenic in the liquor he was certain to drink when they stopped to pick up carbines at the tavern in Surrattsville.

Baker was confident that Stanton could see the advantage to himself of having Lincoln killed and sure that the secretary would not interfere if forewarned. On April 10, therefore, Baker told Stanton about his "fears" that there was a conspiracy to kill the president at Ford's Theater on the 14th. Stanton professed to doubt the reality of the plot, but he understood what Baker had in mind, and Baker departed for New York. According to Shelton, the memoir of David H. Bates—which described Lincoln's visit to the War Department telegraph office the morning of April 14—showed Stanton "virtually ordering" Lincoln not to go to Ford's Theater that evening, "a neat bit of negative psychology that made Lincoln determined to go." Of course, Stanton gave the president no specific warning and took no steps to give him effective protection.

Carefully organized down to the last detail, the plan should have worked, and would have but for two factors. First, some insider—Shelton thinks it was probably Stanton's assistant Thomas Eckert—"saw an opportunity to kill at least two birds with one stone." He made a contract with Powell to kill Secretary Seward, timing the attack so it would appear to be by the same man who had shot the president. But Powell's timing was off; the attacks occurred almost simultaneously, and that revealed the existence of a conspiracy. Second, at Surrattsville Herold put the arsenic in a bottle of whiskey, and Booth, who preferred brandy, did not drink enough to kill him. It did make him very ill, however. At Dr. Samuel A. Mudd's home and in the pine thicket where they hid, Herold waited helplessly for Booth to die. Instead he got better, and they continued into Virginia.

In the meantime, Eckert, Stanton, and others who knew the truth about what had happened were in a panic for fear their roles in the conspiracy would become known. But Baker made sure that Booth would not be captured by any but his own hand-picked men. It was Boston Corbett who shot Booth, but the actor would never have made it alive back to Washington anyway. To satisfy the public's demand for the exposure of the assassination conspiracy and the prompt punishment of all involved in it, Baker engineered the conspiracy trial, "one of history's great achievements in treachery." Eight accomplices of Booth, framed by Baker, were tried, convicted, and punished with a maximum of publicity, and the public was given a false but plausible explanation of the assassination.

The chances for the success of this audacious cover-up, Shelton concludes, were remote. "But unvarying human nature equalized the odds. This was the sequence of crime and punishment the people *wanted* to see. These were the explanations they *wanted* to see. These were the explanations they *wanted* to believe. L. C. Baker, the supreme psychologist, won the gamble." His conspiracy trial had successfully masked his treason.[20]

It would not be worthwhile to explain the lengthy and convoluted reasoning by which Shelton arrived at the theory of this new and ridiculous grand conspiracy. Nor need we consider his explanation of why Mrs. Surratt and Herold allowed themselves to be hanged without informing their attorneys that they had been put up to their parts in the conspiracy by Powell, and that the man in the dock with them who was thought to be Powell was somebody else. It is not even necessary to comment upon Shelton's insane idea that the Brutus referred to in Baker's first cipher message—and therefore one of the three instigators of Lincoln's assassination—was not Booth, but none other than Secretary of State Seward. But attention must be paid here (and more will be paid later on) to a document essential to the thesis of *Mask for Treason* that Shelton was the first writer on the assassination to utilize.

The document was a letter addressed to John H. Surratt from one R. D. Watson. At the 1865 conspiracy trial Judge Advocate General Joseph Holt had shown it to the government's witness, Louis Weichmann, and asked him if it was in the handwriting of John Wilkes Booth. Weichmann examined the letter and said he did not believe it was in Booth's hand, and the interrogation continued on another subject. This is the letter.[21]

New York, March 19, 1865

Mr. J. H. Surratt

Dear Sir

I would like to see you on important business, if you can spare the time to come to New York. Please telegraph me immediately on the reception of this, whether you can come on or not & oblige

Yours tr—

P. S. Address Care Demill & Co.   R. D. Watson
178 1/2 Water St.

Shelton's suspicion was aroused by the fact that, although the letter was reproduced in the record of the trial published in Philadelphia by T. B. Peterson and Brothers, it was omitted from the officially approved trial record compiled by Benn Pitman. Since he assumed that the document had been withheld from Pitman's volume because the government wished to conceal its existence, Shelton ordered a photocopy of the original from the National Archives. (Apparently he never asked himself why the letter had been so carefully preserved with the other "Investigation and Trial Papers" if the War Department wished to conceal it.)[22]

Months later Shelton prepared to send another document, which he thought might have been written by Assistant Secretary Eckert, to a handwriting analyst in California. On an impulse, he also sent his copy of the Watson letter, on the chance that it too might have been written by Eckert. The report was negative; neither document was in Eckert's handwriting. But the analyst, who was also a graphologist—i.e., capable of "detecting and interpreting the personality traits revealed by an individual's handwriting"—included in her report a lengthy description of the kind of man Watson was. The description fit Lafayette Baker perfectly! Shelton thereupon rushed authenticated copies of Baker's script to the expert, who compared them to the Watson letter and stated positively that the letter had been written by Baker, though he had attempted to disguise his hand.[23] Here, then, was the origin of Shelton's inspiration that Baker was the architect of Lincoln's assassination.

Could there have been any innocent reason for Baker, a leading War Department detective, to write to Confederate agent Surratt using an assumed name? Shelton thought not. "The letter would be incriminating regardless of what it said. Being dated March 19, 1865—just after the collapse of Booth's kidnap scheme, and just before the events preceding the assassination began to unfold—there is no reasonable alternative to believing that the 'important business' Baker referred to was the murder of President Lincoln."[24]

Shelton's theory rested upon the opinion of one handwriting expert that Baker was the author of the Watson letter. But experts disagree. Prior to the publication of *Mask for Treason*, the magazine *Civil War Times Illustrated* (successor to *Civil War Times*) publicized Shelton's "New Evidence in [the] Lincoln Murder Conspiracy" and described its own efforts to authenticate it. Editor Fowler had submitted a copy of the Watson letter and samples of Baker's handwriting to another expert, an individual frequently called upon to testify in court. This analyst reported that there were insufficient similarities to conclude that Baker had written the Watson letter, a fact that Fowler found "disturbing" and that Shelton omitted from his book.[25] There is so much utter nonsense in *Mask for Treason* that one's inclination is to accept the verdict of the second analyst and reject that of the first, together with the absurd conspiracy that Shelton based upon it. Surely someone in the War Department would have destroyed the letter had it really been written by Baker.

But because of *Civil War Times Illustrated* the Watson letter cannot be so easily and sensibly dismissed. For, if the magazine seemed to undermine Shelton's theory by coming up with an expert who did not believe Baker had written the letter to Surratt, it acted as a conduit to reenforce the theory by putting

Shelton in touch with Neff. And Neff produced evidence that appeared to show that Baker was probably the writer of the Watson letter, after all.

With some pride, *Civil War Times Illustrated* noted that its publication of the Baker ciphers three and one-half years before had resulted in so much publicity that Neff had been deluged with new information about Baker and with several collections of papers of individuals and businesses involved with him. From one of these collections, Neff supplied Shelton with copies, which he himself certified as true, of the records of a Canadian shipping line, J. & J. Chaffey Co. These documents revealed that Baker had acted as an agent of the company as far back as the 1840s, and that in the year 1864 alone the company had made payments to him totalling a colossal $148,894. Even more surprising, the documents showed that John Wilkes Booth was also on the company payroll. Between August and October, 1864, he had received a $10,000 advance "for services," and an additional $4,500 had been deposited to his credit. Baker and Booth secretly employed by the same company! Most startling of all was the address for the Chaffey Co. given on Neff's copies of its papers: 178 1/2 Water Street, New York City. The same address as that given to Surratt by Watson![26] It was all the confirmation Shelton needed to conclude that the California handwriting analyst had been correct: Baker and Watson were one and the same. "Demill & Co.," in care of which Watson had asked to be addressed, Shelton reasoned, was simply a blind established by Baker in order to avoid the use of the Chaffey name in his secret and treasonable correspondence.[27]

Shelton had additional reason to be grateful to Neff. In his twin capacities as historical investigator and consultant chemist and toxicologist, Neff also supplied Shelton with a formal "Investigation Report," in which he gave his professional opinion that Booth could indeed have been poisoned when he drank the whiskey at Surrattsville on assassination night. "This would explain the 'yellow and discolored' condition of his skin," as reported by the physician who examined Booth's body on April 27, 1865, Neff's report declared. The condition was known as "arsenic bronzing" and "is due to jaundice discoloration, the liver being greatly damaged as well as the kidneys (explaining back pain). In addition the symptoms include anorexia, weakness, diarrhea (or sometimes constipation), and occasional nausea and vomiting, selective edemas (ankles, eyelids), conjunctivitis, sore nose and throat, dermatitis, including bronzing and jaundice. As you can see, this is similar to the Booth symptoms."[28]

Although there was nothing in the documents furnished by Neff to substantiate Shelton's theory that Baker was the mastermind of the assassination, the Chaffey papers did appear to confirm what had been indicated for the first time in the cipher messages: that in some capacity or other, Baker was involved in the assassination conspiracy. By the time of his death in 1963— before Neff produced the Chaffey records—even Eisenschiml seems to have thought so. When asked how Secretary Stanton could possibly have conspired with Booth without being found out, Eisenschiml answered that he would have used a go-between. Who could it have been? the questioner wanted to know. Without hesitation Eisenschiml replied, "I think L. C. Baker would be the logical suspect. He had the character for such low business and of course he had plenty of opportunity."[29]

Shelton's grand conspiracy theory was so absurd that it is unlikely to have made many converts. What it did do, and what Neff's ciphers and his copies of the Chaffey Co. records did, was to bolster the faith of those who had believed—even before the discovery of "evidence"—that the assassination conspiracy had originated in the War Department.

Eisenschiml was dead, but among true believers his thesis was stronger than ever.

It is natural that the writers of books should believe that their new evidence or new insights contribute significantly to the understanding of a subject. Sometimes this assumption may be only implicit in the fact of the book's existence; sometimes it may be explicit, stated with modesty (either real or false) in a preface; sometimes it may be expressed in an outburst of reckless and extravagant self-congratulation. The assumption of David Balsiger and Charles E. Sellier, Jr., about the importance of their *The Lincoln Conspiracy* (1977) falls into the last of these categories.

"We have advanced the Lincoln assassination study more in one year," Balsiger announced, "than it has been advanced in the previous 112 years." Balsiger and Sellier claimed to have exposed a "massive cover-up effort by government officials to prevent the American public from ever learning the real truth about the assassination." As with the Warren Commission's investigation into the Kennedy assassination in the 1960s and the Watergate cover-up of the 1970s, it was a case of "our government not telling us the truth" about Lincoln's murder.[30] Balsiger and Sellier were able to discover the truth, so they tell us, because of their devotion to original sources. "In research a primary document provides greater authenticity and accuracy than the secondary source materials most often used by the traditionalists." Indeed, they believed that traditional historians had helped to perpetuate the cover-up of the Lincoln conspiracy "by using 1865 government data and documents as gospel, in addition to quoting previously published books on the subject."[31]

The two young non-traditionalists engaged in a whirlwind search for the original sources overlooked by professional historians and, with remarkable ease, uncovered documents staggering in number and significance. Most significant—most astounding—of all were the eighteen pages missing from the diary of John Wilkes Booth! In addition, they secured from the industrious Neff copies of several collections of papers, including those of Baker himself, the Chaffey Co. (supplementing the records Neff had earlier furnished to Shelton), and Andrew Potter, a member of the National Detective Police and thus once a subordinate of Baker.[32]

As a result of the extraordinary information found in these never-before-studied sources, Balsiger and Sellier asserted that they could give positive answers to many of the questions originally asked by Eisenschiml. Was Stanton—"Lincoln's power-obsessed Secretary of War"—a conspirator? Why was the president's bodyguard who left his post at Ford's Theater never punished or even questioned? "Why were all the escape routes out of Washington closed except the route Booth used? Who, for hours after the murder, blacked out commercial telegraph lines from Washington? . . . Why was the existence of Booth's diary hidden until long after the famous 1865 Conspiracy Trial, and when revealed, why had 18 pages been cut out? . . . Were the convicted and hanged Booth co-conspirators scapegoats for higher figures in a massive cover-up?"[33] In answering these and other questions, Balsiger and Sellier promised a triumphant vindication of the Eisenschiml thesis.

But it turned out otherwise. Despite a very large sale for the book (and honorary doctorates for its authors), despite a major media blitz for a simultaneously released motion picture version of the story (which won the Freedoms Foundation's George Washington Medal of Honor for the film's producers), the impact of the *Lincoln Conspiracy* was much less than might have been expected, and much different. Far from producing the triumphant capstone to the work of Eisenschiml, Balsiger and Sellier may have finished off the Eisenschiml thesis for good. For the *Lincoln Conspiracy* was not just a fraud based upon twisted reasoning, like so many other books on the assassination. It was a fraud based upon apparent hoaxes, and this time professional historians—most notably William C. Davis for *Civil War Times Illustrated* and Harold M. Hyman for the Abraham Lincoln Association—fulfilled their critical responsibilities and exposed it for what it was.

In their book Balsiger and Sellier professed to be so impressed by their newly discovered documents and so shocked by the nature of the conspiracy the documents revealed that they called upon Congress to establish a joint Senate-House committee to reopen the Lincoln murder case. "Until that congressional committee is formed," they instructed their readers, "you are the judge of the evidence."[34] The trouble is they do not give their readers any evidence to judge, they simply state that it exists. Indeed, Balsiger and Sellier had not seen most of their new sources themselves, only copies and excerpts. The missing pages from Booth's diary, for example, were allegedly found among papers owned by unnamed descendants of Stanton by one Joseph Lynch, identified as an appraiser and dealer in Americana but unknown to leaders in the field.[35] Efforts by Balsiger and Sellier to secure access to the pages broke down over what Lynch explained was the owners' "desire for total anonymity, a disagreement on a dollar amount for using the papers, excessive contractual restrictions on their use, and numerous legal questions." The best that Balsiger and Sellier were able to do was to acquire—for $6,500—a 3,000-word transcript that implicated many prominent businessmen, various Union and Confederate political leaders, and, of course, Secretary Stanton. "Everything possible was done to authenticate the Booth diary transcripts," the authors assure us, "including performing voice analyses on numerous interviews [apparently with Lynch], using the psychological stress evaluator (PSE), used by many law enforcement agencies and the CIA." Based on the PSE results and their own critical evaluation of the contents of the transcript, they believed "the material to be authentic."[36]

One thing is certain: whoever the anonymous members of the Stanton family were who had possession of the missing pages, they were unknown to Ernest Lee Jahncke, Jr., and the secretary's other descendants. In 1961 when the Neff-Baker ciphers were first published, the New York *Times* noted that it was inconceivable that Stanton, who wanted to wipe out the last traces of slavery in the South, and Booth, who believed slavery to be one of God's greatest blessings, could have acted together against Lincoln. Stanton had his faults, the paper conceded, but he deserved to be remembered as a great secretary of war. "It is especially gratifying for me as a great-grandson of Edwin M. Stanton," Jahncke told the *Times*, "to express to you how much all his family appreciate the fair-mindedness of your . . . editorial."[37]

Balsiger and Sellier cannot give proof that the pages missing from Booth's diary have been found, but in the fortuitous discovery of the diary of a Representative in Congress from Indiana, George W. Julian, they seek to prove that the missing pages were once in Stanton's possession. As described in the *Lincoln Conspiracy*, Julian was as anxious as other Radicals to remove Lincoln from the presidency but was not a member of any of the four conspiracies the book claims existed against him. Summoned to the War Department on April 24, 1865, Julian found several Radicals greatly agitated over a little book that was being passed among them. "I asked what was happening," Julian wrote in his diary that night, as reported by Balsiger and Sellier, "and Stanton said, 'We have Booth's diary and he has recorded a lot in it.' . . . Stanton asked me if I wanted to read the diary and I told him that since I had not met the man [Booth] and was not mentioned in his diary, I was better off not reading it. . . . Stanton said, 'It concerns you, for we either stick together, or we will all go down the river together.' But I did not read it nor do I know what was in it."[38]

If authentic, this new document would indeed show that the pages from Booth's diary had once been in Stanton's office, and that would lend some credibility to Lynch's transcript. But once again Balsiger and Sellier do not present a document for the judgment of their readers, but only the transcript of one.

In 1926 Julian's daughter, Grace Julian Clarke, lent her father's diary to the writer Claude G. Bowers, who used it as a source for his popular revisionist book on Reconstruction, *The Tragic Era* (1929). "I fear it will not be up to your expectations," Mrs. Clarke had told Bowers. "And please remember that it was never meant for such critical examination and that my father meant to destroy it. I feel a little guilty in sending it forth, even for your friendly eye."[39] When Bowers returned the manuscript, Mrs. Clarke burned the parts relating to the Civil War and gave the rest to the Indiana State Library. But Bowers, so the story goes, had made a transcript, and it is this that Balsiger and Sellier use.

The alleged transcript of Julian's diary was not found among the Claude G. Bowers Papers at Indiana University but in the bulging archives of the indefatigable Neff. If the transcript is genuine, it means that Mrs. Clarke was completely blind to the importance of her father's diary and that Bowers, whose prejudices against the Radicals were extreme, deliberately closed his eyes to material that would have incriminated many of them in Lincoln's death, suppositions it is impossible to entertain. Further, by a happy circumstance, portions of Julian's diary for the Civil War years had been copied in the *Indiana Magazine of History* in 1915. The entry for April 24 contains no reference to Booth's diary and describes no meeting with Stanton. It is obvious, observed William C. Davis, successor to Fowler as editor of *Civil War Times Illustrated*, that "the fabricator of the more lurid version of the Julian diary didn't do his or her homework."[40]

Instances of failure to do homework on matters great and small abound in the "documents" upon which the *Lincoln Conspiracy* is based (to say nothing of the failure of Balsiger and Sellier to do their own homework in basic Lincoln biography and Civil War history). Among other examples, the documents purport to show that all of the four groups conspiring against Lincoln were working with Booth. All were known to Stanton and Baker—who were themselves involved with one or more of them—and Baker served as liaison man. (Eisenschiml had been right!) After the actor had bungled several attempts to kidnap Lincoln, some of the conspirators insisted that he be replaced. To serve as the new head of the operation, Stanton and Baker chose one James W. Boyd, a Confederate officer from Tennessee, who was then a prisoner in the Old Capitol Prison. Released by Stanton's order in February 1865, Boyd perfected a plan to seize Lincoln, Vice-President Andrew Johnson, and Secretary of State Seward, and take them aboard one of the Chaffey Co. ships for transportation to an island in Chesapeake Bay, where they would be put to death. Just as Boyd was about to execute this plan, Booth shot Lincoln on his own initiative, and in company with one Edward Henson—not David Herold—made good his escape over the route that had been left open for Boyd. Immediately Baker sent Boyd and Herold in pursuit; but they, fearing they would be betrayed by Baker, determined to escape themselves. But they were trapped in the shed at Garrett's farm, where Herold sur-rendered and Boyd, believed to be Booth, was killed.

Documents in the Andrew Potter Papers showed that Boyd very strongly resembled Booth and, of course, shared his ini-tials, which, by a remarkable coincidence he—like Booth—had tatooed on one of his hands. When it was discovered that the wrong man had been killed, Stanton—having already an-nounced the death of Booth—decided to cover up the mistake. He therefore passed Boyd off as Booth, suppressed Booth's diary (which, according to the *Lincoln Conspiracy*, had been recov-ered by the government a few days before from the campsite where the assassin had carelessly left it), and cut out the pages that incriminated himself and so many others.

There was, in fact, a Confederate officer from Tennessee named James W. Boyd who was released from the Old Capitol Prison by Stanton's orders in February 1865. But the papers supplied by Neff outlining the role he had played in the conspiracies against Lincoln and showing that he had been killed instead of Booth were easily proved to be fabrications. So carelessly were they prepared, they even had Boyd's middle name wrong; it was Ward, not William. In reality, Boyd did not look in the least like Booth and could not have been mistaken for him by the friends and acquaintances who identified the body. Boyd's oath of allegiance on file in the National Archives describes him as gray-haired, blue-eyed, six feet two inches tall, and forty-two years of age. A picture in the *Lincoln Conspiracy* identified as Boyd does look like Booth; but the man does not fit the official description of Boyd and was wearing a Union private's uniform. Boyd family documents and a Tennessee newspaper, furthermore, prove conclusively that Boyd died on January 1, 1866, seven months after he was supposed to have been shot at the Garrett farm.[41]

The Chaffey Co. papers that had so impressed Shelton because they showed the company operating out of 178 1/2 Water Street, New York, and thus provided a link between Baker (alias R. D. Watson) and John H. Surratt, were also easily exposed as hoaxes. No city directory for the years 1844-65 listed any firm with the Chaffey name, and there was no reference to such a company in the city tax records. During the Civil War the New York *Times* daily listed the ships entering and leaving the port. Not one of them was registered to Chaffey, despite the fact that the Chaffey papers indicated the company shipped regularly out of New York during the war. These and other discrepancies convinced editor Davis that the Chaffey Co. "never existed, and that the papers of this spectral firm are clumsy fakes."[42]

The relationship between Baker and Stanton recounted in the *Lincoln Conspiracy* is very close to that described in Neff's cipher messages—hardly surprising, since Neff was also the "discoverer" of the Baker papers, copies of which were utilized by Balsiger and Sellier. In their last chapter the authors confirm what the cipher messages and the testimony at the hearing on the codicil to Baker's will had hinted: Baker had died of arsenic poisoning by order of the War Department, the arsenic having been put in Baker's beer over a period of time by his own brother-in-law, Walter Pollock, who worked for the department. Balsiger and Sellier were able to arrive at this conclusion because among the Baker papers was a diary kept by Baker's wife, and in the diary was a lock of Baker's hair. "Using an atomic absorption spectrophotometer analysis," they tell us, apparently with straight faces, "Dr. Neff has been able to show that on each occasion Pollock brought beer to Col. Baker, the arsenic content in his hair shot up until finally . . . he died from the poisoning."[43]

The authors found "even more irrefutable" proof that Baker was killed by his wife's brother in a passage in Mrs. Baker's diary. "Something is amiss," the doomed man's wife was supposed to have written. "Today I was brushing Wally's coat, and his cigar case fell out of his pocket. It is leather bound, quite expensive, and it came open at the bottom. It had in it little bottles of powder and in them a little silver spoon. I wonder what it means? Wally is so mysterious." Awed by the utter conclusiveness of their evidence, Balsiger and Sellier state simply: "Mrs. Baker was describing white arsenic."[44]

Such absolute corroboration so conveniently at hand! One is reminded of the testimony of William Carter at the 1872 hearing that he had seen Lafayette Baker writing those cipher messages in the military journal. Another piece of fiction, of course. Neff had found no record of the hearing on the codicil to Baker's will in the Philadelphia City Hall because there had been no hearing. The document examined at the city hall by the editor of *Civil War Times* in 1961 had apparently been planted there for him to see; it promptly disappeared and has not been seen since. The hearing transcript published in the magazine had been taken from a typewritten copy of the spurious document, which Neff had certified to be true.[45]

But editors have been fooled before and since, and in 1977 *Civil War Times Illustrated* made partial amends for its earlier credulousness, for no one did more to discredit—indeed, to destroy—the *Lincoln Conspiracy*. Finally, in 1981 the magazine issued a formal refutation and repudiation of the twenty-year-old cipher article "and everything contained therein."[46] It acted not only to set the record straight, but also out of a conviction, as Davis put it, that if we lose touch with the truth of our past "there can be no sure grip on the future."[47] The hoaxers who fabricated evidence of one conspiracy to assassinate Lincoln and of another to cover up the first may have thought it great sport to rewrite their country's history, but in reality it was its future they were tinkering with.

The only grand conspiracy theory to have much of a following between the collapse of the government's Confederate grand conspiracy charge in the 1860s and the introduction of the War Department grand conspiracy charge in the late 1930s was the theory that the assassination had been brought about by the Roman Catholic Church. This supposition owed its existence not only to the residual influence of long centuries of Catholic-Protestant conflict, but to a feeling common in the United States in the Jacksonian era that the autocratic church of Rome represented a threat to the fledgling American democracy. Such fears were confirmed and strengthened by the Irish invasion of the 1850s, which increased alarmingly the influence of Catholicism and threatened to bring about major changes in the nature of American society. Among many staunch Unionists during the Civil War, the fact that the Irish were among the most conspicuous opponents of the war and of the policies adopted to win it—especially emancipation—contributed further to a sense that Catholics were no friends of the United States. Thus anti-Catholicism had both religious and patriotic—to say nothing of bigoted—connotations.

Since some Americans were in the habit of blaming whatever they did not like on the Catholics, it was natural that some of them should have blamed Catholics for Lincoln's assassination. The "Investigation and Trial Papers" contain warnings from well-meaning citizens about Romish conspiracies against the government and institutions of the United States and about the danger of more assassinations.[48] The newspaperman George Alfred Townsend contributed to such fears by reporting early in May 1865 that all the conspirators awaiting trial were Catholics.[49] He was wrong, but the error circulated as a fact; only the Surratts and Mudd were Catholics. Later it was stated that Booth himself had been a "Protestant pervert to Catholicism."[50]

When it was discovered that after the assassination John H. Surratt had been hidden for several months by Catholic priests in Canada and that at the time of his arrest he was serving in the Papal guards at the Vatican, many anti-Catholic Americans saw a direct link between Rome and Ford's Theater.

But it was not until 1886, when Charles Chiniquy published his *Fifty Years in the Church of Rome*, that the idea of the assassination as a Catholic grand conspiracy received systematic development. Deeply moved in 1865 by Lincoln's death, Chiniquy prayed for the time and strength to demonstrate to the world what he said he knew to be truth, "that that horrible crime was the work of Popery." Twenty years later he announced that

"I come fearlessly, today, before the American people, to say and prove that the President, Abraham Lincoln, was assassinated by the priests and the Jesuits of Rome."[51]

As a French-Canadian priest, Father Chiniquy in 1851 had led a group of his parishioners to Illinois, where they founded the village of St. Anne's, near Kankakee, fifty miles south of Chicago. Feeling inadequately supported by the Church hierarchy, Chiniquy began to waver in his faith, quarreled bitterly with his bishop, and in the mid-1850s was the defendant in a suit for slander brought by one of the bishop's friends. To defend him, Chiniquy engaged the services of the prominent Illinois attorney, Abraham Lincoln. As he preferred to do in such cases, Lincoln arranged a compromise settlement out of court, and the jury was dismissed. Chiniquy professed to believe, however, that he had been vindicated, and therefore that Lincoln had humiliated the Catholic Church and won its everlasting enmity. He even thought he could read Lincoln's sentence of death in the eyes of some Jesuits present in the courtroom at the time the case was thrown out. In 1860 Chiniquy left the Roman Catholic Church (if he had not already been defrocked), and with his followers affiliated with the Church of Christ.[52]

Chiniquy claimed to have continued his friendship with Lincoln, visiting him three times in the White House. The first time was in August 1861, when he warned the president of a Catholic assassination conspiracy. During the presidential election campaign of 1860, the Democratic press, which, according to Chiniquy, "was then, as it is still now, almost entirely under the control of the Roman Catholics," had not only denounced and ridiculed Lincoln but also had reported that he had been born a Roman Catholic but had left the church. "Let me tell you that I wept as a child when I read that story for the first time," Chiniquy says he told Lincoln. "Do not forget that in the Church of Rome an apostate is an outcast, who has no place in society, and who has no right to live."[53] If Chiniquy wept when he read the story that Lincoln had been born a Catholic, Lincoln did not. "I laughed at that," Chiniquy quotes the president as having said, "for it is a lie. Thanks be to God, I have never been a Roman Catholic."[54]

On his second visit, in June 1862, Chiniquy reports he found Lincoln so busy he stayed only long enough to shake his hand.[55]

The third alleged visit occurred two years later, when Chiniquy says he joined the president and his wife on a tour of some of the Washington hospitals. By this time, Chiniquy discovered, Lincoln was fully aware of the peril from Rome; indeed, he even held Catholicism responsible for the war. "This war would never have been possible," Lincoln is said to have exclaimed, "without the sinister influence of the Jesuits. We owe it to Popery that we now see our land reddened with the blood of her noblest sons."[56]

Chiniquy reports that back at the White House Lincoln asked him if he had seen the letter which Pope Pius IX had sent the previous December to the "Illustrious and Hon. Jefferson Davis, President of the Confederate States of America." Chiniquy said that he had, and that he had come to Washington to make sure Lincoln understood its significance. "That letter," he said to the president, "is a poisoned arrow thrown by the Pope at you personally; and it will be more than a miracle if it be not your irrevocable warrant of death." For, by addressing Davis as president of the Confederate States, the pope had in effect recognized the legitimacy of the Confederate government and that meant that in addition to being an apostate Lincoln was fighting a bloody war against the will of God.

Lincoln indicated to Chiniquy that he had understood the letter's meaning. Before they read the pope's letter, "the Roman Catholics could see that I was fighting against Jeff Davis and his Southern Confederacy," he explained. "But now they must believe that it is against Christ and His holy vicar, the Pope, that I am raising my sacrilegious hands." Assassination plots were being discovered almost daily, Lincoln added, and they all apparently originated with the Jesuits. He had come to believe that Catholics were such a threat to the nation that they could no longer be tolerated. "I am for liberty of conscience," he was quoted as having said. "But I cannot give liberty of conscience to the Pope and his followers."[57]

From Chiniquy's lengthy reports of his conversations with Lincoln, it is evident that, as far as Chiniquy was concerned, the two men were in complete agreement about the menace of Roman Catholicism.

Although Chiniquy's theory of the assassination was the climax of his autobiographical fulmination against the Church, he did not devote much space to it. Who lived in and visited the Surratt boardinghouse where the assassination was plotted, he asked, and then he answered his own question: "The most devoted Catholics in the city!" At the conspiracy trial the testimony given by priests themselves demonstrated that they visited the house frequently and that they used it as a kind of rendezvous. "What does the presence of so many priests in that house reveal to the world? No man of common sense, who knows anything about the priests of Rome, can entertain any doubt that, not only did they know all that was going on inside those walls, but that they were the advisers, the counsellors, the very soul of that infernal plot. . . . Everyone of those priests was a rabid rebel in heart."

Chiniquy was convinced that

Booth was nothing but the tool of the Jesuits. It was Rome who directed his arm, after corrupting his heart and damning his soul. . . . Who does not see the lessons given by the Jesuits to Booth, in their daily intercourse in Mary Surratt's house, when he reads those lines written by Booth [in his diary] a few hours before his death: 'I can never repent, God made me the instrument of His punishment!' Compare these words with the doctrines and principles taught by the councils, the decrees of the Pope, and the laws of the Holy Inquisition . . . and you will find that the sentiments and belief of Booth flow from those principles as the river flows from its source. . . . There is not the least doubt that the priests had perfectly succeeded in persuading Mary Surratt and Booth that the killing of Lincoln was a most holy and deserving work, for which God had an eternal reward in store. There is a fact to which the American people have not yet given sufficient attention. It is that, without a single exception, the conspirators were Roman Catholics.[58]

In case there were still doubters after five hundred of such pages, Chiniquy presents what he calls conclusive proof of "the complicity of the priests of Rome in the murder of the martyred President." It was the sworn affidavit of a Protestant clergyman that on the day of the assassination at about 6:00 P.M.—hours before the assassination—he was in the Catholic village of St. Joseph, Minnesota, and was told by a Catholic in front of witnesses that the priests in the local monastery were saying that Lincoln and Seward were dead. Where could the priests have heard such news? the clergyman had wondered at the time; the nearest railroad was forty miles away, the nearest telegraph eighty.[59]

Chiniquy had the explanation, no doubt the same as the clergyman's. The priests of St. Joseph often visited Washington, where they probably stayed at the Surratt house. There they were in daily communication with their brother priests.

There were no secrets among them, as there are no secrets among priests. They are the members of the same body, the branches of the same tree. The details of the murder, as the day selected for its commission, were as well known among the priests of St. Joseph as they were among those of Washington. . . . There is not a man of sound judgment who will have any doubt about that fact. The 14th of April, 1865, the priests of Rome knew and circulated [news of] the death of Lincoln four hours before its occurrence, in their Roman Catholic town of St. Joseph, Minnesota. But they could not circulate it without knowing it, and they could not know it without belonging to the band of conspirators who assassinated President Lincoln.[60]

Other writers immediately picked up Chiniquy's theme—and Chiniquy's material. One of the first to do so was Justin D. Fulton, a Baptist minister and prolific writer of anti-Catholic literature, whose *Washington in the Lap of Rome* (1888) summarized much of *Fifty Years in the Church of Rome*. Under the heading "Behind the Purple Curtain," the parts of the book dealing with Lincoln and the assassination were reprinted in the anti-Catholic magazine *Christian Heritage* in 1958, when John F. Kennedy was seeking to become the first Catholic President of the United States. "The details of the tragedy of April 14, 1865," stated the magazine's editor, "have long since been suppressed by the Roman hierarchy." Fulton's work should be taken as "a warning to all Americans who see no danger in having a Roman Catholic in the White House. *Caveat elector*—let the voter beware!"[61]

Another early writer on the assassination as a Catholic grand conspiracy was Thomas M. Harris, the former member of the 1865 military commission. In his *The Assassination of Lincoln* (1892), Harris had given his wholehearted endorsement to the long-discredited Confederate grand conspiracy theory. He did point out that Surratt had been protected by Catholic priests in Canada and, after escaping with their help to Europe, had enlisted in the "army of the Pope." Such assistance was not likely to have been given Surratt for mere personal reasons, he felt sure, so it must have been out of sympathy for the purpose of Surratt's crime"—the subversion of our free institutions." Harris also said of Surratt's 1870 lecture about Booth's kidnapping scheme (which Harris believed had never existed) that it "bears throughout the marks of the 'fine Italian hand' of the Jesuit."[62] But he said nothing about a Catholic plot.

In 1897, inspired by Chiniquy and angered by the constantly reiterated charge that Mrs. Surratt had been hanged because she was a Catholic, Harris "lost his temper completely," his biographer tells us, and said exactly what he thought about *Rome's Responsibility for the Assassination of Abraham Lincoln*.[63] Actually he had little to say about Rome's responsibility, though he was impressed by the frequency of priestly visits to the Surratts, and by the fact that the assassination was being talked about in St. Joseph before it occurred. Like Chiniquy and Fulton, Harris saw the murder of Lincoln as but part of a larger conspiracy against America's free institutions. In fact, he believed Rome was plotting to take over the whole country; the church's encouragement of Catholics in Europe to emigrate to the United States and its stockpiling of weapons in the basements of parochial schools and churches were proof of it. The press and the army, Harris feared, were succumbing to Catholic influences, and the pope was "rapidly getting control of all the sources of power in the United States."[64] Harris's book was reprinted by Heritage Manor in 1960, the year of Kennedy's successful presidential campaign.

Equally rabid was Burke McCarty's *The Suppressed Truth about the Assassination of Abraham Lincoln* (1924). Like all other anti-Catholic writers on the subject, McCarty leaned heavily upon Chiniquy, but she added some imaginative details of her own: the chapter of the Knights of the Golden Circle—a forerunner of the copperhead organization, the Sons of Liberty—which Booth was said to have joined in Baltimore in 1860 was located across the street from a Catholic cathedral; its password was "Rome. Beware the Negroes"; Booth was chosen to be Lincoln's assassin while playing in the Roman Catholic city of New Orleans during the winter of 1863–64, and the presentation of the assassination as a simple conspiracy originating with Booth was conceived in Rome. McCarty held the church responsible not only for the murder of Lincoln, but for the deaths of presidents William Henry

Harrison and Zachary Taylor and for the attempted murder by poisoning of James Buchanan as well.[65] These were the same crimes for which fanatics of an earlier time had held the "Slave Power" responsible.[66] Guilt swings easily from one group to another when the case rests upon argumentation and inspiration instead of evidence.

Emmett McLoughlin's *An Inquiry into the Assassination of Abraham Lincoln* (1963) is distinguished from other books by the fact that it states the case for a Catholic grand conspiracy without stridency and excessive emotion. Like Chiniquy a former Catholic priest, McLoughlin praises Chiniquy and defends him (and himself) against the widely held supposition that because he had left the church he was necessarily biased and incapable of telling the truth about it. With justification he points out that in the 1950s the revelations of Communists who left the party were not greeted with a similar skepticism; on the contrary, what they said was generally accepted as the truth about Communism because "they had been there."[67]

McLoughlin believes that the church was "deliberately and culpably involved" in Lincoln's death because of its sympathy for slavery and southern civilization, and because of what he declares was its long acceptance of assassination as a means of eliminating dangerous heads of state. Lincoln was considered to be dangerous because he personified Protestantism. "The alignment of forces . . . is clear," writes McLoughlin. "On one side were dictatorship, slavery, secession, monarchy, European imperialism, Jesuit chicanery and a Church-dominated assault upon the Monroe Doctrine [in the French occupation of Mexico in the 1860s]. . . . On the other side were freedom, emancipation, Freemasonry, democracy, [and] Latin American struggle against foreign domination." It was Pope Pius IX versus Abraham Lincoln, and it led "inexorably to the tragic moment of assassination."[68]

The church, however, was not the only conspirator in the assassination. McLoughlin sees it acting as a silent partner of anti-Lincoln conspiracies in Richmond, Maryland, and Canada. It stayed in the background and observed the principle "What is likely to bring disfavor get others to do." Booth and his Confederate and Copperhead friends were manipulated into doing

Rome's dirty work,[69] but McLoughlin gives no hint about how this neat trick was accomplished.

Naturally McLoughlin ends his book with a warning and a call to action. "The Papacy is just as totalitarian in the nineteen sixties," he warns us, "as it was a century ago. . . . In 1865 a man was assassinated. In 1963 the free human mind is being assassinated."[70] In 1963 a Roman Catholic president was assassinated, and it may be that there will be no more books about Lincoln's assassination as a Catholic conspiracy. Anti-Catholicism is no longer the force it once was, and most Americans are too worldly wise to believe that the threat to their free institutions comes from Rome.

Of course, there never had been any evidence of the Catholic Church's complicity in the assassination, and none that Lincoln himself feared Catholicism. Professor Joseph George, Jr., has shown that in all probability Chiniquy never talked to Lincoln in the White House, and it is certain that there were no theological discussions.[71] The anti-Catholic sentiments Chiniquy put in Lincoln's mouth were only a propagandist's trick. To the editor of the Catholic magazine *Columbia,* Robert Todd Lincoln wrote that he knew of no anti-Catholic statement or writing of his father and reminded the editor that through the years his father's name had been "a peg on which to hang many things."[72]

The history of Lincoln's assassination is full of lunacies. One of the oldest and most persistent is that—David Herold's statements about the man in the barn with him notwithstanding—Booth was not killed at Garrett's farm that fiery early morning. Booth escaped. In later years a bewildering number of men at home and abroad confessed that they were Lincoln's assassin. One student of the assassination reported that he had collected data on seventeen different Booths and that he knew of someone who had information on twenty-two.[73] In 1936 the custodian of Lincoln's tomb in Springfield noted that five different Booth skulls were then being exhibited, each with its supporting affidavits, and for years a Booth mummy was an attraction at county fairs across the country, along with fat ladies and two-headed chickens.[74]

In the nineteenth century numerous women claimed to be

Booth's widow or his daughter, and in 1937 Izola Forrester revealed in *This One Mad Act,* an entertaining piece of fiction purporting to be *The Unknown Story of John Wilkes Booth and His Family,*[75] that she was his granddaughter. Her mother, Booth's daughter, was born just before the Civil War. (In the novel Booth escaped after killing Lincoln and fathered a son.) The author was so persuasive she fooled even Stanley Kimmel, historian of the Booth family.[76] Of course, there is no way to prove that Booth, who was so attractive to women, did not father a child—or dozens of them—before and during the war, and Forrester's mother could have been the daughter of one of them. But in *The Great American Myth* George S. Bryan points out so many errors and inconsistencies in her narrative and supporting "documents" that it is impossible to take her claim seriously.[77] Nevertheless, her descendants have taken it very seriously indeed; one of them, Eric Booth (born Eric Booth Miller) was in the 1980s pursuing a career on the stage as the great-great-great-grandson of John Wilkes Booth.[78]

The rumor that Booth escaped and that some other man's body was brought to Washington early on the morning of April 27, 1865, grew out of Stanton's determination that no respect be paid to the assassin's remains. At the secretary's order, Booth's body was unceremoniously buried in the dirt floor of a storeroom in the Old Penitentiary on the Washington Arsenal grounds, the same building in which the conspiracy trial would soon take place.[79] No announcement about the place of interment was made, and in the excitement of the times the silence seemed to imply mystery, and what could the mystery be but that it was somebody else, not Booth, who had been captured and killed? "There was nothing about the identity of Booth that entered your consideration in making the burial a secret?" Stanton was asked by a Congressional committee in 1867. "Nothing whatever," he replied. "It was done simply and solely for the purpose of preventing him from being made the subject of rebel rejoicing."[80]

There is perhaps an even more fundamental reason why the rumor of Booth's escape originated and why it has persisted. Since antiquity, Lloyd Lewis writes in *Myths After Lincoln,* "ordinary death was never felt . . . to be punishment enough for the various betrayers of great heroes. The Cains and Judases have been too monumental in their villainies to suffer man's conventional penalties. They must always wander on, tortured by remorse, shunned by the world, to wretched deathlessness."[81] So it has been for some Americans with Booth.

Booth's body was identified beyond any possibility of a mix-up at a coroner's inquest on April 27, 1865. It was identified again in February 1869, when it was exhumed for final burial in Baltimore.[82] Writers as hostile to each other's ideas as Bryan and Eisenschiml—both of whom studied the question carefully—agree: Booth did not escape.[83]

Another lunacy with devoted partisans is that Lincoln was done in by a conspiracy of international bankers, led by the Rothschilds, who objected to his protectionist policies and wanted him removed so they could establish their domination of the American economy.[84]

David Rankin Barbee, a revisionist writer who devoted much of his life to the study of the assassination, rejected Eisenschiml's thesis about Stanton, but believed nevertheless that other Radicals wanted Lincoln out of the way enough to kill him. "My own researches have led me to the conclusion," he wrote, "that Lincoln knew he was going to be assassinated, and that if Booth had not killed him some fanatic in the North, belonging to the group which wished to put the South under the heel of the Negro, would have done so. In fact, Lincoln told his son Robert, on the very day of his assassination, that Thad Stevens had that day threatened him with death if he tried to put through any pacific plan of Reconstruction."[85] Stevens's biographer, Fawn Brodie—a post-revisionist—finds it "inconceivable that Stevens would ever have made such a threat," for he had "an abiding respect for Lincoln" and would have recognized that a threat would have "ruined their political relationship as well as their somewhat arms-length social friendship. Stevens, after all, didn't even want death for Jefferson Davis." Besides, the last time Stevens saw Lincoln was late in March 1865, and on the day of the assassination the Radical leader was at his home in Lancaster, Pennsylvania.[86]

A hypnotist discovered in the early 1970s that a farm boy under her treatment was a reincarnation of Booth. Among the things she learned from him under deep hypnosis was that Booth had been paid by Copperheads to kill Lincoln, that he had escaped to Europe, married, and died in 1875. The hypnotist found a significant parallel between the eighteen pages missing from Booth's diary and the eighteen minutes erased from President Richard Nixon's famous tape.[87]

Booth was an innocent victim of circumstances, another assassination buff insists. The real assassin was Major Henry R. Rathbone, Lincoln's guest in the box at the theater. Nor was this individual's faith in Booth's innocence shaken by the manner of the actor's entrance into the box, by his jump to the stage, by his cry of "*Sic Semper Tyrannis!*," or by his flight from Washington. Such matters were easily explained: "Booth didn't sneak into that box, he went in with a pass. He was in there and just got scared and left. Wouldn't you? Naaaw, naaaw, he didn't say anything except 'get me out,' maybe. He didn't know any Latin. That was something made up by the Secretary of War."[88]

Absurd and amusing explanations of Lincoln's murder far outnumber (but do not out-influence) the dishonest and deceitful ones. But whether farcical or foul, or simply superficial and uninformed, most interpretations teach us more about their authors and about human nature than they do about why what happened at Ford's Theater happened.

A Few Last Words . . .

AMONG THE REASONS WHY the sensationalists, the charlatans, and the crackpots have been able to make such a big thing out of Abraham Lincoln's assassination is that the assassin never had his day in court, not even military court: he denied it to himself by refusing to be captured alive. Had he lived to answer questions and explain his motivations, much of the mystery of his murder conspiracy would have been dispelled, no matter whom he implicated or failed to implicate. Two other chances for him to explain away some of the mystery of his deed were frustrated, one by the cowardice of a friend, one by the implacable determination of an enemy that he be denied any opportunity to appeal for public sympathy.

Early in the afternoon of the Friday evening shooting, John Wilkes Booth wrote a two-page letter—"a long article," he later called it—to an editor of the Washington *National Intelligencer*, setting forth the reasons for "our proceedings." On his way to mail it about 3 P.M., he met a friend, John Mathews, who had a small part in the play being performed at Ford's Theater, and on an impulse gave the already-stamped envelope to him for delivery at the newspaper office the following morning. Perhaps he feared that the letter, left in the mail, would not reach its destination before Monday, and he was anxious that the world should not have to wait for an explanation of what he had done. That night, in a panic that he would be implicated in the assassination, Mathews tore open the envelope, read the letter through twice, and then burned it.[1]

For days in the pine thicket in southern Maryland where he had taken refuge with David Herold, Booth searched eagerly for his statement in the newspapers brought by Confederate agent

Thomas A. Jones. At last, on April 21, he wrote despairingly, "The little, the very little I left behind to clear my name, the Govmt will not allow to be printed. So ends all."[2]

But there was still one more way to take his case to the public. Twice while waiting in the thicket for a chance to cross the Potomac into Virginia, Booth opened the 1864 diary he carried in his pocket and used in 1865 for memoranda and wrote about the assassination in terms familiar to all who had lived through the Civil War. People on both sides, he began, had justified the sacrifice of human lives for the sake of what they believed; he had worked for six months to capture the author of his country's wrongs, but the cause was almost lost and "something decisive & great" had to be done; and Lincoln had been a greater tyrant than either of those whom Brutus and William Tell had been honored for killing. There is much that is personal as well as political in the second, April 21, passage, for by this time Booth was only too well aware that the assassination was being execrated as a foul crime, and he needed to reassure himself that he had acted as the decent man he believed himself to be. "I hoped for no gain," he wrote. "I knew no private wrong. I struck for my country and that alone."

Expecting to cross the river that night, Booth declared he was almost of a mind to return to Washington and clear his name, which he felt, "in a measure," he could do. He wanted to clear his name, but he had played too much Shakespeare to be able to cast himself in the role of prisoner mounting the gallows, and it is doubtful that he ever seriously considered returning to Washington. He finished writing by stating that he did not wish to shed any more blood, but "'I must fight the course' 'Tis all thats left me." Like Macbeth, he would go down fighting.[3]

The diary was delivered to Secretary of War Edwin M. Stanton on April 26 and not seen again for two years, when a bitter Lafayette C. Baker revealed its existence. It was Stanton, too, who ordered Booth's body secretly buried beneath the floor of the old penitentiary on the Washington arsenal grounds, where no Lincoln hater could pause to leave flowers or say a prayer. It was Stanton who closed Ford's Theater so that no one would be entertained at the site where Lincoln was shot, and it was he who saw to the building's purchase by the United States and its conversion to federal offices. It was Stanton who forbade the sale of Booth's picture in Washington.[4]

By the 1980s the "American Judas" whom Stanton so abhorred had emerged as something of a folk hero. As early as 1937, the owner of the old Booth home, Tudor Hall, outside Bel Air, Maryland, reported that visitors to the shrine regarded Booth as "a sacrifice to the Lost Cause"—just what he himself would have wished if he could not be known as saviour of the South. Conceding that much of the recent interest in Booth is rooted in the same morbid fascination that has for years turned solid citizens into fans of Jesse James and Billy the Kid, Professor Constance Head has nevertheless found that many people are attracted to Booth because he was a handsome and glamorous star of the stage, a Confederate patriot and spy, and a tremendously likable young man. Modern "Boothies," as they call themselves without embarrassment, are not aggressively anti-Lincoln; they have simply discovered that it is possible to like both Lincoln and the man who killed him.[5]

A similar revision in the popular reputation of Stanton may be in the offing; if so, it will be considerably more general. Instead of the frightened incompetent portrayed by David M. Dewitt or the traitor invented by Otto Eisenschiml, Stanton may yet receive public recognition as a superbly effective secretary of war and as Lincoln's true friend. Stanton made enemies easily, but, as John Hay told him at the end of the war, "No honest man has cause of quarrel with you." Hay believed that, as one of "the very few who stood by the side of him who has gone to his better reward," Stanton deserved and would receive a major share of credit for the Union victory.[6]

Mary Lincoln was in Germany in 1869 when she learned that "that noble & patriotic man" had died. "What a misfortune his death!" she exclaimed. "How nobly, he served his country. . . . The news, almost overwhelms me. My husband & himself, were very warmly attached to each other & we can well believe, that they are *now* together—I do."[7] On the same occasion, Robert Todd Lincoln wrote to Stanton's son: "I know it is useless to say anything . . . and yet when I recall the kindness of your father to me, when my father was lying dead and I felt utterly desperate, hardly able to realize the truth, I am as little able to keep my eyes from filling with tears as he was then."[8]

A generation after Lincoln's death, the newspaperman and former Civil War correspondent, John Russell Young, imagined Lincoln imploring his old friends to save him from the public's unrealistic and unrestrained idolatry. "Save me," Young thought Lincoln might say, "save me, friends, from this slush called history."[9] In his appreciation of Lincoln, Young became rather slushy himself, perhaps because, like other writers, he found it a way to compensate the president for having been murdered. But he was right, of course; Lincoln would not have enjoyed the extravagant and pseudoreligious praise being offered in his name by so many Americans. Possibly he would have been reminded of some anecdote by which to deflate the absurdities of such exaggerations. But one suspects that if he could learn of the slush written about the suggested involvement of his secretary of war in his own death he would simply become angry.

Notes

Notes to "By Way of Introduction . . ."

1. As quoted in Dorothy Meserve Kunhardt and Philip B. Kunhardt, Jr., *Twenty Days* (New York: Harper & Row, 1965), foreword, n.p.

2. As quoted in Neely, "The Lincoln Theme since Randall's Call: The Promises and Perils of Professionalism," *Papers of the Abraham Lincoln Association* (Springfield: Abraham Lincoln Association, 1979), 1: 41–42.

3. Nevins, *The War for the Union* (New York: Charles Scribner's Sons, 1979), 4: 319.

Notes to "They Hated Lincoln"

1. Quoted in Avery Craven, "Southern Attitudes toward Abraham Lincoln," *Papers in Illinois History, 1942* (Springfield: State Historical Society, 1944), 2.

2. *Messages and Papers of Jefferson Davis and the Confederacy, 1861–1865*, ed. James D. Richardson, new ed. (New York: Chelsea House–Robert Hector, 1966), 1: 32–33.

3. Wendell Phillips, *Speeches, Lectures, and Letters* (Boston: Lee & Shepard, 1892), 350.

4. *Messages and Papers of the Presidents*, comp. James D. Richardson (Washington: Bureau of National Literature and Art, 1907), 5: 636.

5. R. G. Horton, *A Youth's History of the Great Civil War* (New York: Van Evrie, Horton & Co., 1867), 72.

6. Scott to William H. Seward, Mar. 3, 1861, Abraham Lincoln Papers, Library of Congress, Washington, Scott's italics. Seward forwarded the letter to Lincoln on Mar. 4.

7. *The Conflict of Convictions. American Writers Report the Civil War*, ed. Jack Lindeman (Philadelphia: Chilton Book Co., 1968), 211.

8. Lucius E. Chittenden, *Invisible Siege. The Journal of . . .* (San

Diego: Americana Exchange Press, 1969), iii-iv, 32; William E. Doster, *Lincoln and Episodes of the Civil War* (New York: G. P. Putnam's Sons, 1915), 171.

9. John Russell Young, *Men and Memories,* ed. May D. Russell Young (New York: F. Tennyson Neely, 1901), 56; Constance McLaughlin Green, *Washington, Village and Capital, 1800–1878* (Princeton: Princeton University Press, 1962), 21.

10. Harold M. Hyman, *A More Perfect Union* (New York: Alfred A. Knopf, 1973), 85–86.

11. As quoted in Horace Greeley, *The American Conflict* (Hartford: O. D. Case & Co., 1866), 2: 497–98.

12. Ibid., 500.

13. *Union Pamphlets of the Civil War,* ed. Frank Freidel (Cambridge, Mass.: Belknap Press of Harvard University Press, 1967), 1: 535–37.

14. Edward Bates, *The Diary of . . . ,* in Howard K. Beale, ed., *Annual Report of the American Historical Association* (1930), 4 (Washington: Government Printing Office, 1933), 331.

15. *Diary,* ed. Allan Nevins and Milton Halsey Thomas (New York: Macmillan, 1952), 3: 204.

16. "Life Behind Confederate Lines in Virginia: The Correspondence of James D. Davidson," ed. Bruce S. Greenawalt, *Civil War History,* 16 (Sept. 1970), 214.

17. As quoted in Rufus Rockwell Wilson, *Lincoln Among His Friends* (Caldwell, Idaho: Caxton Printers, 1942), 243.

18. Maria Lydia Daly, *Diary of a Union Lady, 1861–1865*, ed. Harold Earl Hammond (New York: Funk & Wagnalls, 1962), 240.

19. "Are Handkerchiefs Superfluous? Lincoln Thought So," *Tyler's Quarterly Historical and Genealogical Magazine,* 15 (July 1933), 24–25, reprinting an article from *Blackwood's Magazine,* Dec. 1864.

20. *Memoirs of American Jews,* ed. Jacob Rader Marcus (Philadelphia: Jewish Publication Society, 1955–56), 2: 101.

21. Martin Abbott, "Southern Reaction to Lincoln's Assassination," *Abraham Lincoln Quarterly,* 7 (Sept. 1952), 319; Michael Davis, *The Image of Lincoln in the South* (Knoxville: University of Tennessee Press, 1971), 63–66.

22. *Union Pamphlets,* 2: 639.

23. William Dusinberre, *Civil War Issues in Philadelphia, 1856–1865* (Philadelphia: University of Pennsylvania Press, 1965), 157.

24. Joseph George, Jr., "'Abraham Africanus I': President Lincoln through the Eyes of a Copperhead Editor," *Civil War History,* 14 (Sept. 1968), 232–34.

25. As quoted in Robert S. Harper, *Lincoln and the Press* (New York: McGraw Hill, 1951), 151–52.

26. William Wilkins Glenn, *Between North and South. A Maryland Journalist Views the Civil War,* ed. Bayly Ellen Marks and Mark Norton Schatz (Rutherford: Fairleigh Dickinson University Press, 1976), 145.

27. Apr. 18, 1863. The clipping is in Papers Relating to Suspects in the Lincoln Assassination, Record Group 110, Records of the Provost Marshal General's Office (Civil War), Entry 79, National Archives, Washington.

28. John G. Nicolay and John Hay, *Abraham Lincoln. A History* (New York: Century Co., 1890), 8: 8, 13.

29. *Official Records of the Union and Confederate Navies* (Washington: Government Printing Office, 1894–1914), Series II, 3: 1035–36.

30. Ibid., 174.

31. Judah P. Benjamin to John Slidell, Apr. 30, 1864, ibid., 1105–6.

32. Robin W. Winks, *Canada and the United States. The Civil War Years* (Baltimore: Johns Hopkins University Press, 1960), 296–97, 306. See also Oscar A. Kinchen, *Confederate Operations in Canada and the North* (North Quincy, Mass.: Christopher Publishing House, 1970), ch. II.

33. *Collected Works,* ed. Roy P. Basler (New Brunswick: Rutgers University Press, 1953), 7: 451.

34. Edward McPherson, *The Political History of the United States of America during the Great Rebellion,* 3rd ed. (Washington: Solomons & Chapman, 1876), 301–3; Edward Chase Kirkland, *The Peacemakers of 1864* (New York: Macmillan, 1927), 79–84.

35. Lincoln, *Collected Works,* 7: 514; Neely, "The Lincoln Theme," 19–21. For all subjects relating to Lincoln, Mark E. Neely, Jr., *The Abraham Lincoln Encyclopedia* (New York: McGraw-Hill, 1982) is indispensable.

36. Daly, *Diary of a Union Lady,* 160.

37. Anna Ridgely, "A Girl in the Sixties: Excerpts from the Journal of . . . ," *Journal of the Illinois State Historical Society,* 22 (Oct. 1929), 437–38.

38. Harper, *Lincoln and the Press,* 151.

39. From a series of extracts from Chicago *Times* editorials, Papers Relating to Suspects, Record Group 110.

40. Frank L. Klement, "A Small-Town Editor Criticizes Lincoln: A Study in Editorial Abuse," *Lincoln Herald,* 54 (Summer 1952), 28–32.

41. *The Assassination of President Lincoln and the Trial of the Con-*

spirators, comp. Benn Pitman, facsimile ed. (New York: Funk & Wagnalls, 1954), 28. Hereafter cited as Pitman, *Trial of the Conspirators*.

42. Ibid., 54.

43. Stanley Kimmel, *The Mad Booths of Maryland*, 2nd ed. rev. and enlarged (New York: Dover Publications, 1969), 191–92.

44. Pitman, *Trial of the Conspirators*, 54.

45. John W. Headley, *Confederate Operations in Canada and New York* (New York: Neale Publishing Co., 1906), 402–5, 409–10.

46. Elbert J. Benton, *The Movement for Peace without Victory during the Civil War* (New York: Da Capo Press, 1972), 69–72. See also [Benjamin J. Sweet], "The Chicago Conspiracy," *Atlantic Monthly*, July 1865, 108–20, and James D. Horan, *Confederate Agent. A Discovery in History* (New York: Crown Publishers, 1954).

47. Felix G. Stidger, *Treason History of the Order of Sons of Liberty* (Chicago: Felix G. Stidger, 1903), 120; William Zornow, "Treason as a Campaign Issue in the Re-election of Lincoln," *Abraham Lincoln Quarterly*, 5 (June 1949), 360. For a balanced treatment of the Copperhead menace, see Mark E. Neely, Jr., "Treason in Indiana. A Review Essay," *Lincoln Lore*, Feb. and Mar. 1974.

48. *Official Records of the Union and Confederate Armies, the War of the Rebellion* (Washington: Government Printing Office, 1880–1901), Series II, 7: 543–49.

49. Dec. 3, 1864, ibid., Series I, 48, Pt. 2: 930–36.

50. Holcombe to Judah P. Benjamin, Nov. 16, 1864, *Official Records, Navies*, Series II, 3: 1238.

51. *Collected Works*, 4: 190.

52. Victor Searcher, *Lincoln's Journey to Greatness* (Philadelphia: Winston, 1960), 18, 59; John Mason Potter, *Thirteen Desperate Days* (New York: Obolensky, 1964), 32.

53. Harper, *Lincoln and the Press*, 90–91.

54. Oct. 20, 1860, Lincoln Papers.

55. J. G. Holland, *Life of Abraham Lincoln* (New York: Paperback Library, 1961), 210–14; Searcher, *Lincoln's Journey*, 40, 59–60.

56. *Collected Works*, 4: 240; Searcher, *Lincoln's Journey*, 250–60.

57. Feb. 25, 1861, p. 1, col. 1.

58. Rufus Rockwell Wilson, *Lincoln in Caricature* (New York: Horizon Press, 1953), 102–9; William Hanchett, *Irish. Charles G. Halpine in Civil War America* (Syracuse: Syracuse University Press, 1970), 33.

59. *Recollections of Abraham Lincoln*, ed. Dorothy Lamon Teillard (Washington: Teillard, 1895), 266.

60. Leonard Swett, "The Conspiracies of the Rebellion," *North American Review*, Feb. 1887, 187–88.

61. Hanchett, *Irish*, 56.

62. *Greeley on Lincoln*, ed. Joel Benton (New York: Baker & Taylor, 1893), 36–37.

63. William O. Stoddard, *Inside the White House in War Times* (New York: Charles L. Webster, 1890), 30–31.

64. Gideon Welles, "Recollections of Events Immediately Preceding and Following the Assassination and Death of Lincoln," n. d. (ca. 1870), manuscript, Welles Papers, Huntington Library, San Marino, Calif.

65. Lamon dated the incident Aug. 1862, *Recollections*, 268. John A. Logan, *The Great Conspiracy* (New York: A. R. Hart & Co., 1886), 646n–47n, dated it Aug. 1864.

66. Robert W. McBride, "Lincoln's Body Guard. The Union Light Guard of Ohio," *Indiana Historical Society Publications*, 5 (1911), 20–21; Lamon, *Recollections*, 270.

67. McBride, "Lincoln's Body Guard," 21–24.

68. William H. Crook, *Through Five Administrations*, comp. and ed. Margarita Spalding Gerry (New York: Harper & Brothers, 1910), 1–4.

69. *Abraham Lincoln*, 10: 286.

70. As quoted in Henry J. Raymond, *The Life and Public Services of Abraham Lincoln* (New York: Derby and Miller, 1865), 779.

71. Letters from the correspondent were published in the New York *Tribune* on Jan. 13, p. 1, col. 1; Jan. 25, p. 1, cols. 4–6; Mar. 19, p. 1, cols. 1–3; and Apr. 23, 1864, p. 1, cols. 1–3.

72. Ibid., Apr. 23, 1864, p. 1, col. 1.

73. Ibid., col. 2.

74. The correspondent's letters from Canada were published in ibid., Dec. 16, 1864, p. 1, cols. 4–5; Jan. 7, p. 1, cols. 1–2; Jan. 11, p. 1, cols. 1–3; and Jan. 20, 1865, p. 1, cols. 1–2. That information received from the correspondent was passed on to authorities in Washington is in ibid., June 6, 1865, p. 4, col. 2.

75. J. B. Jones, *A Rebel Clerk's Diary*, new and enlarged ed. (New York: Old Hickory Bookshop, 1935), 2: 24; Pitman, *Trial of the Conspirators*, 52, 375; Davis to C. J. Wright, May 11, 1876, in Carl Sandburg, *Lincoln Collector* (New York: Harcourt, Brace, 1949), 292–93.

76. Pitman, *Trial of the Conspirators*, 51; Otto Eisenschiml, "Did He, Too, Try to Kill Lincoln?" *Lincoln Herald*, 48 (June 1946), 30–33; Davis, *Lincoln Image in the South*, 98n.

77. Margaret Leech, *Reveille in Washington* (Garden City, N.Y.: Garden City Publishing Co., 1945), 53.

78. William W. Goldsborough, *The Maryland Line in the Confederate States Army* (Baltimore: Kelly, Piet & Co., 1869), 246–48. A

relationship between Johnson's plan and that of John Wilkes Booth is suggested in John C. Brennan, "General Bradley T. Johnson's Plan to Abduct President Lincoln," *Chronicles of St. Mary's*, 22 (Nov. 1974), 413–20, and ibid. (Dec. 1974), 421–25, and in *Surratt Society News*, Mar. 1981.

79. *A Confederate Spy* (New York: J. S. Ogilvie Publishing Co., 1892), 69–70, and *The Rebel Scout* (Washington: National Publishing Co., 1904), 119, 131. Conrad consistently misspelled Secretary Seddon's name, even in the letter he claimed to have received from him. See also John C. Brennan, "Confederate Spy—Captain Thomas Nelson Conrad," *Surratt Society News*, June/July 1977, and Percy E. Martin, "John 'Bull' Frizzell," ibid., Jan. 1980. Frizzell was one of the men recruited by Conrad.

80. A. K. McClure, "Jefferson Davis and Abraham Lincoln," *Confederate Veteran*, June 1908, 245–47.

81. *Official Records, Armies*, Series I, 14: 599.

82. Emory M. Thomas, "The Kilpatrick-Dahlgren Raid," *Civil War Times Illustrated*, 17 (Apr. 1978), 31.

83. Ibid.; Robert E. Lee, *The Wartime Papers of . . .*, ed. Clifford Dowdey and Louis H. Manarin (Boston: Little, Brown, 1961), 678.

84. Thomas, "Kilpatrick-Dahlgren Raid," 32. Meade's comment is quoted in Douglas Southall Freeman, *R. E. Lee. A Biography* (New York: Charles Scribner's Sons, 1935), 3: 219n.

Notes to "Sic Semper Tyrannis!"

1. Richmond *Dispatch*, Feb. 7, as reprinted in the New York *Times*, Feb. 10, 1865.

2. Leech, *Reveille*, 366–67; Stanley Kimmel, *Mr. Lincoln's Washington* (New York: Bramhall House, 1957), 164.

3. George S. Bryan, *The Great American Myth* (New York: Carrick & Evans, 1940), 121–22.

4. *Lincoln Day by Day*, ed.-in-chief Earl Schenck Miers (Washington: Lincoln Sesquicentennial Commission, 1960), 3: 322–25.

5. *Official Records, Armies*, Series I, 46, Pt. 3: 509.

6. *Lincoln Day by Day*, 3: 325; Crook, *Through Five Administrations*, 52–54. Carl Sandburg, *Abraham Lincoln. The War Years*, Sangamon ed. (New York: Charles Scribner's Sons, 1949), 4: 176–77.

7. *Abraham Lincoln*, 10: 218.

8. *The Unlocked Book. A Memoir of John Wilkes Booth . . .* (New York: G. P. Putnam's Sons, 1938), 139.

9. Paine reported the incident to Thomas T. Eckert. See "Impeachment of the President," *House Report 7*, 40 Cong., 1 Sess (1867), 674.

Herold spoke of Booth's reaction to his attorney, Frederick Stone, who gave the information to George Alfred Townsend. See Townsend's *Katy of Catoctin* (New York: Appleton, 1886), 490, 490n.

10. This theme is stressed by Michael Kauffman in "Booth, Republicanism and the Lincoln Assassination" (Special Scholars Thesis, University of Virginia, 1980).

11. Asia Booth Clarke, *The Elder and the Younger Booth* (Boston: James R. Osgood, 1882), 66–70, 113; Ella V. Mahoney, *Sketches of Tudor Hall and the Booth Family* (Bel Air, Md.: Franklin Printing Co., 1925), 11–12.

12. Clarke, *Unlocked Book*, 63, 71–72, 105.

13. Edwina Booth Grossmann, *Edwin Booth. Recollections by His Daughter* (New York: Century, 1894), 227–28.

14. Kimmel, *Mad Booths*, 157.

15. Ibid., 158; Eleanor Ruggles, *Prince of Players* (New York: W. W. Norton, 1953), 100.

16. Grossmann, *Edwin Booth*, 227–28.

17. A search of the Philadelphia newspapers of the period by Julie Babcock Duppstadt failed to turn up any reference to John Wilkes Booth.

18. The still unpublished manuscript is in the Walter Hampden Memorial Library, New York City.

19. Clarke, *Unlocked Book*, 114.

20. E.g., Mrs. Thomas Bailey Aldrich, *Crowding Memories* (Boston: Houghton Mifflin, 1920), 72.

21. Unidentified clipping dated Baltimore, Oct. 4, 1861, in Investigation and Trial Papers Relating to the Assassination of President Lincoln, Microcopy 599, Roll 3, frame 0123, National Archives.

22. The provost marshal's statement is in ibid., Roll 4, frame 0075.

23. Clarke, *Unlocked Book*, 114–17.

24. *House Report 104*, 39 Cong., 1 sess. (1866), 13.

25. Clarke, *Unlocked Book*, 119.

26. Affidavit of Junius Brutus Booth, May 6, 1865, in Investigation and Trial Papers, Roll 2, frames 2061–68.

27. Clarke, *Unlocked Book*, 124.

28. Ibid., 115.

29. Samuel Bland Arnold, *Defence and Prison Experiences of a Lincoln Conspirator* (Hattiesburg, Miss.: Book Farm, 1943), 38.

30. Pitman, *Trial of the Conspirators*, 45. See also Kimmel, *Mad Booths*, 350–51.

31. Bryan, *Great American Myth*, 111–12.

32. The hotel register showed his name for that date. Kimmel, *Mad Booths*, 188.

33. Kimmel is sure that he did see these men. See ibid., 188–89. A summary of the testimony about Booth in Canada given at the conspiracy trial is in Clara E. Laughlin, *The Death of Lincoln* (New York: Doubleday, 1909), 203–4.

34. Kimmel, *Mad Booths,* 189.

35. Ibid., 189–90.

36. Clarke, *Unlocked Book,* 125–26.

37. After being published in the newspapers by the reporter to whom Clarke had given it, the original copy of this letter was passed on to a federal marshal in Philadelphia. It then disappeared until 1977, when it was tracked down by James O. Hall, of McLean, Virginia, in the files of the Attorney General's office, the National Archives. The manner in which Booth signed the letter had not previously been known. Hall to the writer, July 22, 1977. See also *The Lincoln Log,* May/June 1977, 1–4.

38. Like the "To Whom It May Concern" letter, Booth's letter to his mother was discovered by James O. Hall in the files of the Attorney General's office, the National Archives. It was published for the first time in ibid., 2.

39. Investigation and Trial Papers, Roll 3, frame 0657, and Roll 5, frame 0084.

40. Statement of Samuel Cox, Jr., in Osborn H. Oldroyd, *The Assassination of Abraham Lincoln* (Washington: O. H. Oldroyd, 1901), 267–68; Bryan, *Great American Myth,* 117, 124.

41. Pitman, *Trial of the Conspirators,* 71; Kimmel, *Mad Booths,* 190–91.

42. *The Life of Dr. Samuel A. Mudd,* ed. Nettie Mudd (New York: Neale, 1906), 42–48; Pitman, *Trial of the Conspirators,* 114.

43. Conrad, *Confederate Spy,* 127–28.

44. A Confederate States document listing it as such was discovered in the National Archives by Erick F. Davis, of Baltimore, in 1979. I am indebted to John C. Brennan, of Laurel, Maryland, for a copy. See also David W. Gaddy, "The Surratt Tavern—A Confederate 'Safe House'?" *Surratt Society News,* Apr. 1979.

45. Laurie Verge, "Mrs. Surratt's Other Son," ibid., Aug. 1977; John H. Surratt, "Lecture on the Lincoln Conspiracy," *Lincoln Herald,* 51 (Dec. 1949), 24–25.

46. Pitman, *Trial of the Conspirators,* 123, 131–32.

47. An interesting account of one such agent is James O. Hall, "The Lady in the Veil," *Maryland Independent,* June 25 and July 2, 1975.

48. *House Report 7,* 40 Cong., 1 sess. (1867), 674; Washington *Daily Morning Chronicle,* July 8, 1865, p. 1, col. 2. In the records of the

conspiracy trial Paine's name was spelled "Payne," but he himself spelled it with an "i."

49. Arnold, *Defence of a Lincoln Conspirator,* 22; Surratt, "Lecture," 25.

50. Arnold, *Defence of a Lincoln Conspirator,* 23–24; Surratt, "Lecture," 26.

51. Surratt, "Lecture," 27.

52. Arnold, *Defence of a Lincoln Conspirator,* 24.

53. Pitman, *Trial of the Conspirators,* 223.

54. *Lincoln Day by Day,* 3: 321.

55. Investigation and Trial Papers, Roll 6, frame 0491.

56. *While Lincoln Lay Dying. A Facsimile Reproduction of the First Testimony Taken in Connection the Assassination of Abraham Lincoln as Recorded by Corporal James Tanner* (Philadelphia: Union League, 1968), n.p.

57. Francis Wilson, *John Wilkes Booth* (Boston: Houghton Mifflin, 1929), 81–84.

58. Investigation and Trial Papers, Roll 5, frame 0466.

59. Albert A. Woldman, *Lincoln and the Russians* (New York: Collier Books, 1961), 233.

60. Nicolay and Hay, *Abraham Lincoln,* 10: 200–201.

61. Alexandra Lee Levin, "The Canada Contact: Edwin Gray Lee," *Civil War Times Illustrated,* 18 (June 1979), 44.

62. Ibid.; Surratt, "Lecture," 28–29.

63. M. B. Ruggles, "Pursuit and Death of John Wilkes Booth," *Century Magazine,* 33 (Jan. 1890), 445.

64. New York *Herald,* Apr. 30, 1865, p. 1, col. 6.

65. Kimmel, *Mad Booths,* 216–19.

66. Crook, *Through Five Administrations,* 65.

67. John P. Usher, *President Lincoln's Cabinet* (Omaha: Nelson H. Loomis, 1925), 12.

68. New York *Times,* Apr. 19, 1865, p. 4, col. 4.

69. Lamon, *Recollections,* 274–75, 280–81.

70. Pitman, *Trial of the Conspirators,* 76.

71. Ibid., 123; Bryan, *Great American Myth,* 219.

72. Dr. Samuel R. Ward, "Present When Lincoln Was Shot," *Kessinger's Mid-West Review,* Apr. 1931, 23.

73. Booth made the declaration in his diary. See William Hanchett, "Booth's Diary," *Journal of the Illinois State Historical Society,* 72 (Feb. 1979), 40; Pitman, *Trial of the Conspirators,* 78.

74. Pitman, *Trial of the Conspirators,* 154–60; Charles F. Cooney, "Seward's Savior," *Lincoln Herald,* 75 (Fall 1973), 93–96.

75. Benjamin P. Thomas and Harold Hyman, *Stanton. The Life and Times of Lincoln's Secretary of War* (New York: Alfred A. Knopf, 1962), 396–97; Moorfield Storey, "Dickens, Stanton, Sumner, and Storey," *Atlantic Monthly,* Apr. 1930, 463–65.

76. Pitman, *Trial of the Conspirators,* 149, 152; Julia Dent Grant, *Personal Memoirs,* ed. John Y. Simon (New York: G. P. Putnam's Sons, 1975), 156–57; Jesse R. Grant, *In the Days of My Father* (New York: Harper & Bros., 1925), 40; Lamon, *Recollections,* 279.

77. Pitman, *Trial of the Conspirators,* 307; New York *Times,* Jan. 19, 1869, p. 8, col. 2; Doster, *Lincoln and Episodes of the Civil War,* 269.

78. Hanchett, "Booth's Diary," 39.

Notes to "The Assassination as a Confederate Grand Conspiracy"

1. Strong, *Diary,* 3: 582–83; Washington *Daily Morning Chronicle,* Apr. 15, 1865, p. 1, cols. 4–5; Helen Nicolay, *Lincoln's Secretary* (New York: Longmans, Green, 1949), 232–33; William H. DeMotte, "The Assassination of Abraham Lincoln," *Journal of the Illinois State Historical Society,* 20 (Oct. 1927); Henry L. Burnett, *Some Incidents in the Trial of President Lincoln's Assassins,* (New York: D. Appleton, 1891), 4.

2. As quoted in Thomas Reed Turner, *Beware the People Weeping. Public Opinion and the Assassination of Abraham Lincoln* (Baton Rouge: Louisiana State University Press, 1982), 46.

3. Bates, *Diary,* Apr. 15, 1865, 473.

4. David McDonald, "Hoosier Justice. The Journal of . . . ," ed. Donald O. Dewey, *Indiana Magazine of History,* 62 (1966), 199.

5. Sherman, *Memoirs* (New York: D. Appleton, 1875), 2: 349.

6. Charles H. Lynch, *The Civil War Diary, 1862–1865, of . . .* (Hartford: Privately printed, 1915), 148–49.

7. E.g., see Franklin Pierce in *The Lincoln Memorial. A Record of the Life, Assassination, and Obsequies of the Martyred President,* ed. John Gilmary Shea (New York: Bunce & Huntington, 1865), 86–87; Abott A. Abott, *The Assassination and Death of Abraham Lincoln* (New York: American News Co., 1865), 12; Ridgely, "A Girl in the Sixties," 433; *The Assassination and History of the Conspiracy* (New York: J. R. Hawley, 1865; New York: Hobbs, Dorman, 1965), 36.

8. As quoted in Harper, *Lincoln and the Press,* 351.

9. Gurowski, *Diary* (Boston, 1862–66), 3: 397.

10. Pitman, *Trial of the Conspirators,* 41, 236.

11. William E. Barton, *The Life of Abraham Lincoln* (Indianapolis: Bobbs, Merrill, 1925), 2: 479–80.

12. *Official Records, Armies,* Series I, 46, Pt. 3: 784–85.

13. Ibid., 45, Pt. 3: 847.

14. Mary Bernard Allen, "Joseph Holt, Judge Advocate General, 1862–1875" (Ph.D. diss., the University of Chicago, 1927), 47–52; Henry S. Foote, *Casket of Reminiscences* (Washington: Chronicle Publishing, 1874), 98–99; Nicolay and Hay, *Abraham Lincoln,* 2: 360–63; 3: 130–31, 147–49.

15. Allen, "Joseph Holt," 66–67; *Letter from the Hon. Joseph Holt, upon the Policy of the Government* . . . , 2nd ed. (Washington, 1861), 16; New York *Times,* Aug. 20, 1894, p. 1, col. 2.

16. Joseph Holt Papers, Box 2, Huntington Library, San Marino, Calif.

17. Hyman, *A More Perfect Union,* 190–91.

18. Allen, "Joseph Holt," 44–45, 90–92.

19. *Official Records, Armies,* Series I, 47, Pt. 3: 301.

20. New York *Times,* May 13, 1865, p. 4.

21. Stanton to Holt and Holt to Stanton, May 2, 1865, Andrew Johnson Papers, Library of Congress, Washington; Thomas and Hyman, *Stanton,* 424.

22. *Messages and Papers of the Presidents,* 6: 307–8.

23. Gideon Welles, *Diary of* . . . , ed. Howard K. Beale (New York: W. W. Norton, 1960), 2: 299–300.

24. Pitman, *Trial of the Conspirators,* 91; Bryan, *Great American Myth,* 262–63. The soldier, Willie Jett, was ostracized by many Virginians. Conrad, *Confederate Spy,* 109.

25. The best account of the shooting and death of Booth is John K. Lattimer, *Kennedy and Lincoln. Medical and Ballistic Comparisons of Their Assassinations* (New York: Harcourt Brace Jovanovich, 1980), 60–87; Pitman, *Trial of the Conspirators,* 92–93.

26. New York *Times,* Apr. 30, 1865, p. 1, col. 6, May 2, 1865, p. 1, col. 4.

27. Mike Kauffman, "Fort Lesley McNair and the Lincoln Conspirators," *Lincoln Herald,* 80 (Winter 1978), 176–81.

28. Pitman, *Trial of the Conspirators,* 18–21.

29. Sketches of the lives of these attorneys are carried in the standard biographical references. See also Doster, *Lincoln and Episodes of the Civil War,* 255–82.

30. Pitman, *Trial of the Conspirators,* 21–22; David Miller Dewitt, *The Assassination of Abraham Lincoln, and Its Expiation* (New York: Macmillan, 1909), 106–10.

31. Thomas Ewing III to David Rankin Barbee, Feb. 5, 1934, Thomas

Ewing Papers, Columbia University, New York City; Doster, *Lincoln and Episodes of the Civil War*, 264.

32. Ibid., 259.

33. Otto Eisenschiml, *In the Shadow of Lincoln's Death* (New York: Wilfred Funk, 1940), 305.

34. *Abraham Lincoln*, 10: 312n.

35. *Lincoln and Episodes of the Civil War*, 265–67.

36. June 26, 1865, Lew Wallace Papers, William Henry Smith Memorial Library, Indiana Historical Society, Indianapolis.

37. Doster, *Lincoln and Episodes of the Civil War*, 281.

38. Hamilton Gay Howard, *Civil War Echoes* (Washington: Howard Publishing, 1907), 199–200.

39. On the eve of his execution, Herold also spoke of a plan to capture Lincoln in the theater. Washington *Daily Morning Chronicle*, July 8, 1865, p. 1, col. 3.

40. Pitman, *Trial of the Conspirators*, 390.

41. Ibid., 44–45.

42. Ibid., 382.

43. Ibid., 247–49.

44. Investigation and Trial Papers, Roll 16, frames 0356–64.

45. Pitman, *Trial of the Conspirators*, 250.

46. July 7, 1865, p. 2, cols. 1–2.

47. Doster, *Lincoln and Episodes of the Civil War*, 276. Doster's statement that upon leaving the arsenal he encountered a large crowd shouting that Mrs. Surratt had been judicially murdered—ibid., 277—is not to be taken literally.

48. Pitman, *Trial of the Conspirators*, 380.

49. Ibid., 35–37.

50. David Homer Bates, *Lincoln in the Telegraph Office* (New York: Century Co., 1907), 78–83.

51. Pitman, *Trial of the Conspirators*, 24–25.

52. Documents in the Holt Papers (Huntington Library) reveal that Conover forged Confederate Secretary of War James A. Seddon's signature to letters written on department stationery and other printed forms identifying himself as a secret agent entitled to draw upon the funds entrusted to Thompson. It is probable that these documents fooled some of the Confederate representatives in Canada and that they later helped to convince Holt that Conover did indeed have inside knowledge of a Confederate grand conspiracy against Lincoln. I am indebted to James O. Hall of McLean, Virginia, for photographic evidence that the documents were forgeries. Note, too, that although Conover's first name is spelled "Sanford" in the trial records, he himself spelled it with a "d."

53. Pitman, *Trial of the Conspirators*, 28–29.

54. New York *Tribune*, June 6, 1865, p. 4, col. 2.

55. Ibid., p. 4, col. 4. See also ibid., p. 4, col. 1.

56. Pitman, *Trial of the Conspirators*, 37–41.

57. Ibid., 51–57.

58. Investigation and Trial Papers, Roll 7, frames 0120–31.

59. Stuart Robinson, *Infamous Perjuries of the 'Bureau of Military Justice,' Exposed* (Toronto, 1865), 9, and passim; W. W. Cleary, "The Attempt to Fasten the Assassination of President Lincoln on President Davis and Other Innocent Parties," *Southern Historical Society Papers*, 9 (July and Aug. 1881), 313–25; *Testimony of Sandford Conover, Dr. J. B. Merritt, and Richard Montgomery, before Military Court at Washington* . . . (Toronto: Lovell & Gibson, 1865), 1–65.

60. *Official Records, Armies*, Series II, 8: 931–34.

61. Dec. 15, 1865, Holt Papers (Huntington Library).

62. *Official Records, Armies*, Series II, 8: 934–45.

63. Welles, *Diary*, 2: 339.

64. Varina Howell Davis, *Jefferson Davis, a Memoir* (New York: Belford Co., 1890), 2: 780–82.

65. *Official Records, Armies*, Series I, Vol. 49, Pt. 2: 1116; *House Report 33*, 39 Cong., 2 sess. (1867), 3. Stanton's testimony was given Jan. 10, 1867.

66. Virginia Clay-Clopton, *A Belle of the Fifties* (New York: Da Capo Press, 1969), 313–14.

67. Ibid., 321–25.

68. *Official Records, Armies*, Series II, 8: 812–14.

69. Holt's report dated Dec. 6, 1865, with a postscript dated Jan. 18, 1866, is in ibid., 855–61; Holt to Stanton, Mar. 20, 1866, ibid., 890–92; Clay-Clopton, *Belle of the Fifties*, 374.

70. Fawn Brodie, *Thaddeus Stevens, Scourge of the South* (New York: W. W. Norton, 1959), 214.

71. *Official Records, Armies*, Series II, 8: 844–45. See also Hanchett, *Irish*, 143–48.

72. *House Executive Document 9*, 39 Cong., 2 sess. (1866), 3–7.

73. Jan. 18, 1866. *Official Records, Armies*, Series II, 8: 847–55.

74. *Messages and Papers of the Presidents*, 6: 378.

75. *Congressional Globe*, 39 Cong., 1 sess., 1854–55.

76. *Official Records, Armies*, Series II, 8: 942.

77. Davis, *Jefferson Davis*, 2: 469–70.

78. *Official Records, Armies*, Series II, 8: 921–23.

79. Ibid., 943. Holt's deposition, June 18, 1866, is in Joseph Holt Papers, Scrapbook 93, p. 173, Library of Congress.

80. *House Report 104*, 39 Cong., 1 sess. (1866), 1–29.

81. Ibid., 30–41.

82. New York *Herald*, Aug. 12, 1866, p. 5, cols. 1–2, and Aug. 24, 1866, p. 2, cols. 3–4.

83. *Vindication of Judge Advocate General Holt, from the Foul Slanders of Traitors*, 2nd ed. (Washington, 1866), originally published in Washington *Daily Morning Chronicle*, Sept. 3, 1866.

84. Welles, *Diary*, 2: 610, 604, 616; Orville Hickman Browning, *Diary*, ed. James G. Randall (Springfield: Illinois State Historical Library, 1933), 2: 95, 96.

85. Sept. 11, 1866, *Official Records, Armies*, Series II, 8: 964–65.

86. Ibid., 973–74, 978–80.

87. Ibid., 973–74. In 1881 Cleary and in 1883 Thompson wrote articles stating that the perjury and suborning of perjury for which Conover was tried and convicted took place at the 1865 conspiracy trial, instead of before the Judiciary Committee in 1866. Holt attempted to set the record straight in *Reply of J. Holt to Certain Calumnies of Jacob Thompson* (Washington, 1883), a copy of which is in the Holt Papers (Huntington Library). However, the misrepresentations of Cleary and Thompson are often accepted as truth. See, e.g., Seymour J. Frank, "The Conspiracy to Implicate the Confederate Leaders in Lincoln's Assassination," *Mississippi Valley Historical Review*, 40 (Mar. 1954), 639–40.

88. *Official Records, Armies*, Series II, 8: 976–78.

89. The fullest treatment of this subject is Roy Franklin Nichols, "United States vs. Jefferson Davis, 1865-1869," *American Historical Review*, 31 (Jan. 1926), 266–84.

90. Pitman, *Trial of the Conspirators*, 70.

91. London *Times*, Apr. 28, 1865, p. 9, cols. 4–5.

92. Tucker, "Address," ed. James Harvey Young (Atlanta: Emory University, 1948), 15–21.

93. Justin G. Turner and Linda Levitt Turner, *Mary Todd Lincoln. Her Life and Letters* (New York: Alfred A. Knopf, 1972), 345.

94. *House Report 7*, 40 Cong., 1 sess. (1867), 2–5, 29–32, 458–62.

95. Ibid., 111. Stanton and Holt had already investigated Baker's charge and concluded that it was false. Ibid., 29, 282.

96. Mar. 26, 1867, *Congressional Globe*, 40 Cong., 1 sess., 363.

97. Hanchett, "Booth's Diary," 42.

98. Mar. 26, 1867, *Congressional Globe*, 40 Cong., 1 sess., 363.

99. *Butler's Book* (Boston: A. M. Thayer, 1892), 930. See also Hans Louis Trefousse, "Belated Revelations of the Assassination Committee," *Lincoln Herald*, 58 (Spring and Summer 1956), 13–16.

100. Howard, *Civil War Echoes*, 104–7; W. H. Taylor, "A New Story of the Assassination of Lincoln," *Leslie's Weekly*, Mar. 26, 1908, 302.

101. Hanchett, "Booth's Diary," 43–44.

102. Mar. 26, 1867, *Congressional Globe*, 40 Cong., 1 sess., 364.

103. *House Report 33*, 39 Cong., 2 sess. (1867); New York *Times*, May 28, 1867, p. 2, cols. 1–2.

104. See especially *Trial of John H. Surratt* (Washington: French & Richardson, 1867), 1202–3.

105. Ibid., 1248–49.

106. New York *Tribune*, Aug. 5, 1867, p. 8, col. 1.

107. New York *Times*, Aug. 6, 1867, p. 5, col. 1.

108. *Trial of John H. Surratt*, 1379.

109. Washington *Star*, Feb. 8, 13, 15, 1869. The return of the prisoners was noted by the Baltimore *Sun* but ignored by most other papers. See *Surratt Society News*, May 1979.

Notes to "The Assassination as a Simple Conspiracy"

1. Townsend, *The Life, Crime, and Capture of John Wilkes Booth* (New York: Dick & Fitzhugh, 1865), 40–41.

2. Abott, *Assassination and Death*, 12.

3. Utica (New York) *Daily Observer*, May 4, 1865, clipping in Ewing Papers.

4. Richard Taylor, *Destruction and Reconstruction. Personal Experiences of the Late War* (New York: Longmans, Green, 1955), 299; Bryan, *Great American Myth*, 388.

5. Raymond, *Life and Public Services*, 712–13.

6. Greeley, *American Conflict*, 2: 748–49.

7. E. D. Townsend, *Anecdotes of the Civil War* (New York: D. Appleton, 1884), 140–41, 275–78; Thomas and Hyman, *Stanton*, 638–39.

8. *Harper's Weekly*, 713, and Sept. 21, 1872, 733–34.

9. Ingersoll, *Works* (New York: Ingersoll Publishers, 1900), 9: 157–58.

10. D. X. Junkin, *The Life of Winfield Scott Hancock* (New York: D. Appleton, 1880), 272–77. Clampitt's letter is reproduced in Frederick E. Goodrich, *Life of Winfield Scott Hancock* (Boston: B. B. Russell, 1886), 217–30. See also John W. Clampitt, "The Trial of Mrs. Surratt," *North American Review*, 131 (Sept. 1880), 237–38.

11. In hundreds of Republican campaign documents, Herbert J. Clancy in his *The Presidential Election of 1880* (Chicago: Loyola University Press, 1958), 171–72, found no references to Mrs. Surratt. Glenn Tucker does not treat the issue as significant in *Hancock the Superb* (Indianapolis: Bobbs, Merrill, 1960), 300–305.

12. As quoted in Lately Thomas, *The First President Johnson* (New York: William Morrow, 1968), 625.

13. Joseph Holt, *Vindication* (Washington: Chronicle Publishing Co., 1873), 1–13. The article first appeared in the Washington *Daily Morning Chronicle*, Aug. 27, 1873.

14. Aug. 29, 1873, Holt Papers (Huntington Library). Hay published an article sustaining Holt in the New York *Tribune*, Aug. 27, 1873, p. 4, cols. 2–3.

15. Washington *Daily Morning Chronicle*, Nov. 12, 1873.

16. "Miscellaneous Pieces," Box 8, Holt Papers (Huntington Library).

17. Quoted in Joseph Holt, "New Facts about Mrs. Surratt," *North American Review*, 147 (July 1888), 92.

18. Typed copy of letter from Holt to John A. Bingham, dated 1888, John A. Bingham Papers, Ohio Historical Society, Columbus.

19. Speed was a reluctant correspondent and called an abrupt end to the exchange of letters. Holt, "New Facts," 92–93.

20. John Speed, "The Assassins of Lincoln," *North American Review*, 147 (Sept. 1888), 314–15.

21. New York *Times*, Aug. 20, 1894, p. 1, col. 3; Allen C. Clark, *Abraham Lincoln in the National Capital* (Washington: W. F. Roberts, 1925), 149–50; James Schouler, *History of the United States*, rev. ed. (New York: Dodd, Mead, 1894–1913), 7: 26.

22. Nicolay and Hay, *Abraham Lincoln*, 10: 288–93.

23. Ibid., 312–13.

24. Harris, *Assassination of Lincoln* (Boston: American Citizen Co., 1892), 180–81.

25. Ibid., 176.

26. Ibid., 175. Harris was perhaps influenced by a letter from Bingham, Mar. 12, 1892, which made this point at some length, Thomas M. Harris Papers, West Virginia University, Morgantown.

27. Harris, *Assassination*, 114.

28. Ibid., 282.

29. David Miller Dewitt, *The Judicial Murder of Mary E. Surratt* (Baltimore: John Murphy, 1895), 4–6. In this discussion subsequent page numbers appear in the text.

30. Thomas and Hyman, *Stanton*, 431–32. Thomas and Hyman erroneously state that Stanton backed Holt's request for a court of inquiry on this issue. He did so on another issue. See the discussion above, 80–81.

31. Dewitt, *Assassination of Lincoln*, 131–32.

32. Thomas Ewing, Jr., to David Rankin Barbee, Feb. 5, 1934, Ewing Papers.

33. William Burton Benham, *Life of Osborn H. Oldroyd* (Washington: O. H. Oldroyd, 1927), 1–31; *An Interview with Osborn H. Oldroyd* (New York: The Sun, 1908), 3–11; *Lincoln Lore*, Dec. 22, 1930.

34. Oldroyd, *Assassination*, vi, 130–31.

35. Townsend, "How Wilkes Booth Crossed the Potomac," *Century Magazine*, Apr. 1884, 822–32.

36. For interesting guides, see James O. Hall, *Notes on the John Wilkes Booth Escape Route* (Clinton, Md.: The Surratt Society, 1980), and John C. Brennan, *Pictorial Primer Having To Do with the Assassination of Abraham Lincoln and with the Assassin, John Wilkes Booth* (Laurel, Md.: Minuteman Press, 1979).

37. Laughlin, *Traveling Through Life* (Boston: Houghton Mifflin, 1934), 101–2.

38. Ibid., 103.

39. Crook, "Lincoln's Last Day," *Harper's Monthly,* Sept. 1907, 519–30; Laughlin, *Death of Lincoln*, 94–95.

40. Laughlin, *Death of Lincoln*, 288, and *Travelling Through Life*, 109–10.

41. Laughlin, *Death of Lincoln*, 178–80.

42. Stewart, *Reminiscences*, ed. George Rothwell Brown (New York: Neale Publishing Co., 1908).

43. Laughlin, *Death of Lincoln*, 114, 180–81.

44. Ibid., 190, 327–31. Laughlin cites Dewitt's *Judicial Murder* only once in passing and on a subject unrelated to the petition (182n).

45. Laughlin, *Death of Lincoln*, 331. Many writers confuse the testimony suborned by Conover before Holt's Bureau of Military Justice and the House Judiciary Committee in 1866 with the testimony he presented at the 1865 conspiracy trial.

46. Dewitt, *Assassination*, 25–26, 35–36.

47. Ibid., 56–57. Stanton could not have cabled news of the assassination to Europe, for, although the Atlantic cable operated briefly in 1858, it was not again in operation until 1866.

48. Ibid., 57–58.

49. Peck, "Dewitt's 'Assassination of Abraham Lincoln,'" *Bookman*, Apr. 1909, 192.

50. Lewis, *Myths After Lincoln* (New York: Readers Club, 1941), 49–50, 63, 105, 187. The book was originally published in 1929.

51. Ibid., 50, 53.

52. E.g., Otto Eisenschiml, *Why Was Lincoln Murdered?* (New York: Grosset & Dunlap, 1937), 420; Phillip Van Doren Stern, *The Man Who Killed Lincoln* (New York: Literary Guild, 1939), 171; James McKinley, *Assassination in America* (New York: Harper & Row, 1977), 19.

53. Lewis, *Myths After Lincoln*, 162–63.

54. Ibid., 162, 203.

55. "The Four Who Were Hanged," *Liberty Magazine*, Feb. 11, 1928, 16.

56. "This Is To Certify," ibid., Feb. 4, 1928, 14; Lewis, *Myths After Lincoln*, 232. The document has disappeared and is presumed lost. Louis J. Weichmann, *A True History of the Assassination of Abraham Lincoln*, ed. Floyd E. Risvold (New York: Alfred A. Knopf, 1975), editor's comment, 405.

57. Lewis, "This Is To Certify," 15.

58. Bryan, *Great American Myth*, xi.

Notes to "They Hated—and Loved—John Wilkes Booth"

1. Apr. 18, 1865, p. 2, col. 4; Apr. 28, 1865, p. 2, col. 1.

2. For early explanations of the assassination see *Our Martyr President, . . . Voices from the Pulpit of New York and Brooklyn* (New York: Tibbals & Whiting, 1865); *Sermons Preached in Boston* (Boston: J. E. Tilton, 1865); Chester Forrester Dunham, *The Attitude of the Northern Clergy toward the South* (Philadelphia: Porcupine Press, 1974), 172–77. For comments on Booth at the conspiracy trial, see Pitman, *Trial of the Conspirators*, 274, 304, 308–14.

3. *The Assassination and History of the Conspiracy*, 49–57. Poore is presumed to be one of the anonymous contributors to this book because part of the passage on Booth was repeated verbatim in Poore, *Perley's Reminiscences of Sixty Years* (Philadelphia: Hubbard Brothers, 1896), 2: 174–75.

4. Townsend, *Life, Crime, and Capture*, 19–27.

5. Ibid., 21; Clarke, *Unlocked Book*, 94–97, 133–34.

6. *Life, Crime, and Capture*, 42.

7. Ibid., 27.

8. Hylton, *The Praesidicide*, 2nd ed. (New York: Howard Challen, 1884).

9. Washington *Daily Morning Chronicle*, Apr. 24, 1865, p. 2, col. 2.

10. For "Parricide," see *Poems of American History*, ed. Burton Egbert Stevenson (Boston: Houghton Mifflin, 1922), 542–43; for "Pardon," ibid. (1970) 539; Laura E. Richards and Maud Howe Elliott, *Julia Ward Howe* (Boston: Houghton Mifflin, 1916), 1: 220–21.

11. Horton, *Youth's History*, 33, 46–47, 379.

12. June 1867, 479, and Aug. 1868, 320. See also George, "Abraham Africanus I."

13. Unidentified clipping, ms LI 4096, Francis Lieber Papers, Huntington Library, San Marino, Calif.

14. Dean, *Crimes of the Civil War* (Baltimore: Wm. T. Smithson, 1868), 39–40. On Dean, see Suzanne Beisel, "Henry Clay, 'Dirty,' Dean," *Annals of Iowa*, 36 (1963), 505–24.

15. *Crimes of the Civil War*, 170–71.

16. Marshall, *American Bastille*, 23rd ed. (Philadelphia: Thomas W. Hartley, 1877), xiv–xv. Marshall himself was arrested in 1862 for carrying information to the Rebels and spent two months in the Old Capitol Prison. *Official Records, Armies*, Series II, 2: 278.

17. Abbott, "Southern Reaction to Lincoln's Assassination," 126.

18. Stone, *Brockenburn. The Journal of . . .*, ed. John Q. Anderson (Baton Rouge: Louisiana State University Press, 1955, 1972), 333, 341.

19. Crozier, *Bloody Junto* (Little Rock: Woodruff & Blocher 1869), 13, 43.

20. Thomas A. Jones, *J. Wilkes Booth. An Account of His Sojourn in Southern Maryland* (Chicago: Laird & Lee, 1893), 7.

21. Wise, *The End of an Era* (Boston: Houghton, Mifflin, 1899), 454–55.

22. Paul H. Buck, *The Road to Reunion* (New York: Vintage Books, 1959), 57; Davis, *Image of Lincoln in the South*, 99–100, 122, 125; Charles L. C. Minor, *The Real Lincoln*, 4th ed., rev. and enlarged (Gastonia, N.C.: Atkins-Rankin, 1928).

23. Garrett, "A Chapter of Unwritten History," *Virginia Magazine of History and Biography*, 71 (Oct. 1963), 393.

24. Ibid., 398–99.

25. *Confederate Veteran*, Apr. 1913, 170; Clarke, *Unlocked Book*, 145–47.

26. James O. Hall, "'Pink' Parker's Tombstone," *Civil War Times Illustrated*, 18 (July 1979), 8–9.

27. John S. Goff, *Robert Todd Lincoln* (Norman: University of Oklahoma Press, 1969), 259.

28. Morse, *Abraham Lincoln* (Boston: Houghton Mifflin, 1893, 1921), 2: 347–48, 353.

29. Logan, *Great Conspiracy*, 643.

30. Schouler, *History of the United States*, 6: 632.

31. Nicolay and Hay, *Abraham Lincoln*, 10: 291, 297–98.

32. Oldroyd, *Assassination*, 94.

33. Dewitt, *Judicial Murder*, 92–93.

34. Dewitt, *Assassination*, 10, 40.

35. Townsend, "How Wilkes Booth Crossed the Potomac," 829–30.

36. Stern, *The Man Who Killed Lincoln*, 383.

37. Wilson, *John Wilkes Booth*, 234; unidentified clipping reprint-

ing story in Boston *Herald,* 1890, Louis A. Warren Lincoln Library and Museum, Fort Wayne, Ind.

38. Quoted in Wilson, *John Wilkes Booth,* 234.

39. Clara Morris, *Life on the Stage* (New York: McClure & Co., 1901), 107–8, and "Some Recollections of John Wilkes Booth," *McClure's Magazine,* Feb. 1901, 299–304.

40. Mrs. McKee Rankin (Kitty Blanchard), "The News of Lincoln's Death," *American Magazine* (Jan. 1909), 259–62.

41. Kimmel, *Mad Booths,* 399–400.

42. Emerson, "How Wilkes Booth's Friend Described His Crime," *Literary Digest,* Mar. 6, 1926, 58, 60.

43. Ellsler, *Stage Memories* (Cleveland: The Rowfant Club, 1950), 125.

44. Ferguson, *I Saw Booth Shoot Lincoln* (Austin, Tex.: Pemberton Press, 1969), 13. For further examples, see Richard J. S. Gutman and Kellie O. Gutman, *John Wilkes Booth Himself* (Dover, Mass.: Hired Hand Press, 1979), 13–17.

45. Clarke, *Unlocked Book,* 138.

46. *Collier's Magazine,* Feb. 15, 1908, n.p.

47. In "John Wilkes Booth in American Fiction," *Lincoln Herald,* 82 (Fall 1980), 455–62, Constance Head shows that in a majority of novels on the assassination published between 1865 and 1979 Booth was treated sympathetically as a well-intentioned tragic hero.

48. Laughlin, *Death of Lincoln,* 5.

49. Ibid., 6, 10–11.

50. Feb. 1909, 54.

51. *Death of Lincoln,* 151–53.

52. Wilson, *Booth,* 19.

53. Ibid., 35, 142–43, 308.

54. Lewis, *Myths After Lincoln,* 348, 353. In the following discussion page references are given in the text.

55. Sandburg, *Letters,* ed. Herbert Mitgang (New York: Harcourt, Brace & World, 1968), 369.

56. Sandburg, *Abraham Lincoln,* 6: 340–41.

57. Ibid., 317, 319.

58. Hertz, "At Ford's Theatre 75 Years Ago," *New York Times Magazine,* Apr. 14, 1940, 18.

59. *Twentieth Century Authors,* 1st Supplement, ed. Stanley J. Kurtz (New York: H. W. Wilson Co., 1955), 957.

60. Stern, *Man Who Killed Lincoln,* 381.

61. Ibid., 93, 95; Kimmel, *Mad Booths,* 63–65, 340–41.

62. *Man Who Killed Lincoln,* 95–96.

63. Ibid., 96–97.

64. Ibid., 96.

65. Wilson, "John Wilkes Booth: Father Murderer," *American Imago*, 1 (1940), 58–59.

66. Weissman, "Why Booth Killed Lincoln. A Psychoanalytic Study of a Historical Tragedy," *Psychoanalysis and the Social Studies*, 5 (1958), 100–101.

67. Ibid., 104–5.

68. Ibid., 102.

69. Ibid., 103. Booth made the comment about Edwin as Hamlet to some actors who had praised his own performance in the role, not to his brother Junius. Bryan, *Great American Myth*, 92–93.

70. Kempf, *Abraham Lincoln's Philosophy of Common Sense. An Analytical Biography* (New York: New York Academy of Sciences, 1965), 1372, 1372n.

71. Badeau, "Edwin Booth On and Off the Stage," *McClure's Magazine*, Aug. 1893, 257.

72. Winter, *Vagrant Memories* (New York: George H. Doran, 1915), 169.

73. Kimmel, *Mad Booths*, 66.

74. "IIis Schooldays, by a Classmate," in Clarke, *Unlocked Book*, 152.

75. (New York: Carleton, 1866). In 1882 an affectionate memoir of Edwin was added, and the book was republished in Boston as *The Elder and the Younger Booth*.

76. Clarke, *Unlocked Book*, 183.

77. Kimmel, *Mad Booths*, 168. Subsequent page references are given in the text.

78. Bryan, *Great American Myth*, 389.

79. *Trial of John H. Surratt*, 1: 407.

80. Arnold, *Defence of a Lincoln Conspirator*, 50.

81. Bryan, *Great American Myth*, 139–40.

82. Ibid., 96, 144, and chs. 5 and 6.

Notes to "Otto Eisenschiml's Grand Conspiracy"

1. Wilson, *History* (New York: Harper & Brothers, 1901–2), 4: 259–61.

2. Oberholtzer, *Abraham Lincoln* (Philadelphia: George W. Jacobs, 1904), 371; Masters, *Lincoln the Man* (New York: Dodd, Mead, 1931), 477.

3. Eisenschiml, *Why Was Lincoln Murdered?*, 379–80.

4. Otto Eisenschiml, *Without Fame. The Romance of a Profession*

(Chicago: Alliance Book Corp., 1942), 4–7; *Who's Who in America, 1963.*

5. *Without Fame,* 200–205, 211–12, 316–18.

6. Ibid., 318, 253–58.

7. Ibid., 224. *The Story of Shiloh* was published in Chicago by the Civil War Round Table.

8. *Why Was Lincoln Murdered?,* 434, 438; *Without Fame,* 253, 345; *O. E., Historian without an Armchair* (Indianapolis: Bobbs-Merrill, 1963), 212.

9. *Why Was Lincoln Murdered?,* 62–63; *Without Fame,* 342; *O. E., Historian,* 94–95.

10. *Without Fame,* 342.

11. *O. E., Historian,* 94–95.

12. *Without Fame,* 177–78.

13. *O. E., Historian,* 95, 112–15; *Without Fame,* 343–44.

14. *O. E., Historian,* 95–96.

15. Ibid., 97.

16. *Why Was Lincoln Murdered?,* 32–33. Subsequent page references are given in the text.

17. *O. E., Historian,* 164, and Otto Eisenschiml, "Addenda to Lincoln's Assassination," *Journal of the Illinois State Historical Society,* 43 (Autumn 1950), 219.

18. See also *Why Was Lincoln Murdered?,* 153–55.

19. *O. E., Historian,* 164.

20. *Shadow of Lincoln's Death,* 127.

21. "Addenda," 207–8.

22. The prison at Albany was federal, not state.

23. See also *Why Was Lincoln Murdered?,* 205–6.

24. Bates, *Lincoln in the Telegraph Office,* 365–68.

25. New York *Sun,* Apr. 27, 1913, as quoted in *Why Was Lincoln Murdered?,* 63.

26. Ibid., 20.

27. Bryan, *Great American Myth,* 221–22; James O. Hall, "The Mystery of Lincoln's Guard," *Surratt Society News,* May 1982.

28. Hall, "The Mystery of Lincoln's Guard."

29. *Why Was Lincoln Murdered?,* 102. Telegraph stations were opened at Port Tobacco and elsewhere in the vicinity by April 24 by tapping the line that ran from Washington to Point Lookout, Maryland. Bates, *Lincoln in the Telegraph Office,* 372–73; Townsend, *Life, Crime, and Capture,* 51–52; *Official Records, Armies,* Series I, 46, Pt. 3: 937, 964.

30. *Official Records, Armies,* Series I, 46, Pt. 3: 754.

31. *Why Was Lincoln Murdered?*, 94.

32. Ibid., 103–4.

33. Ibid., 133.

34. As quoted in ibid., 79. Shortly after the assassination, the superintendent of one of the commercial lines cut off civilian telegraph service in order to avoid interference with military efforts to capture the assassin. See Arthur F. Loux, "The Mystery of the Telegraph Interruption," *Lincoln Herald*, 81 (Winter 1979), 235–36.

35. Harper, *Lincoln and the Press*, 348.

36. Investigation and Trial Papers, Roll 15, frame 0252.

37. Baker in *Trial of John H. Surratt*, 317, and *House Report 7*, 40 Cong., 1 sess. (1867), 481, 487; Doherty, "Pursuit and Death of John Wilkes Booth," *Century Magazine*, Jan. 1890, 447.

38. Catalog No. 8 (1977), 51, George H. LaBarre Galleries, Hudson, N.H.

39. *Why Was Lincoln Murdered?*, 125–29.

40. Ibid., 128–29.

41. Ibid., 123–24, 128–29.

42. *Official Records, Armies*, Series I, 46, Pt. 3: 937, 964.

43. *Why Was Lincoln Murdered?*, 134–35. Nevertheless, O'Beirne ultimately received $2,000 in reward money.

44. Doherty, "Pursuit and Death," 449.

45. In *Kennedy and Lincoln*, 73–87, Lattimer shows convincingly that Booth could not have killed himself. There is some uncertainty as to whether the soldiers were actually under orders not to fire.

46. *Official Records, Armies*, Series I, 46, Pt. 1: 1317–22; Pitman, *Trial of the Conspirators*, 95; Doherty, "Pursuit and Death," 448–49.

47. The affidavit is reprinted in L. C. Baker, *History of the United States Secret Service* (Philadelphia: L. C. Baker, 1867), 532–38. For Baker, see *Trial of John H. Surratt*, 318–19, and *House Report 7*, 40 Cong., 1 sess. (1867), 485, 487.

48. *House Report 7*, 40 Cong., 1 sess. (1867), 327–28; Pitman, *Trial of the Conspirators*, 93; *Trial of John H. Surratt*, 307–8.

49. *House Report 7*, 40 Cong., 1 sess. (1867), 486.

50. Ibid., 479, 486, 488, 490; L. B. Baker, "An Eyewitness Account of the Death and Burial of J. Wilkes Booth," *Journal of the Illinois State Historical Society*, 39 (Dec. 1946), 425, 428.

51. George L. Porter, "The Tragedy of the Nation," typescript of lecture by the physician in charge of the health of the prisoners, n.d., accessioned Feb. 26, 1896, Library of Congress, Washington. The statements of other contemporaries indicate that the hoods were removed, but Eisenschiml denies that they were. *Why Was Lincoln Murdered?*, 178.

52. Ibid., 205.

53. Ibid., 436.

54. Eisenschiml's books made him a celebrity and, ironically, brought him some recognition as a chemist. In 1949 the Chicago chapter of the American Institute awarded him its Honor Scroll. *Chemical and Engineering News*, 27 (Oct. 24, 1929), 3118–19, 3165.

55. *Why Was Lincoln Murdered?*, 310.

56. Ibid., 357.

57. Ibid., 405, 411.

58. Ibid., 405.

59. Ibid., 411–14. Stanton was never a popular figure and cared nothing for popularity.

60. Ibid., 419.

61. *Without Fame*, 349.

62. See especially his *Reviewers Reviewed. A Challenge to Historical Critics* (Ann Arbor: William L. Clements Library, 1940), 7–22, and *O. E., Historian*, 120–22.

Notes to "Following the Leader"

1. *O. E., Historian*, 112–15.

2. Stern, *Man Who Killed Lincoln*, 389, 405.

3. Stern, "A Vivid Scene—and Then Mystery," *New York Times Magazine*, May 8, 1938, 18.

4. *Man Who Killed Lincoln*, 404.

5. Hanchett, "Booth's Diary," 40–42.

6. Eisenschiml to Stern, Jan. 7, 1939, Philip Van Doren Stern Papers, Library of Congress, Washington.

7. Hertz in *Nation*, Feb. 11, 1939, and "At Ford's Theatre," 18.

8. Hertz, *The Hidden Lincoln, from the Letters and Papers of William H. Herndon* (New York: Blue Ribbon Books, 1940), 15–17. Regarding the arrangement between Lincoln and Nicolay and Hay, S. L. Carson writes, "Evidence exists that these writers felt the hot breath of the President's son all during their research and that it affected their writing." "The Other Tragic Lincoln: Robert Todd," *Manuscripts*, 30 (Fall 1978), 252.

9. *The Hidden Lincoln*, 17–19.

10. *Man Who Killed Lincoln*, 406–7, and reprint ed. (New York: Dell Publishing Co.), 316. Stern also told the story in "A Vivid Scene," 18.

11. Mearns, *The Lincoln Papers* (Garden City, N.Y.: Doubleday, 1948), 1: 128.

12. Carson, "The Other Tragic Lincoln," 257.

13. Ibid., 257–58; Carson to the author, Nov. 20, 1979.

14. Nicolay and Hay, *Abraham Lincoln*, 5: 139–40.

15. Paris, July 26, 1865, Edwin M. Stanton Papers, Library of Congress.

16. "Lincoln and Son," *Saturday Evening Post*, Feb. 11, 1939, 23.

17. *The Lincoln Papers*, 1: 89–136. See also Carson, "The Other Tragic Lincoln," 255–59.

18. Eisenschiml, *O. E., Historian*, 189; *Reader's Digest*, Mar. 1939, 77, and Feb. 1960, 284.

19. Mearns, *The Lincoln Papers*, 1: 101, 121.

20. Bryan, *Great American Myth*, 190–91, 389.

21. Jim Bishop, *A Bishop's Confession* (Boston: Little, Brown, 1981), 263–66.

22. *The Day Lincoln Was Shot* (New York: Harper & Bros., 1955), 69. The first paperback edition was published in New York by Bantam in February 1956.

23. Ibid., 243–44.

24. Ibid., 245, 281.

25. Ibid., 234, 241.

26. Ibid., 273.

27. Angle, *A Shelf of Lincoln Books* (New Brunswick: Rutgers University Press, 1946), 124.

28. Roscoe, *The Web of Conspiracy; the Complete Story of the Men Who Murdered Lincoln* (Englewood Cliffs, N.J.: Prentice-Hall, 1959), 195.

29. Ibid., vii-ix, 27–30.

30. *O. E., Historian*, 111–13.

31. William G. Shepherd, "They Tried to Stop Booth," *Collier's Magazine*, Dec. 27, 1924, 12.

32. Roscoe, *Web of Conspiracy*, vii.

33. Ibid., 23–25, 513–14. The circumstance of Mrs. Lincoln's signature is explained in Turner and Turner, *Mary Todd Lincoln*, 211n.

34. Pitman, *Trial of the Conspirators*, 236.

35. "Lecture," 25, 29–30.

36. Laughlin, *Death of Lincoln*, 165–66.

37. Eisenschiml, *Why Was Lincoln Murdered?*, 45.

38. Ibid., 46.

39. D. H. L. Gleason, "Conspiracy against Lincoln," *Magazine of History*, 13 (Feb. 1911), 59–65.

40. Eisenschiml, *Why Was Lincoln Murdered?*, 46.

41. Kimmel, *Mad Booths*, 203; Bryan, *Great American Myth*, 121.

42. Bishop, *Day Lincoln Was Shot*, 80–82.

43. Roscoe, *Web of Conspiracy*, 16–17.

44. Thomas and Hyman, *Stanton*, 394.

45. Shelton, *Mask for Treason* (Harrisburg: Stackpole Books, 1965), 31, 39.

46. Kunhardt and Kunhardt, *Twenty Days*, 187, 188.

47. Fowler, *Album* (Harrisburg: Stackpole Books, 1965), 10.

48. Cottrell, *Anatomy* (London: Frederick Muller, 1966), 78.

49. Hyams, *Killing No Murder* (London: Panther Modern Society, 1970), 93–94.

50. McKinley, *Assassination*, 21, 33.

51. Lattimer, *Kennedy and Lincoln*, 8, 106.

52. Investigation and Trial Papers, Roll 4, frames 0373–80.

53. As quoted in Weichmann, *A True History*, 110.

54. Oldroyd, *Assassination of Abraham Lincoln*, 172.

55. Wilson, *John Wilkes Booth*, 172.

56. This is proved by letters from Weichmann to Oldroyd in the Osborn H. Oldroyd Papers, Manuscripts Department, Lilly Library, Indiana State University, Bloomington. I am indebted to John C. Brennan of Laurel, Maryland, for knowledge and copies of these letters.

57. Weichmann, *A True History*, 109.

58. Ibid., 178, 179–80, 218–19.

59. Eisenschiml, *Why Was Lincoln Murdered?*, 46.

60. Investigation and Trial Papers, Roll 7, frames 0399–402.

61. *Trial of John H. Surratt*, 814–15.

62. Ibid., 454–55.

63. McPhail's telegram was discovered in the archives of the Maryland Historical Society, Baltimore, by Percy E. Martin, who tells of it in his "Surprising Speed in the Identification of Two Baltimore Conspirators," *Surratt Society News*, Oct. 1978. An exchange of telegrams between McPhail and the War Department on April 16 and 17 regarding the arrests of Arnold and O'Laughlin is in *Official Records, Armies*, Series I, 46, Pt. 3: 806, 821.

64. *House Report 325*, 43 Cong., 1 sess. (1874), 1, and *House Report 742*, ibid. (1874), 3.

65. As quoted in Eisenschiml, *Why Was Lincoln Murdered?*, 7–8.

66. Ibid., 49.

67. Ibid., 45.

68. *Trial of John H. Surratt*, 399–400; Kimmel, *Mad Booths*, 203; Hall, "Saga of Sarah Slater," *Surratt Society News*, Feb. 1982.

69. McKinley, *Assassination*, 34.

70. Kimmel, *Mad Booths*, 357.

71. Shelton, *Mask for Treason*, 354.

72. Lattimer, *Kennedy and Lincoln*, 21.

Notes to "Reductio ad Absurdum"

1. Eisenschiml, *O. E., Historian,* 172.

2. Ibid., 174, and Eisenschiml, "Addenda," 94–96.

3. *O. E., Historian,* 177.

4. Eisenschiml, "Addenda," 92–93; *Dictionary of American Biography.*

5. Eisenschiml, "Addenda," 94–96.

6. *Official Records, Armies,* Series I, 46, Pt. 3: 723. On Apr. 5, 1865, Lincoln gave Campbell written instructions to the same effect. *Collected Works,* 8: 386–87.

7. Ibid., 149, 254–55.

8. Ibid., 389, 406–7.

9. Robert H. Fowler, "Was Stanton Behind Lincoln's Murder?" *Civil War Times,* Aug. 1961, 10.

10. The complete text of the transcript is in *ibid.,* 16–23.

11. Ibid., 13.

12. *Civil War Times,* Oct. 1961, 2.

13. Ibid., 2–3.

14. Neely, "The Lincoln Theme," 13–14.

15. *Civil War Times,* Oct. 1961, 3, 5.

16. Neely, "The Lincoln Theme," 43.

17. Shelton, *Mask for Treason* (Harrisburg, Pa.: Stackpole Books, 1965).

18. Ibid., 9.

19. Ibid., 24–26, 54–65, 239–40.

20. Ibid., 401–3.

21. A photograph of the letter is in Robert H. Fowler, "New Evidence in Lincoln Murder Conspiracy," *Civil War Times Illustrated,* Feb. 1965, 8.

22. Ibid., 6. The letter is also printed in Ben: Perley Poore, ed., *The Conspiracy Trial for the Murder of the President . . . ,* (1865–66; reprinted New York: Arno Press, 1972), 1: 371.

23. Fowler, "New Evidence," 6–9; Shelton, *Mask for Treason,* 421–24. That the expert said Baker had tried to disguise his handwriting was omitted from *Mask for Treason.*

24. *Mask for Treason,* 323.

25. Fowler, "New Evidence," 9.

26. Ibid., 10.

27. Ibid., 11. For a reasonable interpretation of the R. D. Watson letter, see Hall, "Saga of Sarah Slater."

28. *Mask for Treason,* 419–21.

29. Fowler, "New Evidence," 11.

30. Balsiger and Sellier, *Lincoln Conspiracy* (Los Angeles: Schick Sunn Classic Books, 1977), 7, 9; Sunn Classic Pictures publicity release.

31. *Lincoln Conspiracy*, 9, 10.

32. Ibid., 10–11.

33. Ibid., 7–8.

34. Ibid., 13.

35. Ibid., 11; Harold M. Hyman, *With Malice Toward Some: Scholarship (or Something Less) on the Lincoln Murder* (Springfield: Abraham Lincoln Association, 1978), 12.

36. *Lincoln Conspiracy*, 11–12.

37. New York *Times*, Aug. 3, 1861, 22, cols, 1–2; Aug. 9, 1961, p. 32, col. 5.

38. The alleged text of Julian's diary was published in *Lincoln Log*, Mar.-Apr. 1977, 5; it was inaccurately quoted and freely paraphrased in *Lincoln Conspiracy*, 219–21.

39. July 22, 1926, Manuscript Department, Lilly Library, Indiana University, Bloomington, as reprinted in *Lincoln Log*, Aug. 1977, 3–4.

40. Davis, "Caveat Emptor," *Civil War Times Illustrated*, Aug. 1977, 36.

41. Ibid., 34–35; William C. Davis, " 'The Lincoln Conspiracy'— Hoax?" *Civil War Times Illustrated*, Nov. 1977, 47–49. Davis acknowledges the research assistance of James O. Hall and Peggy Robbins.

42. "Caveat Emptor," 35.

43. *Lincoln Conspiracy*, 295–96.

44. Ibid., 296.

45. William C. Davis, "Behind the Lines," *Civil War Times Illustrated*, Nov. 1981, 26, and letter to the writer Apr. 22, 1981.

46. Davis, "Behind the Lines," 28.

47. "Caveat Emptor," 37.

48. See especially Roll 1.

49. Townsend, *Life, Crime, and Capture*, 42.

50. Charles Chiniquy, *Fifty Years in the Church of Rome*, rev. and complete ed. (London: Robert Banks & Son, n.d. [1886]), 501, is apparently the first to use the expression in connection with Booth. It has subsequently been repeated by many anti-Catholic writers. In "Insights on John Wilkes Booth from His Sister Asia's Correspondence," *Lincoln Herald*, 82 (Winter 1980), 542–43, Constance Head shows that Booth may indeed have been a convert to Catholicism.

51. Chiniquy, *Fifty Years*, 497–98.

52. New York *Times*, Jan. 17, 1899; Joseph George, Jr., "The Lin-

coln Writings of Charles P. T. Chiniquy," *Journal of the Illinois State Historical Society,* 49 (Feb. 1976), 18. Some writers state that Chiniquy affiliated with the Presbyterian Church, but in *Fifty Years,* 571, he himself says it was with the Church of Christ. Chiniquy's account of his trial, ibid., 393–461, is lengthy and untrustworthy.

53. Ibid., 481.

54. Ibid.

55. Ibid., 484.

56. Ibid., 485.

57. Ibid., 485–89. The pope's letter to Davis, translated from the Latin, is in *Official Records, Navies,* Series II, 3: 975.

58. *Fifty Years,* 497, 498, 499, 500–501.

59. Ibid., 505–9.

60. Ibid., 509–10.

61. Apr. 1958, 13. Fulton's articles appeared in the April and May issues, 1958.

62. Harris, *Assassination,* 224, 267.

63. The original edition, privately printed in Pittsburgh, is extremely scarce. H. E. Matheny, *Major General Thomas Maley Harris* (Parsons, W. Va.: McClain Printing Co., 1963), 217, 217n.

64. Harris, *Rome's Responsibility* (Reprinted Los Angeles: Heritage Manor, 1960), 7–10.

65. McCarty, *Suppressed Truth* (Reprinted Haverhill, Mass.: Arya Varta Publishing Co., 1964), 44–49, 90–91, 104, 212.

66. See John Smith Dye, *History of the Plots and Crimes of the Great Conspiracy to Overthrow Liberty in America* (1866; reprinted Freeport, N.Y.: Books for Libraries Press, 1969).

67. McLoughlin, *Inquiry* (New York: Lyle Stuart, 1963), 8–9.

68. Ibid., 17, 88.

69. Ibid., 18–19.

70. Ibid., 163, 164.

71. George, "Lincoln Writings of Chiniquy," 24–25.

72. Thomas F. Meehan, "Lincoln's Opinion of Catholics," *United States Catholic Historical Society, Historical Records and Studies,* 16 (1924), 88.

73. David Rankin Barbee to Philip Van Doren Stern, June 30, 1938, Stern Papers.

74. Herbert Wells Fay, "Was Mrs. Booth Inhuman?" *Week By Week,* July 18, 1936. The origin of the Booth mummy is described in Finis L. Bates, *Escape and Suicide of John Wilkes Booth* (Memphis: Pilcher Printing Co., 1907). Bates appeared to believe his story. For studies showing he was either mistaken or the perpetrator of a hoax, see William G. Shepherd, "Shattering the Myth of John Wilkes Booth's Es-

cape," *Harper's Magazine*, Nov. 1924, 702–19; F. L. Black, "David E. George as J. Wilkes Booth," Dearborn *Independent*, Apr. 25, 1925, 10–11, 14, and "Identification of J. Wilkes Booth," ibid., May 2, 1925, 19, 27–28, 31; and Bryan, *Great American Myth*, 332–57. The public exhibition of the mummy is described in Alva Johnson, "'John Wilkes Booth' on Tour," *Saturday Evening Post*, Feb. 19, 1938, 16–17, 34, 36–38.

75. Forrester, *Unknown Story* (Boston: Hale, Cushman & Flint, 1937).

76. Kimmel, *Mad Booths*, Supplement 1, 387–90.

77. Bryan, *Great American Myth*, 362–72.

78. Washington *Post*, June 17, 1981, B1, B6.

79. George Loring Porter, "How Booth's Body was Hidden," *Magazine of History*, 38 (1929), 19–35.

80. May 18, in *House Report 7*, 40 Cong., 1 sess. (1867), 409.

81. Lewis, *Myths After Lincoln*, 354.

82. Investigation and Trial Papers, Roll 4, frames 350–69; William M. Pegram, "An Historical Identification. John Wilkes Booth," *Maryland Historical Magazine*, 8 (1913), 327–31.

83. Bryan, *Great American Myth*, 324–81; Eisenschiml, *Shadow of Lincoln's Death*, 53–88.

84. Paul Goldstein, "The Rothschilds' International Plot to Kill Lincoln," *New Solidarity*, Oct. 29, 1976, p. 4, cols. 1–5, presents no evidence of any kind, even circumstantial, to support this theory and takes the details of the assassination plot from Eisenschiml. See also Allen Salisbury, *The Civil War and the American System: America's Battle with Britain, 1860–1876* (New York: Campaigner Publications, 1978), 48–50, and *passim*.

85. David Rankin Barbee, "How Lincoln Rejected Peace Overtures in 1861," *Tyler's Quarterly Historical and Genealogical Magazine*, 15 (Jan. 1934), 137.

86. Brodie to the writer, July 16, 1977, and her *Thaddeus Stevens*, 215, 222.

87. Dell Leonardi, *The Reincarnation of John Wilkes Booth. A Study in Hypnotic Regression* (Old Greenwich, Conn.: Devin-Adair, 1975).

88. Washington *Post/Potomac*, June 29, 1975, 5.

Notes for "A Few Last Words . . ."

1. In 1867 Mathews told his story to the House Judiciary Committee and attempted to reconstruct Booth's letter. See *House Report 7*, 40 Cong., 1 sess. (1867), 782–85.

2. Hanchett, "Booth's Diary," 41–42.

3. Ibid., 40–42.

4. Ibid., 56; New York *Times*, May 6, 1865, p. 4, col. 5, and July 11, 1865, p. 5, col. 1; Thomas and Hyman, *Stanton*, 434–35.

5. Constance Head, "John Wilkes Booth as a Hero Figure," *Journal of American Culture*, 5 (Fall 1982), 26–27.

6. July 26, 1865, Stanton Papers, Library of Congress.

7. Turner and Turner, *Mary Todd Lincoln*, 538.

8. As quoted in Thomas and Hyman, *Stanton*, 638.

9. *Men and Memories*, 53.

Bibliography

Manuscripts

John A. Bingham Papers, Ohio Historical Society, Columbus.
John Wilkes Booth ms, Walter Hampden Memorial Library, New York City.
Thomas Ewing Papers, Columbia University, New York City.
Thomas M. Harris Papers, West Virginia University, Morgantown.
Joseph Holt Papers, Huntington Library, San Marino, California, and the Library of Congress, Washington.
Investigation and Trial Papers Relating to the Assassination of President Lincoln, Microcopy 599, National Archives, Washington.
Andrew Johnson Papers, Library of Congress, Washington.
Ward Hill Lamon Papers, Huntington Library, San Marino, California.
Letters Received by the Office of the Adjutant General (Main Series), 1861–1870, Microcopy 619, National Archives, Washington.
Francis Lieber Papers, Huntington Library, San Marino, California.
Abraham Lincoln Papers, Library of Congress, Washington.
Osborn H. Oldroyd Papers, Indiana State University, Terre Haute.
Papers Relating to Suspects in the Lincoln Assassination. Records of the Provost Marshal General's Office, Record Group 110, National Archives, Washington.
Edwin M. Stanton Papers, Library of Congress, Washington.
Philip Van Doren Stern Papers, Library of Congress, Washington.
Lew Wallace Papers, Indiana Historical Society, Indianapolis.
Gideon Welles Papers, Huntington Library, San Marino, California.

Books, Articles, Dissertations, and Theses

Abott, Abott A. *The Assassination and Death of Abraham Lincoln*. Pamphlet. New York: American News Co., 1865.

Abbott, Martin. "Southern Reaction to Lincoln's Assassination," *Abraham Lincoln Quarterly,* 7 (Sept. 1952).

Aldrich, Mrs. Thomas Bailey. *Crowding Memories.* Boston: Houghton Mifflin, 1920.

Allen, Mary Bernard. "Joseph Holt, Judge Advocate General (1862–1875). A Study in the Treatment of Political Prisoners." Ph.D. diss., University of Chicago, 1927.

Angle, Paul M. *A Shelf of Lincoln Books.* New Brunswick: Rutgers University Press, 1946.

"Are Handkerchiefs Superfluous? Lincoln Thought So," *Tyler's Quarterly Historical and Genealogical Magazine,* 15 (Jan. 1934).

Arnold, Samuel Bland. *Defence and Prison Experiences of a Lincoln Conspirator.* Hattiesburg, Miss.: The Book Farm, 1943.

————. "Lincoln Conspiracy and Its Conspirators," *Ohio State Journal,* Dec. 10, 1902–Dec. 20, 1902.

The Assassination and History of the Conspiracy. Cincinnati: J. R. Hawley, 1865. Reprint ed. New York: Hobbs, Dorman, 1965.

The Assassination of President Lincoln and the Trial of the Conspirators, comp. Benn Pitman. Facsimile ed. New York: Funk & Wagnalls, 1954.

Badeau, Adam. "Edwin Booth On and Off Stage," *McClure's Magazine,* Aug. 1893.

Baker, L. B. "An Eyewitness Account of the Death and Burial of J. Wilkes Booth," *Journal of the Illinois State Historical Society,* 39 (Dec. 1946).

Baker, L. C. *History of the United States Secret Service.* Philadelphia: L. C. Baker, 1867.

Balsiger, David, and Sellier, Charles E., Jr. *The Lincoln Conspiracy.* Los Angeles: Schick Sunn Classic Books, 1977.

Barbee, David Rankin. "How Lincoln Rejected Peace Overtures in 1861," *Tyler's Quarterly Historical and Genealogical Magazine,* 15 (Jan. 1934).

Barton, William E. *The Life of Abraham Lincoln.* Indianapolis: Bobbs, Merrill, 1925. 2 vols.

Bates, David Homer. *Lincoln in the Telegraph Office.* New York: Century Co., 1907.

Bates, Edward. *The Diary of . . . ,* ed. Howard K. Beale. *Annual Report of the American Historical Association* (1930), IV. Washington: Government Printing Office, 1933.

Bates, Finis L. *Escape and Suicide of John Wilkes Booth, Assassin of President Lincoln.* Memphis: Pilcher Printing Co., 1907.

Beisel, Suzanne. "Henry Clay, 'Dirty,' Dean," *Annals of Iowa,* 36 (1963).

Benham, William Burton. *Life of Osborn H. Oldroyd*. Pamphlet. Washington: O. H. Oldroyd, 1927.

Benton, Elbert J. *The Movement for Peace without a Victory during the Civil War*. New York: Da Capo Press, 1972.

Bishop, Jim. *A Bishop's Confession*. Boston: Little Brown, 1981.

————. *The Day Lincoln Was Shot*. New York: Harper & Bros., 1955. Bantam ed., 1956.

Black, F. L. "David E. George as J. Wilkes Booth," *Dearborn Independent*, Apr. 25, 1925.

————. "Identification of J. Wilkes Booth," *Dearborn Independent*, May 2, 1925.

Brennan, John C. "Confederate Spy—Captain Thomas Nelson Conrad," *Surratt Society News*, June 1977.

————. "The Confederate Plan to Abduct President Lincoln," *Surratt Society News*, Mar. 1981.

————. "General Bradley T. Johnson's Plan to Abduct President Lincoln," *Chronicles of St. Mary's*, 22 (Nov. and Dec. 1974).

————. *Pictorial Primer Having to Do With the Assassination of Abraham Lincoln and with the Assassin, John Wilkes Booth*. Laurel, Md.: Minuteman Press, 1979.

Brodie, Fawn. *Thaddeus Stevens, Scourge of the South*. New York: W. W. Norton, 1959.

Browning, Orville Hickman. *The Diary of . . .*, ed. James G. Randall. Volume II. Springfield: Illinois State Historical Library, 1933.

Bryan, George S. *The Great American Myth*. New York: Carrick & Evans, 1940.

Buck, Paul H. *The Road to Reunion*. New York: Vintage Books, 1959.

Burnett, Henry L. *The Controversy between President Johnson and Judge Holt*. Pamphlet. New York: D. Appleton, 1891.

————. *Some Incidents in the Trial of President Lincoln's Assassins*. Pamphlet. New York: D. Appleton, 1891.

Butler, Benjamin F. *Butler's Book*. Boston: A. M. Thayer, 1892.

Butler, Nicholas Murray. "Lincoln and Son," *Saturday Evening Post*, Feb. 11, 1939.

Carson, S. L. "The Other Tragic Lincoln: Robert Todd," *Manuscripts*, 30 (Fall 1978).

Chiniquy, Charles. *Fifty Years in the Church of Rome*. Revised and complete ed. London: Robert Banks & Son, n. d. [1886].

Chittenden, Lucius, E. *Invisible Siege. The Journal of. . . .* San Diego: Americana Exchange Press, 1969.

Clampitt, John W. "The Trial of Mrs. Surratt," *North American Review*, Sept. 1888.

Clancy, Herbert J. *The Presidential Election of 1880*. Chicago: Loyola University Press, 1958.

Clark, Allen C. *Abraham Lincoln in the National Capital*. Washington: W. F. Roberts, 1925.

Clarke, Asia Booth. *Booth Memorials. Incidents and Anecdotes in the Life of Junius Brutus Booth*. New York: Carleton, 1866.

———. *The Elder and the Younger Booth*. Boston: James R. Osgood, 1882.

———. *The Unlocked Book. A Memoir of John Wilkes Booth by His Sister*. New York: G. P. Putnam's Sons, 1938.

Clay-Clopton, Virginia. *A Belle of the Fifties. Memoirs of Mrs. [Clement C.] Clay*. New York: Da Capo Press, 1969.

Cleary, W. W. "The Attempt to Fasten the Assassination of President Lincoln on President Davis and Other Innocent Parties," *Southern Historical Society Papers*, 9 (July and Aug. 1881).

The Conflict of Convictions. American Writers Report the Civil War, ed. Jack Lindeman. Philadelphia: Chilton Book Co., 1968.

Congressional Documents

———. "Committee of the Judiciary . . . Report on John H. Surratt," 39 Cong., 2 Sess., *House Report 33*, 1867.

———. "Impeachment of the President," 40 Cong., 1 Sess., *House Report 7*, 1867.

———. "John H. Surratt," 39 Cong., 2 Sess., *House Executive Document 9*, 1866.

———. "Majority and Minority Reports of the Judiciary Committee Investigating the Assassination of Abraham Lincoln," 39 Cong., 1 Sess., *House Report 104*, 1866.

———. "Memorial in Behalf of James L. McPhail et al." 43 Cong., 1 Sess., *House Report 325*, 1874.

———. "Rejection of Claims of James L. McPhail et al," 43 Cong., 1 Sess., *House Report 742*, 1874.

Conrad, Thomas N. *A Confederate Spy*. New York: J. S. Ogilvie Publ. Co., 1892.

———. *The Rebel Scout*. Washington: National Publishing Co., 1904.

The Conspiracy Trial for the Murder of the President, ed. Ben: Perley Poore. Orig. publ. 1865–66; New York: Arno Press, 1972.

Cooney, Charles F. "Seward's Savior: George F. Robinson," *Lincoln Herald*, 75 (Fall 1973).

Cottrell, John. *Anatomy of An Assassination*. London: Frederick Muller, 1966.

Craven, Avery, "Southern Attitudes toward Abraham Lincoln," *Papers in Illinois History, 1942*. Springfield: State Historical Society, 1944.

Crook, William H. "Lincoln as I Knew Him," *Harper's Monthly*, Feb. 1907.

———. "Lincoln's Last Day," *Harper's Monthly*, Sept. 1907.

———. *Memories of the White House*, comp. and ed. Henry Rood. Boston: Little, Brown, 1911.

———. *Through Five Administrations*, comp. and ed. Margarita Spalding Gerry. New York: Harper & Brothers, 1910.

Crozier, R. H. *The Bloody Junto; or, the Escape of John Wilkes Booth*. Little Rock: Woodruff & Blocher, 1869.

[Daly, Maria Lydig]. *Diary of a Union Lady*, ed. Harold Earl Hammond. New York: Funk & Wagnalls, 1962.

Davidson, James D. "Life behind Confederate Lines in Virginia: the Correspondence of . . . ," ed. Bruce S. Greenawalt, *Civil War History*, 16 (Sept. 1970).

Davis, Michael. *The Image of Lincoln in the South*. Knoxville: University of Tennessee Press, 1971.

Davis, Varina Howell. *Jefferson Davis . . . , a Memoir by His Wife*. New York: Belford Co., 1890.

Davis, William C. "Behind the Lines," *Civil War Times Illustrated*, Nov. 1981.

———. "Caveat Emptor," *Civil War Times Illustrated*, Aug. 1977.

———. "'The Lincoln Conspiracy'—Hoax?" *Civil War Times Illustrated*, Nov. 1977.

Dean, Henry Clay. *Crimes of the Civil War*. Baltimore: Wm. T. Smithson, 1868.

DeMotte, William H. "The Assassination of Abraham Lincoln," *Journal of the Illinois State Historical Society*, 20 (Oct. 1927).

Dewitt, David Miller. *The Assassination of Abraham Lincoln, and Its Expiation*. New York: Macmillan, 1909.

———. *The Impeachment and Trial of Andrew Johnson*. Reprint ed. with introduction by Stanley I. Kutler. Madison: State Historical Society of Wisconsin, 1967.

———. *The Judicial Murder of Mary E. Surratt*. Baltimore: John Murphy & Co., 1895.

Doherty, Edward P. "Pursuit and Death of John Wilkes Booth: Captain Doherty's Narrative," *Century Magazine*, Jan. 1890.

Doster, William E. *Lincoln and Episodes of the Civil War*. New York: G. P. Putnam's Sons, 1915.

Dunham, Chester Forrester. *The Attitude of the Northern Clergy toward the South, 1860–1865*. Philadelphia: Porcupine Press, 1974.

Dusinberre, William. *Civil War Issues In Philadelphia, 1856–1865*. Philadelphia: University of Pennsylvania Press, 1965.

Dye, John Smith. *History of the Plots and Crimes of the Great Conspiracy to Overthrow Liberty in America.* Orig. publ. 1866. Freeport, N.Y.: Books for Libraries Press, 1969.

Eisenschiml, Otto. "Addenda to Lincoln's Assassination," *Journal of the Illinois State Historical Society,* 43 (Summer and Autumn 1950).

———. "Did He, Too, Try to Kill Lincoln?" *Lincoln Herald,* 48 (June 1946).

———. *In the Shadow of Lincoln's Death.* New York: Wilfred Funk, 1940.

———. *O. E. Historian without an Armchair.* Indianapolis: Bobbs-Merrill, 1963.

———. *Reviewers Reviewed. A Challenge to Historical Critics.* Pamphlet. Ann Arbor: William L. Clements Library, 1940.

———. *The Story of Shiloh.* Chicago: Civil War Round Table, 1946.

———. *Why Was Lincoln Murdered?* New York: Grosset & Dunlap, 1937.

———. *Without Fame. The Romance of a Profession.* Chicago: Alliance Book Corp., 1942.

[Emerson, E. A.]. "How Wilkes Booth's Friends Described His Crime," *Literary Digest,* Mar. 6, 1926.

Ellsler, John A. *The Stage Memories of.* . . . Cleveland: The Rowfant Club, 1950.

Fay, Herbert Wells. "Was Mrs. Booth Inhuman?" *Week By Week,* July 18, 1936.

Ferguson, W. J. *I Saw Booth Shoot Lincoln.* Austin, Tex.: Pemberton Press, 1969.

Flower, Frank Abial. *Edwin McMasters Stanton.* Akron: Saalfield Publ. Co., 1905.

Foote, Henry S. *Casket of Reminiscences.* Washington: Chronicle Publ. Co., 1874.

Forrester, Izola. *This One Mad Act. The Unknown Story of John Wilkes Booth and His Family.* Boston: Hale, Cushman & Flint, 1937.

Fowler, Robert H. *Album of the Lincoln Murder.* Harrisburg: Stackpole Books, 1965.

———. "New Evidence in [the] Lincoln Murder Conspiracy," *Civil War Times Illustrated,* Feb. 1965.

———. "Was Stanton behind Lincoln's Murder?" *Civil War Times,* Aug. 1961.

Frank, Seymour J. "The Conspiracy to Implicate the Confederate Leaders in Lincoln's Assassination," *Mississippi Valley Historical Review,* 40 (Mar. 1954).

Freeman, Douglas Southall. *R. E. Lee. A Biography*. New York: Charles Scribner's Sons, 1935. 4 vols.

Fulton, Justin D. "Behind the Purple Curtain: Lincoln's Assassins," *Christian Heritage*, Apr. and May 1958.

Gaddy, David W. "The Surratt Tavern—A Confederate 'Safe House'?" *Surratt Society News*, Apr. 1979.

Garrett, Richard Baynham. "A Chapter of Unwritten History. . . . Account of the Flight and Death of John Wilkes Booth," *Virginia Magazine of History and Biography*, 71 (Oct. 1963).

George, Joseph, Jr. "'Abraham Africanus I': President Lincoln through the Eyes of a Copperhead Editor," *Civil War History*, 14 (Sept. 1968).

————. "The Lincoln Writings of Charles P. T. Chiniquy," *Journal of the Illinois State Historical Society*, 69 (Feb. 1976).

Gleason, D. H. L. "Conspiracy against Lincoln," *The Magazine of History*, 13 (Feb. 1911).

Glenn, William Wilkins. *Between North and South. A Maryland Journalist Views the Civil War*, ed. Bayly Ellen Marks and Mark Norton Schatz. Rutherford: Fairleigh Dickinson University Press, 1976.

Goff, John S. *Robert Todd Lincoln*. Norman: University of Oklahoma Press, 1969.

Goldsborough, William W. *The Maryland Line in the Confederate States Army*. Baltimore: Kelly, Piet & Co., 1869.

Goldstein, Paul. "The Rothschilds' International Plot to Kill Lincoln," *New Solidarity*, Oct. 29, 1976.

Goodrich, Frederick E. *Life of Winfield Scott Hancock*. Boston: B. B. Russell, 1886.

Grant, Jesse R. *In the Days of My Father*. New York: Harper & Brothers, 1925.

Grant, Julia Dent. *The Personal Memoirs of . . .* , ed. John Y. Simon. New York: G. P. Putnam's Sons, 1975.

Greeley, Horace. *The American Conflict*. Hartford: O. D. Case & Co., 1864, 1866. 2 vols.

————. *Greeley on Lincoln*, ed. Joel Benton. New York: Baker & Taylor, 1893.

Green, Constance McLaughlin. *Washington: Village and Capital, 1800–1878*. Princeton: Princeton University Press, 1962.

Grossmann, Edwina Booth. *Edwin Booth. Recollections by His Daughter*. New York: Century Co., 1894.

Gurowski, Adam. *Diary*. Boston: 1862–66. 3 vols.

Gutman, Richard J. S., and Kellie O. Gutman. *John Wilkes Booth Himself*. Dover, Mass.: Hired Hand Press, 1979.

Hall, James O. "The Mystery of Lincoln's Guard," *Surratt Society News,* May 1982.

———. *Notes on the John Wilkes Booth Escape Route.* Pamphlet. Clinton, Md.: The Surratt Society, 1980.

———. "'Pink' Parker's Tombstone," *Civil War Times Illustrated,* July 1979.

———. "The Saga of Sarah Slater," *Surratt Society News,* Jan. and Feb. 1982.

Hanchett, William. "Booth's Diary," *Journal of the Illinois State Historical Society,* 72 (Feb. 1979).

———. *Irish. Charles G. Halpine in Civil War America.* Syracuse: Syracuse University Press, 1970.

Harper, Robert S. *Lincoln and the Press.* New York: McGraw Hill, 1951.

Harris, Thomas M. *Assassination of Lincoln.* Boston: American Citizen Co., 1892.

———. *Rome's Responsibility for the Assassination of Abraham Lincoln.* Los Angeles: Heritage Manor, 1960.

Head, Constance. "Insights on John Wilkes Booth from His Sister Asia's Correspondence," *Lincoln Herald,* 82 (Winter 1980).

———. "John Wilkes Booth as a Hero Figure," *Journal of American Culture,* 5 (Fall 1982).

———. "John Wilkes Booth in American Fiction," *Lincoln Herald,* 82 (Fall 1980).

Headley, John W. *Confederate Operations in Canada and New York.* New York: Neale Publishing Co., 1906.

Hertz, Emanuel. "At Ford's Theatre 75 Years Ago," *New York Times Magazine,* Apr. 14, 1940.

———. *The Hidden Lincoln, from the Letters and Papers of William H. Herndon.* New York: Blue Ribbon Books, 1940.

Holland, J. G. *Life of Abraham Lincoln.* New York: Paperback Library ed., 1961.

Holt, Joseph. *Letter from the Hon. Joseph Holt, upon the Policy of the Government . . . and the Duty of Kentucky.* Pamphlet. Washington, 1861.

———. "New Facts about Mrs. Surratt," *North American Review,* July 1888.

———. *Reply of J. Holt to Certain Calumnies of Jacob Thompson.* Pamphlet. Washington, 1883.

———. *Vindication of Hon. Joseph Holt.* Pamphlet. Washington: Chronicle Publishing Co., 1873.

———. *Vindication of Judge Advocate General Holt, from the Foul Slanders of Traitors.* Pamphlet. Washington, 1866.

Horan, James D. *Confederate Agent. A Discovery in History*. New York: Crown Publishers, 1954.

Horton, R. G. *A Youth's History of the Great Civil War*. New York: Van Evrie, Horton & Co., 1867.

Howard, Hamilton Gay. *Civil War Echoes*. Washington: Howard Publishing Co., 1907.

Hyams, Edward. *Killing No Murder. A Study of Assassination as a Political Means*. London: Panther Modern Society, 1970.

Hylton, J. Dunbar. *The Praesidicide*. New York: Howard Callen, 1884.

Hyman, Harold M. *A More Perfect Union. The Impact of the Civil War and Reconstruction on the Constitution*. New York: Knopf, 1973.

―――. *With Malice Toward Some: Scholarship (or Something Less) on the Lincoln Murder*. Springfield: Abraham Lincoln Association, 1978.

Ingersoll, Robert G. *The Works of . . .* , Vol. 9. New York: Ingersoll, 1900.

Johnson, Alva. "'John Wilkes Booth' on Tour," *Saturday Evening Post*, Feb. 19, 1938.

Johnson, Andrew. "Reply to Joseph Holt's 'Vindication,'" Washington *Daily Morning Chronicle*, Nov. 12, 1873.

Jones, J. B. *A Rebel Clerk's Diary*, new and enlarged ed. New York: Old Hickory Bookshop, 1935.

Jones, Thomas A. *J. Wilkes Booth. An Account of His Sojourn in Southern Maryland . . . and His Death in Virginia*. Chicago: Laird & Lee, 1893.

Junkin, D. X. *The Life of Winfield Scott Hancock*. New York: D. Appleton, 1880.

Kauffman, Michael. "Booth, Republicanism and the Lincoln Assassination." Special Scholars Thesis. University of Virginia, 1980.

Kauffman, Mike. "Fort Lesley McNair and the Lincoln Conspirators," *Lincoln Herald*, 80 (Winter 1978).

Kempf, Edward J. *Abraham Lincoln's Philosophy of Common Sense. An Analytical Biography*. New York: Academy of Sciences, 1965. 3 vols.

Kimmel, Stanley. *The Mad Booths of Maryland*, 2nd rev. and enlarged ed. New York: Dover Publications, 1969.

―――. *Mr. Lincoln's Washington*. New York: Bramhall House, 1957.

Kinchen, Oscar A. *Confederate Operations in Canada and the North*. North Quincy, Mass.: Christopher Publishing House, 1970.

Kirkland, Edward Chase. *The Peacemakers of 1864*. New York: Macmillan, 1927.

Klement, Frank. "A Small-Town Editor Criticizes Lincoln: A Study in Editorial Abuse," *Lincoln Herald*, 54 (Summer, 1952).

Kunhardt, Dorothy Meserve, and Philip B. Kunhardt, Jr. *Twenty Days*. New York: Harper & Row, 1965.

Lamon, Ward Hill. *Recollections of Abraham Lincoln*, ed. Dorothy Lamon Teillard. Washington: Teillard, 1895, 1911.

Lattimer, John K. *Kennedy and Lincoln. Medical and Ballistic Comparisons of Their Assassinations*. New York: Harcourt Brace Jovanovich, 1980.

Laughlin, Clara E. *The Death of Lincoln. The Story of Booth's Plot, His Deed and the Penalty*. New York: Doubleday, Page & Co., 1909.

———. "The Last Twenty-Four Hours of Lincoln's Life," *Ladies' Home Journal*, Feb. 1909.

———. *Traveling through Life*. Boston: Houghton Mifflin, 1934.

Lee, Robert E. *The Wartime Papers of . . .* , ed. Clifford Dowdey and Louis H. Manarin. Boston: Little, Brown, 1961.

Leech, Margaret. *Reveille in Washington, 1861–1865*. Garden City, N.Y.: Garden City Publishing Co., 1945.

Leonardi, Dell. *The Reincarnation of John Wilkes Booth. A Study in Hypnotic Regression*. Old Greenwich, Conn.: Devin-Adair, 1975.

Levin, Alexandra Lee. "The Canada Contact: Edwin Gray Lee," *Civil War Times Illustrated*, June 1979.

Lewis, Lloyd. "The Four Who Were Hanged," *Liberty*, Feb. 11, 1928.

———. *Myths after Lincoln*. New York: Readers Club, 1941.

———. "This Is to Certify," *Liberty*, Feb. 4, 1928.

Lincoln, Abraham. *Collected Works*, ed. Roy P. Basler. New Brunswick: Rutgers University Press, 1953. 9 vols.

Lincoln and the Baltimore Plot, 1861, from Pinkerton Records and Related Papers, ed. Norma B. Cuthbert. San Marino: Huntington Library, 1949.

Lincoln Day by Day, ed. Earl Schenck Miers. Washington: Lincoln Sesquicentennial Commission, 1960. 3 vols.

The Lincoln Log, ed. Richard E. Sloan. Seaford, N.Y.: 1975–81.

The Lincoln Memorial. A Record of the Life, Assassination, and Obsequies of the Martyred President, ed. John Gilmary Shea. New York: Bunce & Huntington, 1865.

Logan, John A. *The Great Conspiracy*. New York: A. R. Hart & Co., 1886.

Loux, Arthur F. "The Mystery of the Telegraph Interruption," *Lincoln Herald*, 81 (Winter 1979).

Luthin, Reinhard. *The Real Abraham Lincoln*. Englewood Cliffs: Prentice-Hall, 1960.

Lynch, Charles H. *The Civil War Diary, 1862–1865, of.* . . . Hartford: Privately printed, 1915.

McBride, Robert W. "Lincoln's Body Guard. The Union Light Guard of Ohio," *Indiana Historical Society Publications*, 5 (1911).

McCarty, Burke. *The Suppressed Truth about the Assassination of Abraham Lincoln.* Reprint ed. Haverhill, Mass.: Arya Varta Publishing Co., 1964.

McClure, A. K. "Jefferson Davis and Abraham Lincoln," *Confederate Veteran*, June 1908.

McDonald, David. "Hoosier Justice. The Journal of. . . ," ed. Donald O. Dewey, *Indiana Magazine of History*, 42 (1966).

McKinley, James. *Assassination in America.* New York: Harper & Row, 1977.

McLoughlin, Emmett. *An Inquiry into the Assassination of Abraham Lincoln.* New York: Lyle Stuart, 1963.

McPherson, Edward. *The Political History of the United States . . . during the Great Rebellion.* 3rd ed. Washington: Solomons & Chapman, 1876.

Mahoney, Ella V. *Sketches of Tudor Hall and the Booth Family.* Bel Air, Md.: Franklin Printing Co., 1925.

Marshall, John A. *American Bastille. A History of the Illegal Arrests and Imprisonment of American Citizens during the Late Civil War,* 23rd ed. Philadelphia: Thomas W. Hartley, 1877.

Martin, Percy E. "John 'Bull' Frizzell," *Surratt Society News*, Jan. 1980.

———. "Surprising Speed of the Identification of Two Baltimore Conspirators," *Surratt Society News*, Oct. 1978.

Masters, Edgar Lee. *Lincoln the Man.* New York: Dodd, Mead, 1931.

Matheny, H. W. *Major General Thomas Maley Harris.* Parsons, W.Va.: McClain Printing Co., 1963.

Mearns, David C. *The Lincoln Papers.* Garden City, N.Y.: Doubleday, 1948. 2 vols.

Meehan, Thomas F. "Lincoln's Opinion of Catholics," *United States Catholic Historical Society, Historical Records and Studies*, 16 (1924).

Memoirs of American Jews, 1775–1865, ed. Jacob Rader Marcus. Philadelphia: Jewish Publication Society, 1955–56. 3 vols.

Messages and Papers of Jefferson Davis and the Confederacy, ed. James D. Richardson. New ed. New York: Chelsea House-Robert Kector, 1966. 2 vols.

Messages and Papers of the Presidents, comp. James D. Richardson. Washington: Bureau of National Literature and Art, 1907. 11 vols.

Minor, Charles L. C. *The Real Lincoln, from the Testimony of his Contemporaries*. Gastonia, N.C.: Atkins-Rankin Co., 1928.

Morris, Clara. *Life on the Stage. My Personal Experiences and Recollections*. New York: McClure & Co., 1901.

———. "Some Recollections of John Wilkes Booth," *McClure's Magazine*, Feb. 1901.

Morse, John T. *Abraham Lincoln*. Boston: Houghton Mifflin, 1893, 1921. 2 vols.

Mudd, Samuel A. *The Life of Dr. . . .* , ed. Nettie Mudd. New York: Neale Publishing Co., 1906.

Neely, Mark E., Jr. *The Abraham Lincoln Encyclopedia*. New York: McGraw-Hill, 1982.

———. "The Lincoln Theme since Randall's Call: The Promises and Perils of Professionalism," *Papers of the Abraham Lincoln Association*, 1 (1979).

———. "Treason in Indiana. A Review Essay," *Lincoln Lore*, Feb. and Mar. 1974.

Nevins, Allan. *The War for the Union*. New York: Charles Scribner's Sons, 1959–1971. 4 vols.

Nichols, Roy Franklin. "United States vs. Jefferson Davis, 1865–1869," *American Historical Review*, 31 (Jan. 1926).

Nicolay, Helen. *Lincoln's Secretary. A Biography of John G. Nicolay*. New York: Longmans, Green, 1949.

Nicolay, John G., and John Hay. *Abraham Lincoln. A History*. New York: Century Co., 1890. 10 vols.

Oberholtzer, Ellis Paxson. *Abraham Lincoln*. Philadelphia: Geo. W. Jacobs, 1904.

Official Records of the Union and Confederate Armies, the War of the Rebellion. Washington: Government Printing Office, 1880–1901. 130 vols.

Official Records of the Union and Confederate Navies. Washington: Government Printing Office, 1894–1914. 30 vols.

Oldroyd, Osborn H. *The Assassination of Abraham Lincoln*. Washington: O. H. Oldroyd, 1901.

———. *An Interview with. . . .* Pamphlet. New York: the Sun, 1908.

Our Martyr President, Abraham Lincoln. Voices from the Pulpit of New York and Brooklyn. New York: Tibbals & Whiting, 1865.

Peck, Harry Thurston. "Dewitt's 'Assassination of Abraham Lincoln,'" *Bookman*, Apr. 1909.

Pegram, William M. "An Historical Identification. John Wilkes Booth—What Became of Him?" *Maryland Historical Magazine*, 8 (1913).

Phillips, Wendell. *Speeches, Lectures, and Letters*. Boston: Lee & Shepard, 1892.

Poems of American History, ed. Burton Egbert Stevenson. Boston: Houghton Mifflin, 1922; Freeport, N.Y.: Books for Libraries, 1970.

Poore, Ben: Perley. *Perley's Reminiscences of Sixty Years in the National Metropolis*. Philadelphia: Hubbard Brothers, 1886. 2 vols.

Porter, George Loring. "How Booth's Body Was Hidden," *Magazine of History*, 38 (1929).

————. "The Tragedy of the Nation," unpublished lecture, accessioned Feb. 1896, Library of Congress, Washington.

Potter, John Mason. *Thirteen Desperate Days*. New York: Obolensky, 1964.

Rankin, Mrs. McKee. "The News of Lincoln's Death," *American Magazine*, Jan. 1909.

Raymond, Henry J. *The Life and Public Services of Abraham Lincoln*. New York: Derby and Miller, 1865.

Richards, Laura E., and Maud Howe Elliott. *Julia Ward Howe*. Boston: Houghton-Mifflin, 1916. 2 vols.

Ridgely, Anna. "A Girl in the Sixties: Excerpts from the Journal of . . . ," *Journal of the Illinois State Historical Society*, 22 (Oct. 1929).

Robinson, Stuart. *Infamous Perjuries of the 'Bureau of Military Justice' Exposed*. Pamphlet. Toronto, 1865.

Roscoe, Theodore. *The Web of Conspiracy; the Complete Story of the Men who Murdered Lincoln*. Englewood Cliffs: Prentice-Hall, 1959.

Ruggles, Eleanor. *Prince of Players*. New York: W. W. Norton, 1953.

Ruggles, M. B. "Pursuit and Death of John Wilkes Booth: Major Ruggles's Narrative," *Century Magazine*, 39 (Jan. 1890).

Salisbury, Allen. *The Civil War and the American System. America's Battle with Britain, 1860–1876*. New York: Campaigner Publications, 1978.

Sandburg, Carl. *Abraham Lincoln. The Prairie Years and the War Years*. New York: Harcourt, Brace & World, 1954.

————. *Abraham Lincoln*, Sangamon ed. New York: Charles Scribner's Sons, 1926–1949. 6 vols.

————. *The Letters of . . .* , ed. Herbert Mitgang. New York: Harcourt, Brace & World, 1968.

————. *Lincoln Collector. The Story of Oliver R. Barrett's Great Private Collection*. New York: Harcourt, Brace, 1949.

Schouler, James. *History of the United States of America under the Constitution*, Vol. 6, 1861–1865. New York: Dodd, Mead, 1899.

Searcher, Victor. *Lincoln's Journey to Greatness*. Philadelphia: Winston, 1960.

Sermons Preached in Boston on the Death of Abraham Lincoln. Boston: J. E. Tilton & Co., 1865.

Shelton, Vaughan. *Mask for Treason. The Lincoln Murder Trial.* Harrisburg: Stackpole Books, 1965.

Shepherd, William G. "Shattering the Myth of John Wilkes Booth's Escape," *Harper's Magazine,* Nov. 1924.

———. "They Tried to Stop Booth," *Collier's Magazine,* Dec. 27, 1924.

Sherman, William Tecumseh. *Memoirs.* New York: D. Appleton, 1875. 2 vols.

Speed, James. "The Assassins of Lincoln," *North American Review,* Sept. 1888.

Starkey, Larry. *Wilkes Booth Came to Washington.* New York: Random House, 1976.

Stern, Philip Van Doren. *The Man Who Killed Lincoln.* New York: Literary Guild, 1939: rev. ed. New York: Dell Publishing Co., 1955.

———. "A Vivid Scene—and Then Mystery," *New York Times Magazine,* May 8, 1938.

Stewart, William M. *Reminiscences,* ed. George Rothwell Brown. New York: Neale Publishing Co., 1908.

Stidger, Felix G. *Treason History of the Order of the Sons of Liberty.* Chicago: Felix G. Stidger, 1903.

Stoddard, William O. *Inside the White House in War Times.* New York: Charles L. Webster & Co., 1890.

Stone, Kate. *Brokenburn. The Journal of . . . , 1861–1868,* ed. John Q. Anderson. Baton Rouge: Louisiana State University Press, 1955, 1972.

Storey, Moorfield. "Dickens, Stanton, Sumner, and Storey," *Atlantic Monthly,* Apr. 1930.

Strong, George Templeton. *The Diary of . . . ,* ed. Allan Nevins and Milton Halsey Thomas. New York: Macmillan, 1952. 4 vols.

[Sweet, Benjamin J.]. "The Chicago Conspiracy," *Atlantic Monthly,* July 1865.

Swett, Leonard. "The Conspiracies of the Rebellion," *North American Review,* Feb. 1887.

Surratt, John H. "Lecture on the Lincoln Conspiracy," *Lincoln Herald,* 51 (Dec. 1949).

Taylor, Richard. *Destruction and Reconstruction.* New York: Longmans, Green, 1955.

Taylor, W. H. "A New Story of the Assassination of Lincoln," *Leslie's Weekly,* Mar. 26, 1908.

The Terrible Tragedy at Washington. Pamphlet. Philadelphia: Barclay & Co., 1865.

Testimony of Sandford Conover, Dr. J. B. Merritt, and Richard Mont-

gomery before [the] Military Court at Washington. Toronto: Lovell & Gibson, 1865.

Thomas, Benjamin P., and Harold Hyman. *Stanton. The Life and Times of Lincoln's Secretary of War.* New York: Knopf, 1962.

Thomas, Emory M. "The Kilpatrick-Dahlgren Raid," Pt. 2, *Civil War Times Illustrated,* Apr. 1978.

Thomas, Lately. *The First President Johnson.* New York: William Morrow, 1968.

Townsend, E. D. *Anecdotes of the Civil War.* New York: D. Appleton, 1884.

Townsend, George Alfred. "How Wilkes Booth Crossed the Potomac," *Century Magazine,* Apr. 1884.

———. *Katy of Catoctin.* New York: Appleton, 1886.

———. *The Life, Crime, and Capture of John Wilkes Booth.* New York: Dick & Fitzgerald, 1865.

Trefousse, Hans Louis. "Belated Revelations of the Assassination Committee," *Lincoln Herald,* 58 (Spring-Summer 1956).

Trial of John H. Surratt. Washington: French & Richardson, 1867. 2 vols.

Tucker, Beverly, "Address to the People of the United States, 1865," ed. James Harvey Young. *Emory University Publications,* Ser. V, no. 1. Atlanta: Emory University, 1948.

Tucker, Glenn. *Hancock the Superb.* Indianapolis: Bobbs-Merrill, 1960.

Turner, Justin G., and Linda Levitt Turner. *Mary Todd Lincoln. Her Life and Letters.* New York: Knopf, 1972.

Turner, Thomas R. *Beware the People Weeping. Public Opinion and the Assassination of Abraham Lincoln.* Baton Rouge: Louisiana State University Press, 1982.

Union Pamphlets of the Civil War, 1861–1865, ed. Frank Freidel. Cambridge, Mass.: Belknap Press of Harvard University Press, 1967. 2 vols.

Verge, Laurie. "Mrs. Surratt's Other Son," *Surratt Society News,* Aug. 1977.

Ward, Samuel R. "Present When Lincoln Was Shot," *Kessinger's Mid-West Review,* Apr. 1931.

Weichmann, Louis J. *A True History of the Assassination,* ed. Floyd E. Risvold. New York: Knopf, 1975.

Weissman, Philip. "Why Booth Killed Lincoln. A Psychoanalytic Study," *Psychoanalysis and the Social Studies,* 5 (1958).

Welles, Gideon. *Diary of . . . ,* ed. Howard K. Beale. New York: W. W. Norton, 1960. 3 vols.

While Lincoln Lay Dying. A Facsimile Reproduction of the First Testimony Taken in Connection with the Assassination . . . as Re-

corded by Corporal James Tanner. Philadelphia: Union League of Philadelphia, 1968.

Wilson, Francis. *John Wilkes Booth. Fact and Fiction of Lincoln's Assassination*. Boston: Houghton Mifflin, 1929.

Wilson, George W. "John Wilkes Booth: Father Murderer," *American Imago*, 1 (1940).

Wilson, Rufus Rockwell. *Lincoln among his Friends*. Caldwell, Idaho: Caxton Printers, 1942.

————. *Lincoln in Caricature*. New York: Horizon Press, 1953.

Wilson, Woodrow. *A History of the American People*. New York: Harper & Brothers, 1901–2. 5 vols.

Winks, Robin W. *Canada and the United States. The Civil War Years*. Baltimore: Johns Hopkins University Press, 1960.

Winter, William. *Vagrant Memories*. New York: George H. Doran, 1915.

Woldman, Albert A. *Lincoln and the Russians*. New York: Collier Books, 1961.

Young, John Russell. *Men and Memories*, ed. May D. Russell Young. New York: F. Tennyson Neely, 1901.

Zornow, William. "Treason as a Campaign Issue in the Re-election of Lincoln," *Abraham Lincoln Quarterly*, 5 (June 1949).

Index

Rathbone, Henry R., 55, 56, 144,
165, 244
Raymond, Henry J., 91
Revisionism in the writing of Civil
War history, 104–5, 121, 123,
159, 181–83, 217–19, 243
Rhodes, James Ford, 159
Rogers, Andrew J., 80
Roosevelt, Theodore, 117, 139
Roscoe, Theodore: on the assassina-
tion, 193–95; on the Weichmann-
Gleason talks, 199
Rothschilds, the, 243

Sandburg, Carl: on Booth, 145–47
Sanders, George N., 15, 16, 60, 64,
73, 75
Schouler, James, 99
Scott, Winfield, 9, 24
Secession of the lower South, 7–8
Seddon, James A., 27, 29, 30–31,
192–93
Sellier, Charles E., Jr. See Balsiger,
David.
Seward, Frederick, 57
Seward, William H.: warns Lincoln
about Baltimore plot, 22; believes
assassination not a danger, 25; as
intended assassination victim, 54,
64, 101; attacked by Paine, 56–
57, 58; and the petition of clem-
ency for Mary E. Surratt, 96, 97,
98; mentioned, 11, 29, 59, 60,
149, 219, 222, 237
Seymour, Horatio, 10
Shelton, Vaughan, 199, 209; on the
assassination, 219–23; on the
R. D. Watson letter, 223–26
Sherman, William T., 59, 60, 183
Simonds, Joseph H., 44
Smith, Gerrit, 75, 90
Snevel, Joseph, 79
Sons of Liberty, the, 14, 38, 239.
See also Copperheads
Spangler, Edman: arrest, trial, sentence of, 66, 70; pardon of, 88–
89; mentioned, 84, 114, 180
Speed, James, 70, 76, 77, 78, 96,
98–99, 111, 113
Stanton, Edwin M.: warns Lincoln
of danger, 24–25, 36; as intended
assassination victim, 54, 57, 58,

61; announces the assassination
was part of a Confederate grand
conspiracy, 64, 207; changes mind
about Confederate grand conspiracy, 75–76, 77; writes letter in
support of Holt, 81; criticized for
having made charge of Confederate grand conspiracy, 91–92;
David M. Dewitt on, 105–15,
120–21; Clara Laughlin on, 118;
Lloyd Lewis on, 122; Otto Eisenschiml on, 163–84; Philip Van
Doren Stern on, 186–91; George
S. Bryan on, 191; Jim Bishop on,
191–93; Theodore Roscoe on, 193;
on his alleged knowledge of the
abduction conspiracy, 195–208; in
the Neff-Baker ciphers, 214–18;
David Balsiger and Charles E.
Sellier, Jr., on, 231–33; his hatred
for Booth, 242, 246–47; true
place in history of, 247–48; mentioned, 4, 60, 62, 72, 73, 74, 78,
80, 82, 85, 96, 97, 98, 119, 186,
210, 211, 212, 213, 214, 242
Stephens, Alexander H., 35
Stern, Philip Van Doren: on the assassination, 147–49, 152, 158,
186–88, 198; on Robert Lincoln
burning his father's papers, 189–
91; on the Weichmann-Gleason
talks, 198
Stevens, Thaddeus, 75, 76, 80, 90,
210, 243
Stewart, William M., 118
Stone, Frederick, 66
Stone, Kate, 132
Strong, George Templeton, 11
Surratt, Anna, 47, 48
Surratt, Isaac, 48
Surratt, John H.: and the abduction
conspiracy, 47, 48–50; goes to
Canada, 51, 52; discovered in En-
gland, 76–77; capture and trial of,
86–87, 88, 203–6; visited by
Clara Laughlin, 117–18; his lecture on the abduction conspiracy,
118, 119, 195–96, 198; Vaughan
Shelton on, 220, 223–24; men-
tioned, 51, 52, 61, 66, 72, 75,
101, 107, 149, 155, 176, 180, 181
Surratt, Mary E.: acquaintance with

A Note on the Author

WILLIAM HANCHETT is professor of history at San Diego State University. He received his B.A. from Southern Methodist University and his M.A. and Ph.D. from the University of California, Berkeley. He is the author of *Irish: Charles G. Halpine in Civil War America* (1970) and of numerous articles on Lincoln and the Civil War era.